Heal Yourself

by Clearing

the Chakras

Transcendence Toolbooks, vol 4

Heal Yourself

by Clearing

the Chakras

KIM MICHAELS

Copyright © 2013 Kim Michaels. All rights reserved. No part of this book may be used, reproduced, translated, electronically stored or transmitted by any means except by written permission from the publisher. A reviewer may quote brief passages in a review.

MORE TO LIFE PUBLISHING

www.morepublish.com

For foreign and translation rights,

contact info@ morepublish.com

ISBN: 978-9949-518-45-6

Series ISBN: 978-9949-518-04-3

The information and insights in this book should not be considered as a form of therapy, advice, direction, diagnosis, and/or treatment of any kind. This information is not a substitute for medical, psychological, or other professional advice, counseling and care. All matters pertaining to your individual health should be supervised by a physician or appropriate health-care practitioner. No guarantee is made by the author or the publisher that the practices described in this book will yield successful results for anyone at any time. They are presented for informational purposes only, as the practice and proof rests with the individual.

For more information:

www.ascendedmasterlight.com

www.transcendencetoolbox.com

CONTENTS

Introduction 9

1 | The Ascended Master Approach to Healing 15

2 | The Chakras and the Spiritual Rays 33

3 | What You Need From Outside the Separate Self 57

4 | Karma Is Not What You Think 65

5 | First Ray: A Non-Linear View of Karma 71

6 | Second Ray: Wisdom Is a Vital Force of Healing 89

7 | Third Ray: You Are Always Worthy of Love 107

8 | Fourth Ray: Acceleration Is the Key to Wholeness 125

9 | Fifth Ray: Closing the Gap on the Spiritual Path 143

10 | Sixth Ray: The Unconditional Joy of Service 167

11 | Seventh Ray: Balancing the Scales of Life 189

12 | Clearing the Secret Heart Chakra 207

13 | Clearing the Heart Chakra 225

14 | Clearing the Solar Plexus Chakra 243

15 | Clearing the Throat Chakra 263

16 | Clearing the Soul Chakra 283

17 | Clearing the Third Eye Chakra 303

18 | Clearing the Base Chakra 323

19 | Clearing the Crown Chakra 343

INTRODUCTION

The idea behind *Transcendence Toolbooks* is to give you effective tools for shifting your consciousness. Many spiritual books give you understanding, and while this may be inspiring, it does not necessarily lead to practical change. This book contains a unique combination of teachings and techniques for invoking spiritual light. Both the teachings and the invocations are given by the universal spiritual teachers of humankind, also known as the ascended masters. The combination of teachings and exercises has the potential to help you go through a real transformation that will bring you to a higher level of your personal path.

This book is designed to help you develop an entirely new and spiritually holistic approach to healing both physical and psychological problems. This approach is based on the fact that your physical body is the most dense part of a larger energy field. The body is produced by the total energy field, meaning that what is happening at the higher levels of this field have a profound impact on your physical body.

The teachings and tools in this book are given by representatives for each of the seven spiritual rays. If you are not familiar with the ascended masters and their teachings, it is recommended that you read the book *The Power of*

Self, which explains who the masters are, how they can help you and how you can follow the path to self-mastery offered by the masters. You can find more information on the website: *www.ascendedmasterlight.com.* You will also find a set of powerful tools for healing in the book *The Song of Life Healing Matrix.*

This book is structured in three parts:

- **Part One:** An introduction to how the ascended masters approach healing. An introduction to the seven main centers, called chakras, of your energy body.

- **Part Two:** Discourses by the ascended masters that give you a deeper understanding of the energy field, the chakras and how purifying the chakras can impact your psychological and physical health.

- **Part Three:** Spiritual exercises, called invocations, designed to clear the chakras. By using these invocations, you invoke spiritual energy that has immense power to transform your consciousness and take you beyond old patterns.

The invocations in Part Three are meant to be read aloud by you. You can read them in a slow, meditative way or you can give them faster and with more power in your voice. There is no one right way to give the invocations, but they obviously cannot work unless you read them aloud. If you desire more detailed instructions for how to give invocations, please visit the website: *www.transcendencetoolbox.com.* You might also find it helpful to give the invocations along with a recording. You can purchase and download sound files of the invocations from the website: *www.morepublish.com.*

Introduction

It is suggested that you start using this book by reading Part One so you are familiar with how the ascended masters talk about healing and the chakras. After that, you can take two different approaches. One approach is that you read the chapters in Part Two in the order they are given. This will give you a good understanding of the spiritual rays and the chakras. You can then give the invocations in Part Three. If you are new to ascended master teachings, this approach will be the most productive.

The second option is that you start a vigil of giving the first invocation in Part Three once a day while studying the corresponding dictation in Part Two. It is recommended that you follow the order in which the invocations in Part Three are listed. You would begin by studying the chapter on the Third Ray and giving the invocations for clearing the Secret Chamber of the Heart Chakra and the Heart Chakra. You would then continue with the next invocation and so forth. Before each invocation you will find a reference to the corresponding chapter.

Whether you take the first or the second approach, it is recommended that you spend at least nine days on a particular chakra. You would therefore give the invocation for clearing the Secret Chamber of the Heart once a day for nine days while studying the corresponding dictation. You would then give the invocation for clearing the Heart Chakra once a day for nine days while studying the same dictation (you might just read parts of the dictation each day). You then move on to giving the invocation for clearing the Solar Plexus Chakra once a day for nine days and so forth.

It is recommended that all students would start by going through the chakras in the order given in Part Three, giving each invocation once a day for nine consecutive days. This would be a basic chakra clearance that would give you an intuitive sense of which chakras might need further clearance. You could then focus on one chakra and give the invocation for that chakra once a day for 33 consecutive days. You could also give a larger clearance of all of the chakras by giving each invocation once a day for 33 days.

Depending on your speed, it takes 15-25 minutes to give one invocation. This means you can give all of the invocations (one after the other) in a little over two hours, which is a very powerful ritual. If you decide to do this, you do not have to give the opening prayer or the sealing with each invocation. You give an opening prayer when you start and the sealing after you finish the last invocation.

Feel free to be creative in the use of the tools included in this book. For example, you can give the matrix for another person or persons that you desire to see healed. You can even use the tools for clearing the chakras of the planetary energy field or the energy field of your nation.

If you make the effort to overcome your initial resistance and build a momentum on giving the invocations, you will likely find that it is one of the most powerful and effective spiritual tools you have ever used. By combining this tool with a willingness to look into your own psyche and let go of limiting beliefs, you can turn your life into an upward spiral and heal both psychological and physical ailments. Truly, as the masters say, everything revolves around your free will. If you can accept that transcendence is possible for you, then the results *will* be manifest for you. Invoke, and ye shall receive.

PART ONE

Healing and the Chakras

The purpose of this section is to give an introductory teaching on how the ascended masters approach healing and also to introduce the chakras and their characteristics. If you already know ascended master teachings, there may be little new here, but if you are not familiar with ascended masters, it is important to know the ideas described in the following chapters. Chapter 2 gives a brief overview of the chakras, and this information forms the foundation for getting the best results from giving the invocations in Part Three.

1 | THE ASCENDED MASTER APPROACH TO HEALING

Most readers of this book are probably already familiar with the existence of an energy field around the physical body, normally called the aura. They are probably also aware that the aura has a number of energy centers, including seven main centers, or chakras. The purpose of this chapter is to give a brief summary of the teachings given by the ascended masters about the energy field. It is important for you to know these teachings because they can help you overcome some of the common misconceptions about the aura and the chakras. These misconceptions can block your ability to heal yourself.

The body does not produce the aura

The most common misconception about the aura is caused by the fact that most people were taught about magnets in school. We were taught that a bar magnet produces an invisible magnetic field around itself. When we later hear about an energy field around the physical body, it is easy to assume that the body produces the energy field. This is an image that will directly block your ability to heal yourself because it will make you confuse cause and effect, thinking matter is the cause and energy the effect.

The existence of an energy field around the body has been scientifically plausible since Albert Einstein formulated the theory of relativity. He proved that we do not live in a dualistic universe made of energy and matter—the two being separate. Instead, we live in a unified world where everything is made from energy. What to our senses seems like solid matter is truly vibrating energy. If you take Einstein's famous formula, $E = mc^2$, you can do something we all learned in school, and you get the following:

$$\frac{E}{c^2} = \frac{m c^2}{c^2}$$

Obviously, we now have C^2 twice on the right side of the equal sign, meaning they cancel out each other. We then get the final formula.

$$\frac{E}{c^2} = m$$

This new formula is not in any way in opposition to Einstein's formula; it simply makes a point that is implied in the theory of relativity but that is often overlooked. The point is that mass, or matter, is made from energy of a very high vibration that has been lowered or reduced in vibration into the frequency spectrum that makes up the material universe. Knowing this is essential for healing because it makes it clear that what we call matter is simply energy that has taken on a lower vibration.

This demonstrates that what we call the material world is subservient to a world of pure energy.

Energy is cause; matter is effect. It will probably take some mental retooling before you are able to think of your physical body as made from vibrating energy. The reward for undertaking this shift in perception is that you can begin to see that the physical body is not as "solid" or difficult to change as you have been conditioned to believe. We are all programmed to believe that a physical disease must have a physical cause and thus also a physical cure. The standard approach to healing in the Western world says that it is impossible to heal your body through the powers of the mind. Obviously, you will get no results from this book by defending this view.

By considering the scientific formula above, you can begin to see that even science has challenged the dualistic view of mind being separate from matter. Both your body and your mind are made from energy, and the mind is obviously the highest form of energy, meaning it has a higher vibration than the energy making up the physical body. This means that since Einstein published the theory of relativity, it has been scientifically plausible that the mind can directly affect the health of the physical body—for better and for worse.

Why healing with the mind is possible

The conclusion is clear. The physical body has an energy field around it, but the aura is not produced by the body. Instead, the physical body is a product of the aura. We could also say that the physical body is the most dense aspect of your total energy field. This means that the energy field is cause and the body is the effect. A disease in the physical body begins as a cause in the higher levels of your energy field.

The disease is (in most cases) not caused at the level of the physical body; it is caused in the higher energy field. This is important for two reasons:

- The higher levels of the energy field are obviously less dense than the physical level of the field. This means that it is easier to change the energy "body" than the physical body. Once you change the cause in the energy body, the effect in the physical body will also change. This change is inevitable, but in some cases it may take time before the physical body outpictures the changes in the energy field.

- It may seem as if the mind has little ability to directly change the cells and molecules of the physical body. Yet it is easy to see that the mind has the ability to change the aura because it is less solid. It is therefore far more believable that you can consciously and willfully make changes in your aura. Once you begin to accept that your body is produced by the aura, you will also begin to accept that changing the energy field will inevitably lead to changes in the body as well. Effect must follow cause.

How energy flows into your field

Science has shown us that the universe has a hierarchical structure and the ascended masters confirm this. As mentioned, Einstein's theory of relativity says everything we call matter is made from energy that has been lowered in vibration. This means that the matter we see with our senses, such as our physical bodies, is made from energy and must obey the laws that guide the workings of energy.

1 | The Ascended Master Approach to Healing

As a visible example, consider that you can make many different items out of iron. There is a set of laws for how you can melt and shape iron, but these laws function within the framework of the laws that guide how atoms and subatomic particles work. A blacksmith can do all kinds of things with iron, but cannot change the atomic and subatomic laws. He must work within them because they set parameters for what can and cannot be done at the grosser level of the iron substance, often called the macroscopic level.

The ascended masters teach that what makes us conscious and able to do anything with our minds is that we are receiving a stream of high vibration energy. This energy comes from a higher realm than the material world, and it is normally called the spiritual realm. The energy that you personally receive is directed from a higher part of your mind, what the masters call your I AM Presence.

This I AM Presence exists in a realm that cannot be affected by anything that happens at the macroscopic level of the material universe. The importance of this fact is that no matter what you have experienced here in the material world (in this and past lifetimes), none of it has destroyed your I AM Presence. It has not diminished your potential to receive energy from

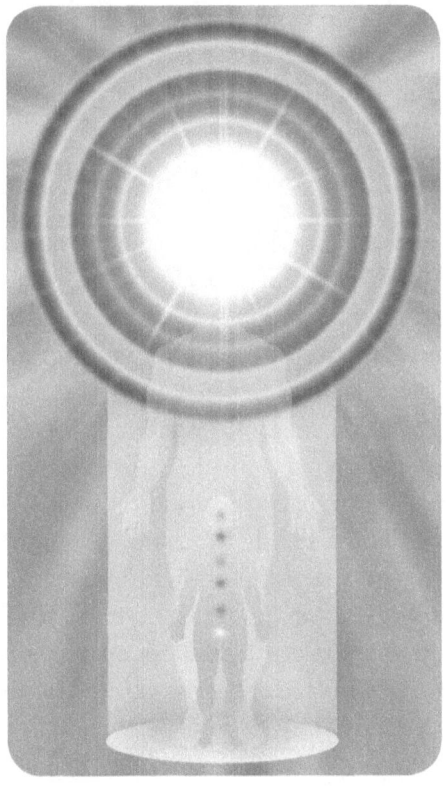

your Presence, but it might have diminished the amount of energy you currently receive. Clearing your chakras will restore the natural energy flow.

It is the spiritual energy that enables you to do something in this world, meaning that in order to heal your physical body or lower mind, you will need to use energy from your I AM Presence. This energy is the cure for all diseases, and because your I AM Presence cannot be affected by what happens to your body, you can never lose the potential to heal your body.

Your I AM Presence will constantly and naturally release energy to your lower being, but the decisions you make with your conscious mind can block this energy. In one sense it can be said that all disease is caused by a blocking of the natural energy flow from your I AM Presence. The master key to healing is to open up this flow. Let us therefore look at how the flow can become blocked.

The four levels of your energy field

The ascended masters teach that our minds have four levels. When you think back to Einstein's finding that everything is energy, you can see that it is possible to set up a scale or continuum that lists energy vibrations from lower to higher. The lower vibrations make up the material world, including our physical bodies. Our thoughts and feelings are obviously forms of energy that are less dense than matter, meaning they take place in a realm of vibration that is higher than the matter world.

The ascended masters say the material world is made from energy that vibrates within a certain spectrum. Above that is energy of a higher vibration, namely the spiritual realm. In between the material spectrum and the spiritual spectrum are three other levels or spectra. The five spectra can be described as follows:

- **The spiritual realm.** This realm has various levels, but the important point is that the energy that makes up all of the material levels comes from the lowest level of the spiritual realm and then "streams" into the material levels. On the personal level, your I AM Presence resides in the spiritual realm and is directing a stream of high frequency energy into the lower levels of your mind.

- **The identity realm.** This is the highest level of the material realm. On the personal level, it is the highest level of your mind or energy field. This is where your deepest sense of identity is stored. Because this is the highest level of your mind, how you identify yourself will set parameters for everything that happens at the lower levels. As the energy from your I AM Presence enters this level of your mind, it is lowered in vibration so that it can enter the next realm. The more it is lowered in vibration, the less powerful will be your creative abilities.

- **The mental realm.** This is the level of your thoughts, especially related to how you can do what you want to do in the matter world. For example, if your identity body contains the belief that you are a material being and that your powers are limited to what you can do with the physical body, this will set limitations for how you seek to heal disease.

- **The emotional realm.** This is obviously the level of your feelings, and again it is subservient to the two higher levels. If you think you are a material being and that your options for healing are limited to material means, you will be susceptible to certain feelings of powerlessness, frustration or anger.

- **The physical realm.** This is the level of the physical body and brain. The ascended masters teach that the body and brain do have certain capabilities that can affect your mental processes. Ideally, we should be in command of this part of the mind, but most people are not.

In the natural scenario, we would have a pure flow of energy from the I AM Presence, and this means we would be consciously aware that we are not material beings. Most people have lost this awareness and that is why we no longer clearly experience that we are spiritual beings with higher powers. Some people have blocked the flow of energy from their Presences so effectively that they function at the level of the body and thus for all practical purposes function as animals.

People who are open to the spiritual side of life have some connection to their I AM Presences. The key to healing is to expand that connection.

What blocks the energy flow

When pure, high-frequency energy from your I AM Presence enters your identity "body," it becomes subject to the conditions found at that level of the mind. The ascended masters have given profound teachings about the purpose of life, and the brief summary is that we are in embodiment on earth in order to have certain experiences which can raise our level of consciousness. What gives us these experiences are the beliefs we form about ourselves, and these beliefs exist at all four levels of the mind. As the energy from your I AM Presence enters the identity mind, its vibration is affected by the beliefs about yourself residing at this level. This has two effects:

- The energy is lowered in vibration. The lower the vibration, the less creative power the energy will have as it flows to the next level down.

- The energy stream is reduced in its volume. The less energy that streams to the lower levels, the less creative power you have.

As an example, say a person is convinced that she is only a human being, an evolved ape, and that she only has the creative power of the physical body. This is actually a highly limiting sense of identity for a spiritual being to take on, which means that upholding this view requires energy. Some of the energy coming from the person's I AM Presence is therefore directed into upholding the view in the identity body. Over time, this energy will accumulate in the identity body and it gradually forms a blockage to the flow of energy from the I AM Presence. Less and less creative energy will be available to flow into the mental body.

At the mental level, the sense of identity that you are a human being will also give rise to a set of beliefs. Anything that limits your creative power will feel unnatural, meaning that it takes energy to uphold it. Again, some of the (already diminished) creative energy will be tied up at the mental level, further reducing the amount that flows into the emotional "body."

The limiting beliefs at the two higher levels will reduce your creative powers, meaning your ability to control and change your situation in the material world. This limited ability to affect change will inevitably make you feel frustrated, meaning you develop the beliefs at the emotional level that in certain situations it is justified or unavoidable to respond with anger. Again, upholding this belief takes energy, further reducing the amount of creative energy reaching the level of the physical body.

As mentioned, when the amount of creative energy that reaches the physical body is reduced to its lowest level, people function as little more than animals. An example of this is the cave man society. The ascended masters teach that when we have descended to this low level of creative power, we become self-fulfilling prophecies. Essentially, we have come to adopt a set of beliefs at the four levels of the mind that portray us as limited beings who are the victims of external circumstances. These very beliefs have reduced the amount of creative energy that can penetrate our minds to such a low level that we can no longer consciously change our physical circumstances. We have indeed become victims of external circumstances.

Our limiting beliefs seem to be validated by everything we experience at the level of the physical body. From a certain perspective we *are* indeed very limited beings. Yet the deeper reality is that we are limited only because the amount of creative energy coming from the I AM Presence has been blocked at the three higher levels of the mind. So little energy reaches the physical level that we simply do not have the vision or the creative power to change our external circumstances.

As said before, nothing that happens in the material universe can affect the I AM Presence. The amount of energy coming from the I AM Presence has not been permanently shut off. We can never lose the ability to restore our creative powers. The way to do so is simple:

- Clear out the energies that have accumulated in the four levels of the mind.

- Consciously dismiss the liming beliefs in the four levels of the mind.

The very fact that human civilization has risen above the level of the cave man proves that a critical mass of people have started restoring the natural flow of creative energy from the spiritual realm. Obviously, this has mainly happened by developing material technology, but even this can take place only when we attain a clearer vision of how the material world works.

The ascended masters teach that in this age millions of people are meant to take civilization to an even higher level where we become more conscious of the creative powers of the mind. This can make us less dependent upon material technology, which is especially important in the field of healing.

A higher form of healing

Your four lower bodies form a hierarchical structure and the physical body is the lowest link in the chain. A disease in the physical body is generated because your physical cells take on an unnatural matrix. This matrix is a psychic matrix that is projected from the three higher levels of the mind. It begins at the identity level, becomes more concrete at the mental level and is then given momentum at the emotional level. As this matrix is projected upon the cells over a period of time (perhaps the matrix has been reinforced over many physical lifetimes), it eventually interferes with the functioning of the cells to the point where they cannot work naturally. Instead, they take on an unnatural form that is determined by the matrix projected upon them.

What mainstream Western medicine has so far done is to deal with disease at the level of the physical body, which is the level of effect. As science has made abundantly clear, dealing with the effect is far less productive than dealing with the cause.

The ascended masters hope that the people who are already open to a holistic approach will be able to take advantage of the teachings they have given on a higher approach to healing. This approach is that instead of dealing with only the physical body, you learn to deal with all four of the lower "bodies." The teachings and the exercises in this book are designed to help you get started on this process.

The ascended master approach to healing has two components. One is that you deal with the energy that has accumulated at the four levels of the mind. The second component is that you resolve the underlying belief that actually generates the lower energy. In many cases, the accumulated energy has reached such a level of intensity that it blocks your ability to see the underlying belief. This is what the masters call a catch-22, a situation that seemingly has no solution.

The solution is to transform some of the accumulated energy until you reduce the amount so much that it no longer blocks your vision of the underlying belief. It then becomes much easier to see and dismiss the belief. As you resolve one limiting belief, you open up greater creative powers, and as you continue to transform energy and resolve beliefs, you will eventually reach a point where a particular disease can be healed through the powers of the mind.

Take note that the ascended masters are not saying that you should refuse medical treatment. On the contrary, they recommend you make use of all healing modalities available to you. The ascended master approach is clearly a more long-term approach and should not be used to refuse treatment that is necessary in order to preserve your life or deal with acute problems.

The masters teach that once you have transformed a sufficient amount of accumulated energy and resolved the underlying beliefs, the psychic matrix projected upon your cells will be dissolved. As this matrix is no longer projected upon the cells, they will – perhaps with the help of physical forms of healing – be able to resume their natural function. Healing is not simply a suppression of symptoms but a removal of the four-layered matrix that is the real cause of all disease.

How ascended master healing works

The first step in the ascended master healing process is to learn how to transform the lower energy that has accumulated in your four lower bodies. You already have a natural ability to do this, and the ascended masters offer tools for helping you use and sharpen this ability.

Transforming low-frequency energy is straightforward and the process is well-documented by science. When two energy waves meet, they form an interference pattern and the result is that a new energy wave is formed. This wave is a combination of the two energy waves.

Imagine that in your emotional body there is an accumulation of low-frequency energy, such as anger. The way to get rid of this energy is to direct an energy wave at it that has a higher vibration than the anger energy. As the high-frequency wave meets the anger energy, an interference pattern is created and the result is a new wave that has a higher vibration than the anger energy. How much higher is a matter of how low is the vibration of the anger energy and how high is the wave you send at it. Obviously, there is also the question of how much anger energy has accumulated, perhaps over many lifetimes. It may take a determined effort to transform all of the accumulated energy by repeatedly invoking and directing high-frequency energy at it.

In your natural state, your four lower bodies would be open to a constant flow of high-frequency energy from your I AM Presence. We can therefore say that, ideally, you should be able to tune in to this stream of energy and direct it with your conscious mind.

Some people are indeed able to do this, but most people have so much accumulated energy that they cannot do this consciously. In order to help us get out of this catch-22, the ascended masters offer us a range of tools for invoking spiritual energy with our present level of awareness.

The most powerful tools for invoking spiritual energy make use of the voice. They take the form of a spoken affirmation or decree that is repeated with great power and sometimes at rapid speed. Some of the techniques given by the ascended masters are called decrees. They are rhymes that are repeated at high speed and therefore allow you to build a powerful momentum of invoking spiritual energy. These decrees are very efficient for invoking energy, and you can find a large selection of them on *www.transcendencetoolbox.com*.

Invoking energy is one aspect, directing it is another. The ascended masters have also released techniques for helping us both invoke energy and direct it into specific conditions. This type of tool is called an invocation, and it combines decrees with affirmative statements. In Part Three, you will find a number of affirmations that are specifically designed to clear each of the eight major chakras.

Transforming energy is only one side of ascended master healing. The other side is to resolve the limiting beliefs that caused you to generate the low-frequency energy. The resolution of such beliefs will to some degree happen spontaneously as you reduce the amount of energy in your four lower bodies. Suddenly, your conscious mind will see a pattern you had never noticed before, and you will see how it is limiting you.

To speed up this process, the ascended masters give teachings in order to help us become aware of the beliefs that limit our creative expression. These teachings are given in the form of dictations, which are messages that are spoken by the masters through a human messenger who has been trained for this purpose. You will find a number of such dictations in Part Two, and studying them will help you become more aware of the beliefs that limit the flow of energy through your major chakras.

To speed up the process even more, the teachings in the dictations have been incorporated in the invocations in Part Three. This means that as you give an invocation, you will invoke high frequency energy, direct it into a specific chakra and you will be prompted to consider the limiting beliefs you might have. These tools are therefore very efficient for clearing the chakras and restoring your creative abilities. Once these abilities are restored, you can direct them into healing your mind and body and changing your outer situation as well.

Understanding chakras and spiritual rays

In order to fully understand ascended master healing, it is necessary to understand that what we have so far called "spiritual light" comes in several qualities. The ascended masters normally refer to these qualities as "spiritual rays." Each ray is made up of high-frequency spiritual energy that vibrates within a certain spectrum of frequencies. The material universe is made by combining the seven major spiritual rays.

On the personal level, the light you receive from your I AM Presence is made up of all seven rays. How does the light enter the four levels of your energy field? It enters through seven centers or portals that are normally called chakras. Each chakra is a portal for the light of a specific ray. A chakra can be seen as an opening, almost like a valve, that allows light to flow through by opening or closing a number of petals or blades. You might picture this as a jet engine where metal blades regulate the airflow.

When we talk about a spiritual ray, we are not simply talking about mechanical energy. In the spiritual realm it is obvious to all beings existing there that there is nothing mechanical about the world. Even the material universe is made by conscious beings, and unless these spiritual beings constantly maintained their creation, the universe would cease to exist. For each of the seven rays, there is a hierarchy of spiritual or ascended beings who serve on that ray. The energy of a given ray that is used to uphold the existence of the material universe is sent from the hierarchy of spiritual beings on that ray. This is important because it helps us understand an essential aspect of ascended master healing.

The techniques given by the ascended masters for invoking light are obviously published in the material world, which means anyone can find them. If the tools had a completely mechanical effect, such as material technology, they could easily be misused. Obviously, nuclear energy is mechanical and can be used to light up or blow up a city. The ascended masters have made sure that their tools cannot be misused by people with selfish or destructive intentions.

The way this works is that in order to invoke light from a given spiritual ray, you must do so through the hierarchy or spiritual beings serving that ray. This means that it is these spiritual beings who release the light that you invoke through an invocation or decree. They can therefore read your intention and shut off the flow of light if your motives are not pure. They can also release just the amount of light that you can handle at your present level of consciousness. In other words, it is difficult to invoke more light than you can handle.

The ascended masters who serve on a given ray can be said to be working at three different levels:

- **The Elohim** are often called the builders of form because the seven Elohim were the beings who created planet earth by combining the energies of the seven rays according to the blueprint they had created. You call to the Elohim in order to invoke the creative energies and in order to increase your creative vision.

- **The Archangel** of a ray is in charge of helping human beings use a ray and also free themselves from the misuses of a ray. You call to the Archangel to send energy that will consume misqualified energy and also to help you become free from external forces or your own ego.

- **The Chohan** of a ray is primarily tasked with teaching human beings about the spiritual path in general and about his or her ray in particular. You call to the Chohan in order to be taught how to make progress on the spiritual path and how to overcome specific blocks in your personal psychology.

The ascended masters generally work in pairs where one master holds the masculine and the other the feminine polarity. The Elohim and Archangels all have such partners, often called twin flames or twin rays, which means you will use two names when calling to them. Most of the Chohans do not have an ascended twin flame, meaning you use only one name when calling to the Chohan.

The key to ascended master healing is to learn how to work with the masters who serve on the seven rays. As you use the tools to transform low-frequency energy, one or more of your chakras will gradually be cleared. As a particular chakra is cleared, you will develop a better intuitive connection to the masters who work on the spiritual ray that corresponds to the chakra. Through this connection you will receive invaluable insights into the limiting beliefs you have and how to transcend them.

As you let go of such beliefs, you will resolve the very cause that has led to physical disease, namely the psychic matrix that has been projected upon your cells through the three higher levels of the mind. Not only will this lead to physical healing, it will also lead to greater emotional well-being, clearer thinking and a deeper sense that you are a spiritual being who is in embodiment with a clear purpose. This will turn your life into an upward spiral that will gradually enrich all aspects of your experience in the material world.

2 | THE CHAKRAS AND THE SPIRITUAL RAYS

The purpose of this chapter is to give a brief introduction to the chakras and how they correspond to the seven spiritual rays. The purpose is to make it easier for you to study the characteristics of the chakra and the ray before you give the invocations in Part Three.

Most spiritually interested people have at least one chakra that is fairly open, which is what allowed us to recognize the need for spiritual growth. We often have at least one chakra that is fairly closed, and this is what causes us to have certain patterns that we seemingly cannot transcend.

When some chakras are more open than others, we tend to express our creative abilities in unbalanced ways. A classical example is a person who has a somewhat open Throat Chakra (the power center) and a closed Heart Chakra (the center for love and compassion). Such a person will tend to express power without having it balanced by love, which inevitably leads to the abuse of power. World history is full of examples of the suffering this can cause.

Each of the main chakras corresponds to one of the seven spiritual rays. The entire material universe is created from a combination of the energy frequencies of these seven rays. The ascended masters teach that planet earth was originally created with a perfect balance between the seven energies. There was balance in nature, with no natural disasters and no lack of food or resources. The human body did not get sick or even age.

What has caused this original state of balance to be lost is that humankind throughout the ages has expressed its creative abilities in unbalanced ways. Each of the seven rays has certain pure qualities. When you receive the light of a given ray through one of your chakras and express it from a state of love, you can be creative without disturbing the balance. When you go below the level of love, you create an imbalance.

The many imbalances you see on earth are created by humankind by perverting the pure qualities of the seven rays. What closes a particular chakra is the perversions of the pure qualities of the corresponding spiritual ray. The following sections describe the main characteristics of the chakras.

Name:
Various systems give slightly different names to the chakras. The following are the names given by the ascended masters:

Crown Chakra
Third Eye Chakra
Throat Chakra
Heart Chakra
Solar Plexus Chakra
Soul Chakra
Base Chakra

Position:
In most teachings, the seven major chakras are shown superimposed upon a picture of the physical body. The chakras are lined up over the spinal column, with the lowest chakra over

the sexual organs and the highest chakra over the top of the head. The central chakra is always the Heart Chakra.

Shape:
The chakras are often depicted with a shape that resembles a flower with varying numbers of petals. They can also be said to resemble a valve, or, as mentioned before, a jet engine that has metal blades opening or closing to regulate the air stream.

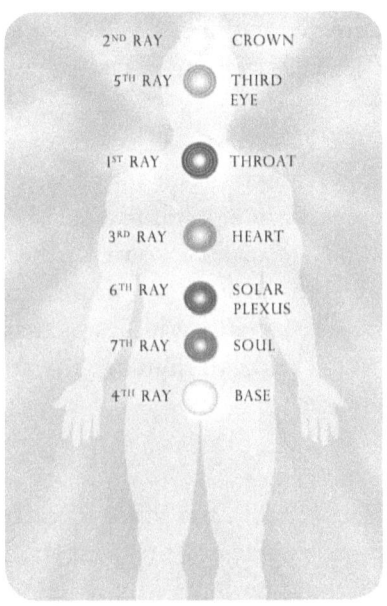

Corresponding spiritual ray:
The ascended masters teach that each chakra corresponds to a particular spiritual ray. Each chakra is meant to be an open door for the spiritual qualities of the ray to be expressed through your lower being. When all of your chakras are functioning optimally, you will have maximum creative flow and you will express it in a balanced way. The balance will ensure a return flow to your higher self, which will then be multiplied and sent back to you, meaning you will exponentially expand your creative powers—as long as you maintain balance.

Color:
Each of the seven main chakras has a corresponding color. In various systems, the colors are depicted differently. One common system depicts the Base Chakra as red and the Heart Chakra as green. It is not the intent here to say that some systems are right and some are wrong. In this book the chakras are

depicted with the same color as the corresponding spiritual ray. Blocked or polluted chakras will have different colors.

Pure qualities:
Each chakra has a set of pure qualities that are defined by the corresponding spiritual ray. If you recognize that you have the ability to express some of these qualities, you can gauge which of your chakras are more pure. If you find that some qualities are lacking, it indicates that the corresponding chakra is not open. You can then use the appropriate tools to purify a given chakra.

Perversions:
Each chakra has a set of qualities that are perversions of the pure qualities of the corresponding ray. If you recognize some of these patterns in yourself, you can use the invocations for a given chakra to call for the purification and balancing of the chakra. You can also begin to make conscious decisions to stop yourself from going into limiting patterns. You can begin to uncover the underlying belief that perverted the pure quality in the first place.

The sequence of the chakras and ray descriptions

One way to list the chakras would be in a linear fashion based on their position in the body, for example starting with the lowest and going up. Another way would be to list the chakras according to the corresponding ray, going from the First Ray to the Seventh Ray. Indeed, the dictations in Part Two are listed according to the order in which they were given, namely from the First Ray to the Seventh Ray.

The following description of the chakras will be ordered differently as will be the invocations. The reason is that the ascended masters teach that the light from your I AM Presence first enters the Secret Chamber of the Heart Chakra, then goes into the Heart Chakra and then into the other chakras in pairs. The chakras above or below the heart are linked in pairs, for example the Crown Chakra and the Base Chakra are linked.

Some Eastern teachings say the key to spiritual growth is to raise the Kundalini energy from the Base Chakra through the other chakras to the Crown Chakra. The ascended masters teach that for people in the Western world, this is not the best approach, especially for people who are new to the spiritual path. As the experiences of many spiritual seekers confirm, seeking to force the Kundalini can lead to various forms of imbalances, even mental illness. Others have experienced that while it is easy to raise the Kundalini, it is very difficult to keep is raised. The reason is a lack of balance.

The ascended masters recommend a balanced approach to clearing the chakras, namely that we begin with the Secret Chamber of the Heart and the Heart Chakra. Then, we clear the Solar Plexus Chakra and the Throat Chakra. After that, we clear the Soul Chakra and the Third Eye Chakra. Finally, we clear the Base Chakra and the Crown Chakra. The purpose is to first clear the entry point of the light and then clear the chakras in the order the light is distributed. This gives you a much more balanced clearance. When all of your chakras are cleared, the spiritual light will more easily be raised and a higher state of consciousness can be maintained over time.

Heart Chakra and Secret Heart Chakra

The three upper chakras are the seat of what we normally call mind, namely the ability to formulate clear and detailed thoughts and explanations. In contrast, the three lower chakras are the seat of feelings that tend to flow without us being able to explain why. They flow according to what feels right or (when perverted) what feels good. The Heart Chakra is located between the higher and lower chakras, and the reason is that it is only through a pure Heart Chakra that you can balance mind and emotions, sometimes called the left and the right brain.

Traditionally, the Heart Chakra has been seen as the seat of love, compassion, charity, appreciation for beauty and selflessness. Yet a deeper understanding is that the Heart Chakra is the seat of balance. Behind the Heart Chakra is an eighth chakra, called the Secret Chamber of the Heart. It is in this chakra that the light from your I AM Presence descends. The light then enters the Heart Chakra from where it is distributed to the other chakras. This means that if the Heart Chakra is polluted by impure expressions of love, then the light that flows to the other chakras will be tainted from the start.

Love can be seen as the balancing force in life, balancing the two basic forces of creation, namely the outgoing (masculine or Father impulse) and the contracting (Feminine or Mother impulse). If these two forces are not balanced, there will be a tendency to take one of them towards the extreme. This means that anything which is created from imbalance will either be taken too far and thus blow apart, or it will not be taken far enough, meaning it will not come to fruition and will eventually self-destruct through contraction.

A pure Heart Chakra gives you the ability to experience unconditionality, namely the one reality that is beyond the two extremes created by the dualistic mind. You can feel when something is dualistic, even though you may not yet have the purified Third Eye and Crown chakras that empower you to give a detailed explanation. You simply sense that conditionality is not "right" because you experience the unconditional nature of God/reality in your heart.

A pure Heart Chakra leads to a deep inner sense of oneness with all life. This gives rise to the ability to discern when something feels uplifting (because it seeks to raise all life) or feels not uplifting (because it seeks to raise one part of life while putting down another). It is in the Heart Chakra that you can know what is the right thing to do, even if you cannot yet explain why through the mind (the upper chakras). It is also in the Heart Chakra that you can sense when the three lower chakras are driven by a selfish impulse, and it gives you the power to balance these chakras.

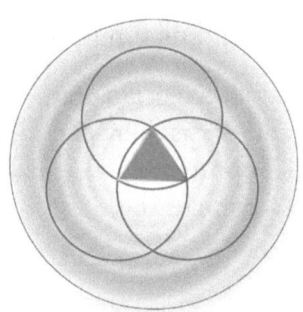

Perversions
The primary perversion of the Heart Chakra is a lack of balance, but this can be expressed in many subtle ways. One way is what many people call love, but which is really a possessive attempt to control others. In extreme forms, this can be expressed as hatred and the desire to punish or destroy those who refuse to be controlled. For example, many people fall in love but then begin to express a sense of ownership towards the person they claim to love.

Another perversion is the firm belief that the ends can justify the means, meaning that because a person loves this superior cause, it is justified to force or kill other people in order to further the cause. This perverted form of love has caused some of the worst atrocities in human history. Few people are harder to convince than those whose Heart chakras have become unbalanced. It is what causes people to believe that in order to demonstrate their love for God, they have to kill other people.

Corresponding ray: Third Ray
Color: Pink
Elohim: Eros and Amora
Archangel: Chamuel and Charity
Chohan: Paul the Venetian

Solar Plexus Chakra and Throat Chakra

The following illustration depicts the figure-eight flow that is meant to exist between the Solar Plexus and the Throat chakras. It is important to visualize this flow while working on clearing these two chakras.

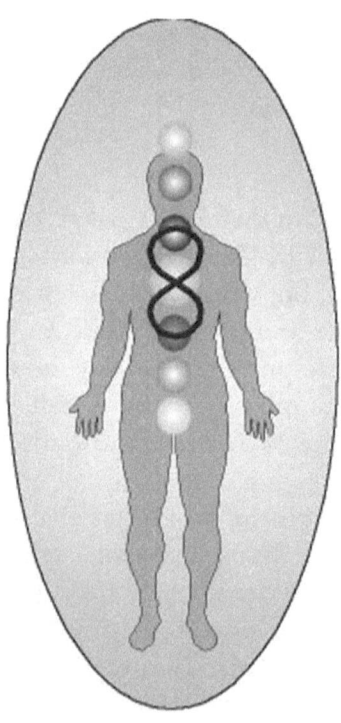

Solar Plexus Chakra

Traditionally, the seat of peace, but it is a "peace that passeth understanding." Understanding is achieved through the chakras above the heart. Peace is an inner sense of being unmoved by the dualistic appearances that are pulling at one from all sides. It is the ability to stand in the midst of a raging conflict and feel the stillness within. It is the ability to feel the pull that seeks to draw you into an unbalanced expression of anger, yet you can remain centered and decide that you do not want to go there.

When you have this peace, you can give truly selfless service because you will intuitively work to bring harmony into every situation. Harmony is the key to helping people see beyond the dualistic struggle and find common ground. A person with a pure Solar Plexus Chakra is always looking for common ground and has an ability (especially when the upper chakras are also pure) to draw people towards consensus and cooperation.

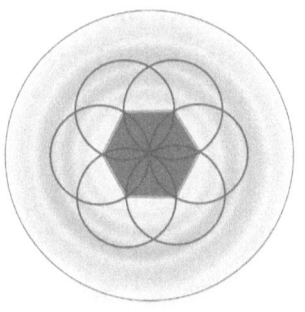

Perversions

The immediate perversions of the Solar Plexus Chakra are anger and agitation, expressed as a very aggressive drive to force others to change or to punish those who resist. It is a non-peace that is also beyond understanding because there is no way to reason with a person who has an agitated Solar Plexus Chakra. They act blindly on their feelings of rage, and they will time and time again do or say things they regret later. They will do what others know to be wrong, yet be completely blind to it at the moment.

Another perversion is what some see as peace, but it is truly passivity, the unwillingness to take a stand for anything. People with this perversion tend to act as victims who can only react to external forces, and they refuse to take responsibility for their lives. There are also people who lose individuality and become part of a "mob mind" that acts blindly or blindly follows a strong leader. Another perversion is a blind sense that violence and warfare can provide viable solutions or that in some situations they are the only way to react, even the justified way to react.

Corresponding ray: Sixth Ray
Color: Purple and gold
Elohim: Peace and Aloha
Archangel: Uriel and Aurora
Chohan: Nada

Throat Chakra

Traditionally, the seat of power and will, yet from a deeper understanding the seat of the creative drive. This is the desire for self-expression—yet in its pure form the expression of your spiritual individuality.

A pure Throat Chakra gives rise to a creative drive that

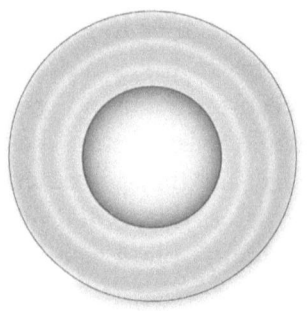

is expressed in a willingness to experiment, even when the outcome of the experiment cannot be known ahead of time. Another example is a willingness to flow with life and learn from every experience. A pure Throat Chakra also gives rise to the sense that everything has a purpose, that life is exciting and that the individual truly can make a positive difference. The Throat Chakra is also the seat of your willingness to work for raising the whole, instead of raising only yourself.

Perversions
The perversion of the creative will is a fear of the unknown that is expressed as an ability to abuse power in order to control one's circumstances, including other people. There is a fear of engaging in activities where the outcome cannot be predicted or guaranteed, which obviously stifles creativity.

People with polluted Throat Chakras are often engaged in a variety of power games with other people, all based on the desire to control the outcome. This is an attempt to quell the very life force itself, which always points towards self-transcendence, and instead protect the separate self and what it thinks it can own in this world. This can lead to a sense of ownership over other people that is one of the major sources of conflict on this planet. In milder cases, people have a fear of being creative and a sense of powerlessness, feeling that nothing really matters and that an individual cannot make a difference—thus, why even bother trying.

Corresponding ray: First Ray
Color: Electric blue
Elohim: Hercules and Amazonia
Archangel: Michael and Faith
Chohan: Master MORE, also known as El Morya, Morya, Master M, M, or Bapu.

Soul Chakra and Third Eye Chakra

The following illustration depicts the figure-eight flow that is meant to exist between the Soul and the Third Eye chakras. It is important to visualize this flow while working on clearing these two chakras.

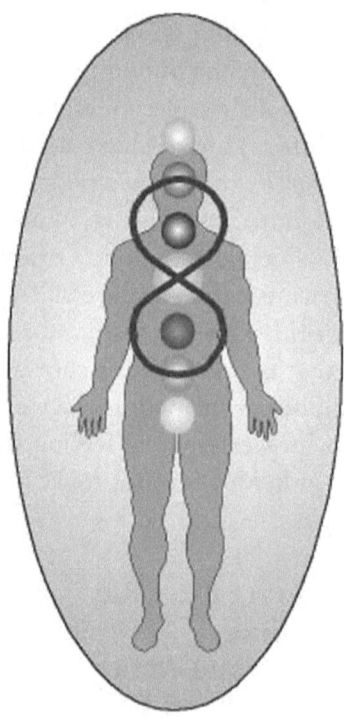

Soul Chakra

Traditionally, seen as the seat of freedom, forgiveness and justice. A deeper understanding is that the Soul Chakra is the seat of your playfulness, your willingness to approach life according to Jesus' statement: "Unless you become as a little child, ye shall in no way enter the kingdom."

A pure Soul Chakra gives people a sense of playfulness about life, especially about creative expression. You feel that you live in a world that is basically good, and you are here to express yourself and play with what is available. You are not worried or anxious about life or the future, and you trust that Spirit will protect you and that the Mother will nurture you. You feel a sense of bubbling freedom and a desire to experience what the world has to offer and to add to it through your own creative expression. You are willing to experiment and learn from every situation.

Perversions

The primary perversion of the Soul Chakra is a tendency to take life very seriously. This can be expressed as a perversion of both freedom and justice. This combines into the sense that you live in a world where everything is a struggle, perhaps even a struggle against a force that is unjustly seeking to take away your freedom.

Take the old saying: "Laugh at the devil, and he runs away from you." There is a truth here, in the sense that if you take something too seriously, you give it power over you. Of course, one might say that there are many things in the world that are seeking to limit your freedom and that are unjust so doesn't that mean you *have* to take them seriously? There is a balance where one realizes the truth in a statement by Jesus: "Be ye wise as serpents, harmless as doves." There is a fine balance between being naive to the temporary conditions in the world and taking them so seriously that you think you cannot feel free until they are changed.

The extreme perversion of the Soul Chakra is the epic mindset where one thinks the world is locked in a battle between good and evil, meaning that anything can be justified in the fight to destroy evil. This leads to complete insensitivity towards life, and this has led to some of the worst examples of human cruelty. As with everything else, insensitivity towards others comes from an insensitivity towards oneself.

When your Soul Chakra is polluted, you tend to think that the problems in the world exist because other people don't take things as seriously as you do. As you overcome this imbalance, you realize that the conditions are still there because people take them too seriously, thus thinking the conditions of the material world have power over their Spirits.

In reality, we are all spiritual beings and one of our ultimate tasks on earth is to demonstrate that we will not allow material conditions to limit our Spirits and their expression in this world. Allowing our higher selves to express themselves through us is the key to freedom, and it is the playfulness of the divine manchild, who knows he or she is one with the Father—and with God all things are possible.

Corresponding ray: Seventh Ray
Color: Violet
Elohim: Arcturus and Victoria
Archangel: Zadkiel and Amethyst
Chohan: Saint Germain and Kuan Yin

Third Eye Chakra

Traditionally, seen as the seat of truth and vision—yet vision of what? The Third Eye is the seat of single vision, as illustrated by Jesus in the remark: "If thine eye be single, thy whole body shall be full of light." The single-eyed vision is the Christ vision that sees beyond duality and separation. This is based on the realization that any expression of "truth" in the material world is less than the Spirit of Truth, and thus one must look beyond any outer expression in order to experience truth.

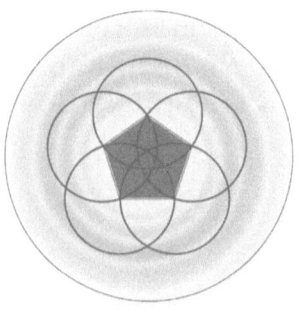

When one looks beyond through a purified Third Eye Chakra, one sees that all divisions are unreal, and one sees the need to raise all life. This gives rise to Christ discernment, the ability to instantly identify and see through the lies of duality that seek to raise up one part of life by putting down another.

This is exemplified in the situation in the Garden of Eden where the Serpent said to Eve: "Thou shallt not surely die," thus inserting the element of doubt into her consciousness. With a purified Third Eye Chakra, you can see through this serpentine logic. You can also see that all appearances in the material world are only temporary, and thus you can hold the immaculate vision for people or conditions to be transformed.

Perversions
The perversions are lack of vision, a lack of ability to discern between the one non-dual Truth and the many dualistic "truths," leading to doubt and a sense of hopelessness or the sense that there is no truth. It is also the belief that there is only one truth and that it is *our* truth.

Another perversion is the sense that because we have the only truth, we are locked in a battle against those who promote another thought system. It is necessary and justified for us to criticize or even destroy their system. People who are critical of other people or ideas have a polluted Third Eye Chakra. Another perversion is the tendency to say that if people do or believe certain things, they are bad people—failing to see beyond temporary appearances.

Corresponding ray: Fifth Ray
Color: Emerald green
Elohim: Cyclopea and Virginia
Archangel: Raphael and Mother Mary
Chohan: Hilarion

Base Chakra and Crown Chakra

The following illustration depicts the figure-eight flow that is meant to exist between the Base and the Crown chakras. It is important to visualize this flow while working on clearing these two chakras.

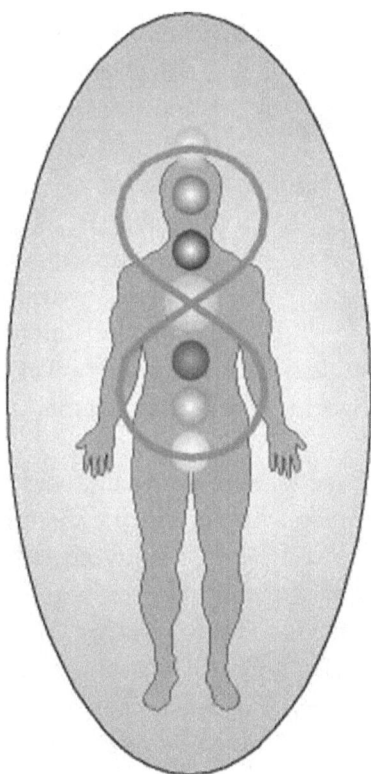

Base Chakra

Traditionally, seen as the seat of purity, hope and self-discipline. At a deeper level, the Base Chakra is the interface between your Spirit and your physical body and the material world.

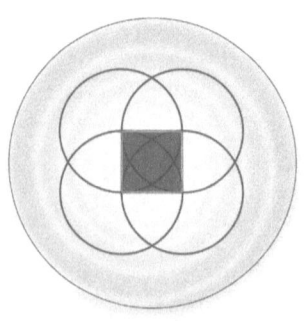

The question asked at the level of the Soul Chakra is whether you will allow the material world to have power over your Spirit so you limit your expression in this world. The question at the level of the Base Chakra is whether you believe the current conditions in the material world are real, permanent and unchangeable. Or are you are willing to unleash your creative power in order to accelerate the material world – the Mother element – beyond current conditions?

With a pure Base Chakra you will avoid being trapped in the illusion that the appearances in the material world are real or permanent. You will be able to avoid being trapped in an endless cycle of seeking to fulfill lower, bodily, carnal or human desires. Instead, you will see this world as a tool for your growth in self-awareness. You will effortlessly avoid activities that do not serve this purpose. This has a deeper layer of understanding, as you will realize it is not a matter of avoiding all human or physical activities—it is a matter of spiritualizing them.

When all of the chakras are pure, you will be able to see that the last illusion to overcome on the spiritual path is the idea that there is a division between the spiritual and the material realm, between spiritual and material activities. Instead, you will be able to remain in oneness, making anything you do a spiritual activity. This will serve to fulfill the purpose for taking embodiment in the first place, namely to accelerate the vibration of the entire material world to a higher level where the universe can become a permanent part of the spiritual realm.

Perversions

Traditionally, the perversions are seen as impurity and chaos. At a deeper level, the perversions are the sense that current conditions are real, are the way they should be or are beyond your power to change. You begin to think this world is separated from the spiritual realm, perhaps even that it belongs to the devil and that you should leave it alone, not seeking to change it. You might believe you have no right to be a spiritual person in this world or that you have no right to express your spiritual powers in this world. Instead, you think you should accept current conditions and adapt to them.

As the ultimate perversion, you might even believe that you are an entirely material being, a product of the material universe—that you have come from dust and that to dust thou shalt return. In this state of mind there is, of course, no hope of acceleration to a higher state. Given that life itself is acceleration into More, this is a state of mind that Jesus called "death," meaning spiritual death.

Corresponding ray: Fourth Ray
Color: White
Elohim: Astrea and Purity
Archangel: Gabriel and Hope
Chohan: Serapis Bey

Crown Chakra

Traditionally, seen as the chakra of wisdom, illumination and self-knowledge. At a deeper level, it is this chakra that empowers you to see that the separate self is unreal and that separation is an illusion.

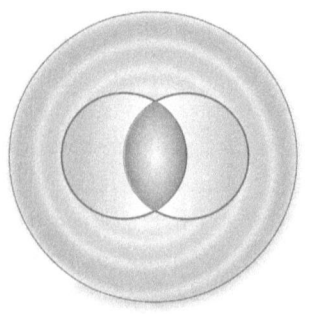

It is through the Crown Chakra that you can experience the underlying reality that all life is one because nothing can be separated from the omnipresent Creator. Openness to a higher understanding is also a quality of a pure Crown Chakra, as is the realization that there are many valid expressions of truth that all point to the same underlying reality of oneness.

Perversions

The perversion of the Crown Chakra is the false wisdom that thinks it knows everything or has an ultimate truth. This illusion is based on the central illusion of duality, namely that "reality" can be divided into separate compartments and that the separate mind has the right and the ability to decide which is true and untrue, good or bad.

Signs of a polluted Crown Chakra can be seen in people who are absolutely sure that they are right – especially those who have become fanatical – and are willing to force others into compliance. Another perversion is intellectualism where people can argue for or against any idea without ever going beyond the idea to a direct experience of the Spirit that is beyond words.

Corresponding ray: Second Ray
Color: Golden yellow
Elohim: Apollo and Lumina
Archangel: Jophiel and Christine
Chohan: Lord Lanto

PART TWO

Claiming Your Power to Heal

The dictations in this section were given by the ascended masters during a conference in Lourdes, France. Lourdes is known as a healing center. In the 19th century, Mother Mary appeared to a young peasant girl and helped her discover a spring where the water is thought to have miraculous healing properties. Since then, the Catholic Church has built a huge basilica that dwarfs the original grotto.

The chapters in Part Two will give you deeper teachings on the seven rays, the main chakras and how clearing your mind from certain imperfect beliefs can open up for a new approach to healing. You will learn many of the beliefs that block the flow of creative energy through the chakras. By coming to consciously see and dismiss these beliefs, you will not only open up the creative flow, you will also feel more connected to your I AM Presence. This sense of oneness is the key to ultimate happiness and inner peace.

3 | WHAT YOU NEED FROM OUTSIDE THE SEPARATE SELF

A dictation by Mother Mary

My beloved hearts, I, Mary, come to greet you in this very auspicious place. "Auspicious" being a concept and word used much in the Eastern teachings of the Buddha, who – although it would seem extremely alien to the many people who come to worship me in the form of the Catholic Virgin Mary – I am nevertheless one with, as the Divine Mother is always one with the Divine Father. The representative of the Divine Mother is one with the representative of the Divine Father for planet earth, the Lord of the World, Gautama.

I desire you to tune in to the unconditional peace of the Buddha. "Unconditional" being the key word. What is it that stands in the way of true healing? Is it not simply the conditions that you have come to accept after you came to accept the one underlying condition, the illusion that you could ever be separated from your Divine Father. You think that the Divine Mother and any expression of her Being could be separated from the Divine Father.

Consider the colors of the many statues that you see in this place. Light blue and white, chosen by me to represent me in this particular apparition, as representing the purity of the Divine Mother and the blue flame of the Will of God, the Divine Father. The light blue to signify that at the time of this apparition – and even beyond that, to the entire history of Christianity up to this point – there has not been the openness and the willingness to truly lock in to and accept the will of the Father. Christianity has promoted the image of the external God in the sky, the remote being up there that you can only reach through an external authority, such as the church hierarchy.

A lesson in humility

Some of you know that you have come here to have a lesson in humility, and this certainly applies to all of you. For each one of you that lesson may be slightly different, depending on your psychology. I ask you to contemplate what lesson in humility that you might personally need to go through and master in order to get the full benefit of this book—in order to reach the full potential that you can reach personally.

Certainly, you all have some lesson of humility, given that you are spiritual people living in the world and there is always the noise that seeks to distract you and take your attention away from that inner, unconditional peace of the Buddha. The demons of Mara are seeking to draw you out of your meditation under the Bo tree of your I AM Presence and make you identify with these material conditions. As you, indeed, will see so many people who come to this place being fully identified with the material conditions that are ravaging their physical bodies or their minds, and from which they seek healing from a miraculous source outside themselves.

I know full well that many spiritual people have a greater understanding, a far greater understanding, than the many

Catholics who come to this place. But I desire all of you to contemplate a general lesson in humility that applies to almost all of you, although of course with individual shadings. You may go down and look at the procession of the people who seek healing here. You may feel, as some of you have already felt, a sense of sorrow—of seeing people so trapped in a certain mindset that makes it very difficult for them to do anything on their own to achieve healing. They seek it only from an outer source, thinking there is no other way. The church that they follow has taken away the true teachings of Christ—that the kingdom of God is within you.

I ask you to contemplate honestly in your hearts whether you have a slight sense of being more advanced, sophisticated, mature, or in some sense superior to the people who come to this place seeking healing. I aim to show you that there is a deeper lesson in humility.

Many of you seek some form of healing for yourselves, perhaps physical, perhaps a deeper psychological-spiritual healing. Some of you have studied and applied these teachings for some time. Although you have made great progress, you know that there is still something that stands between you and your fullest potential, including your inner peace. You might contemplate why it is so difficult for you to overcome that last condition that is holding you back. This is where you might consider the people who come to this place seeking physical and in some cases psychological and spiritual healing.

Why some are healed and some are not

Some who come here are indeed healed, while others – many – come here and are not healed. You might say that there must be something in this place that has the ability to promote healing. Why is it that some people can be healed while others cannot? When you look at this with the wisdom of the heart, you realize that there is only one difference between those who are healed and those who are not. The one difference is that those who are healed can accept – fully – that they are healed. Those who are not healed have some condition that stands in the way of that full acceptance.

You might look at yourselves and what it is that is holding you back from breaking through to being who you truly are. You might see that you are not so different, after all, from the people who come here. Some of you also have a condition that prevents you from fully accepting the healing, accepting that you are healed. What happens in that acceptance is that you switch your sense of identity so that you no longer see yourself as a person who is not whole. You accept yourself as a person who is, indeed, whole. This is the switch in identity that you all need to make in order to be who you fully are. Of course, it does not happen in one grand moment, but in many small moments of accepting a new identity.

I ask you to consider that so many of you have the potential to truly experience a major healing from the use of this book. For that healing to come about, you must switch your identity so that you can accept yourself as a whole being. For that, you might need to look for some condition, some belief, that you have not seen before. I know all of your hearts. There is not one person who would not let go of their conditions if they could truly see them. The only thing that can stand in the way of you letting go of the condition is that you have not seen it, or seen it for what it is.

Be willing to humble yourself and see what you cannot now see. Be willing to look for the guru – that comes often in the form of an ant – to tell you what you cannot see on your own. Only by making that switch can you attain wholeness. You know enough to know that it will not come from some miraculous source outside yourself.

What you can and cannot heal on your own

There is a subtlety that I desire you to ponder. You may go and look at the people who are here, and you may see that they have a vastly different image of God than you have. They hold on to the image of the external God in the sky who can bestow upon them some miracle – perhaps through the Office of the Divine Mother, as they know me in a particular form – but looking outside themselves. You, of course, have been open to the reality, as Jesus said, that the kingdom of God is within you. You know that you can take an active part in seeking to change your consciousness.

Beware of the subtle temptation presented to Eve by the serpent in the garden, the temptation of thinking that you can become as God, knowing good and evil, meaning that you are sufficient in yourself. You think you do not need God, or other people, or an external guru or teacher to show you what you cannot see. The many people who come here to seek healing think they need it from a source outside themselves, meaning themselves as the total beings that they are, however they conceive it. You, of course, have a deeper understanding of yourself, but be aware that in order to become whole, you still need something from outside yourself. Only, that something is not from outside your total being. It is – pay attention now – from outside your separate sense of identity.

You will never be whole by doing anything from that separate sense of identity. You cannot come into *whole*-ness through the self that sees itself as separate from the whole, from the *all*-ness, from the River of Life. How can you become whole through the consciousness of separation? This is why you do need to reach beyond that separate self, and I suggest you ponder that you need several things from outside the separate self.

First, there is the Divine Father and the Will of God—but you cannot see it as an external will, but as your own higher being, the will of your own higher being, the will of who you truly are. You need the love of the Divine Mother that is truly the only force in this universe that can consume your conditions. In order to have them consumed, you must let go of those conditions, and for that, you need the wisdom of Christ, the vision of the Christ mind.

Natural, unconditional giving

What will it take to gain the full wisdom of the Christ mind? It will take a switch where you stop seeking growth, or healing, or wholeness, for yourself as the separate self. You see beyond the separate self and see the vision of the All—and thus seek to raise all life. You immerse yourself in the River of Life and seek to do for someone else unconditionally—not to raise up the separate self, but as a matter of nature.

There is a kind of natural selfless act that may seem insignificant. But it is significant in the sense that it is not done for any purpose of raising up the separate self or making it seem important in the eyes of others, or making it seem good in its own eyes. It springs from the effortlessness, the naturalness.

If you look at your lives, you can all see that you have had at least some experiences of this natural, unconditional giving. You will then see that this is what it is like to be in the River of Life. When you are in the River of Life, effortlessly extending a hand – giving a cup of cold water in Christ's name as a smile, as sharing your joy, as speaking a truth to someone you have never met before and will never meet again and thus expect nothing in return – that is when the universe smiles back at you. You may not get a return from the material world, at least not a direct return. But you will get a return from the universe. In that act of seeking to help another, you are helped with what you could not see, what you could not heal while you were still so wrapped up in the separate self.

The illogical logic of the outer mind

May I suggest to you that you also consider how sometimes that outer mind, that outer self, can have a logic that – when you look closer – is quite contradictory and illogical from a higher sense. Some of you have physical burdens in your bodies. This is a place where many people come for healing. How do they seek that healing? They seek so by walking through the pool of healing waters.

Some of you have said with your outer minds: "I am not going there, I am not doing *that*." Think about the logic of the outer mind so that you may step outside of it. Some of you have experienced what the medical profession will do to you and your bodies. Consider that you have let the doctors cut out parts from your bodies, expose you to radiation, toxic chemicals, inject medicines that have side effects. All this you have gone through, but then when you consider an act where you have to take off your clothes and walk through a pool of cold water, then that suddenly seems more difficult to do than what you have been exposed to from the doctors.

I am not thereby saying that you *should* go through the pool. I am simply saying that you should follow your heart—the answers from within. In order to hear that answer for you personally, you must neutralize the outer mind that has already ahead of time said: "Oh no, I am not doing *that*." You may learn that perhaps there are other aspects of your life where you have a tendency to say: "Oh no, I could not possibly do *that*." Therein lies the key to discovering your personal illusion.

What is the condition that is holding you back from wholeness? When you say: "Oh no, *that* could not possibly apply to me. I could not be worthy. I could not do that," or whatever it may be that you say to yourself. This is your particular condition that reinforces the image that you are separated from your source, separated from other people, separated from the whole, separated from the River of Life.

I am not separated from you. I am not only *in* the River of Life, but as one with the Divine Mother, *I AM* the River of Life. When you set yourself apart from the River of Life, you set yourself apart from *me*. By the Law of Free Will, I cannot help you. I cannot help you unless you are willing to accept that help from outside the separate self. Even the people who come here that are healed, they too have – certainly without knowing it consciously, certainly without having the understanding you have – switched their sense of identity so that they could accept something outside the separate self. In that acceptance is the healing.

Ponder these words. And ponder them, as I ask you to give the *Eightfold Healing Invocation* [See *www.transcendencetoolbox.com*] in a way you may not have given it before, by truly tuning in to the words. I assure you that for each one who may ever hear or read this release from my heart, there is one sentence in that invocation that can help you see your particular illusion and unlock that illusion. Then you may step out of separation and realize that you are not stepping into oneness, you are now accepting the oneness that was always there.

It is indeed with great joy that I, and the rest of the ascended masters, welcome you to this book. May it be all that it can be for each one of you. Be sealed in the unconditional joy of the heart of the Mother and the unconditional peace in the heart of the Buddha.

4 | KARMA IS NOT WHAT YOU THINK

By Kim Michaels

I once had a discussion with a person who was saying he had thought about whether he was a bad or evil person. I asked: "So what if you are?" The way he reacted was: "Well then at least I would have certainty about it instead of worrying about it."

I understood that, because the reality is that we cannot overcome our fears until we face them. If we have a fear about a certain condition, and the condition is so terrible we actually try to run away from even acknowledging we have the fear, then we cannot face the fear and so we cannot overcome it. We are stuck in this no-man's land of wondering: "Am I really a bad person? Am I this or am I that?"

In the following discussion with the person I could see that there was something odd about his self-image and his perspective. He was looking at himself and the world from a certain vantage point. My belief is that it is a shift in perception that is needed before we are free. For a long time I was trying to change his perception, give him a different perspective, get him to snap out of his way of looking at it, and get him to look at it from a different perspective. I was doing everything I could think of, but after a half hour or so, it finally dawned on me: "I am not getting anywhere!"

I did not know what to do at that point. I just centered in my heart and what came to me was: "You know what? Enough of this, I want you to know that I am not trying to change you at all. I love and accept you unconditionally for who you are right now."

He said: "Well, but that makes me feel like this..." I said: "Good. I love and accept you unconditionally for feeling that way." He said: "Yeah, but now I am feeling like this." I said: "Good. I love and accept you unconditionally for feeling this way." After we had done this I don't know how many times, he finally said: "Oh, now I see I am going around in circles."

Why we beat ourselves up

What I took away from that experience is that there are two kinds of people on the spiritual path:

- Some people are not yet willing to look at themselves and the beam in their own eye. They are trying to avoid seeing that maybe they are not perfect or maybe they are not good enough. In a sense, they might seem prideful or arrogant, but the reality is they have very low self-esteem. They are trying to use the spiritual path and teachings to build up their self-esteem. You actually have to have a certain amount of self-esteem before you can look at the beam in your own eye and consider that maybe you are not perfect or that maybe you need to change.

- Most spiritual people are more than willing to look at the beam in our own eye, and we have been doing so for a long time, even to the point where we are beating ourselves up and feel we are at fault and there is this and that wrong with us. The consciousness is that you are so willing to look for what is wrong with you that you are always looking for what is wrong with you.

After I had been pondering this, it suddenly hit me, and here is the statement that came to me: "The only thing that is wrong with you is the consciousness that there is something wrong with you."

We are conscious beings, extensions of God. We are, in our inner beings, pure. We are as pure now as when we were originally created by God. God cannot create anything impure. We have taken on a certain belief that there is a specific thing that is wrong with us. We are trying to fix the thing that is wrong with us, in order to get back to the purity. We are focused on the specific flaw, but it is not the flaw that is wrong. What is wrong is the belief that we are not pure in the first place—that there is something wrong with us.

This is what the ego and the false teachers want us to do. They want us to focus on that outer thing so we think that if we can fix *that*, then we are going to be perfect and God is going to have to accept us. But God has already accepted us. In the beginning, God created us—and then, as the Bible says: "And he saw that it was good."

He created us good, and in God's mind, we are good. We are as pure as when we were created. There is a consciousness in the world that says we are not good. That consciousness has camouflaged itself by saying we are not good because of this or that condition in the world, this or that standard that we are not living up to. That takes our attention away from the reality that we can never become impure.

What we really are

That is why the masters have given us the concept of the Conscious You, who is what it was created to be. In your mind – right now – you are who you think you are.

There are all these kinds of consciousnesses created in the world by the illusion of separation or the consciousness of duality. It is almost like you are walking into a theater, and they have these little metal racks that are holding up the costumes for the different roles you can play in the theater. You can choose to take on whatever costume you want, if that is what you want to experience.

We are created as conscious beings, and as conscious beings we experience. That is what we are here for—to experience. God has given us complete free will. We can choose to create any experience we want for ourselves, and God loves and accepts us no matter what we experience. He has given us free will and told us we are free to experience whatever we want to experience. He has given us the material universe, which is a mirror that reflects back to us whatever we project out that we want to experience.

What we have done is we have said: "Oh, I want to experience *this*," or "I am putting on *this* costume." But then comes the falsity – the serpent – which says: "Oh, there is something wrong with you for putting on that costume. You should not have done that, you have fallen from grace, you have eaten the forbidden fruit, now there is something wrong with you."

Let us say you are in a costume for Hamlet. You focus on that character of Hamlet and you say: "What is wrong with Hamlet? What did he do wrong? I have got to fix Hamlet! I have got to fix him."

You will never get out of the costume by trying to fix what is wrong with the costume. You will only get out of it by realizing: "This is not who I am. I have just taken on the costume.

There was nothing wrong with me taking on the costume. God gave me free will. I took on the costume because I wanted to experience what it was like to see the world from inside that costume, that state of consciousness. I wanted to know what it is like to play that role in the 'All The World's a Stage' play—the drama of life. What does it feel like to see the world from that particular vantage point?"

There is nothing wrong with it. If you recognize that you actually no longer enjoy having that experience, you no longer enjoy seeing the world from that vantage point, then you have to realize that if you want to get out of it, you do not get out of it by trying to fix what is wrong with the costume, by fixing the problem or the outer condition. You get out of it by realizing: "This is not who I am. This is just something I have taken on. Just as God gave me the right to take it on, he has given me the right to take it off any time and to leave it behind!"

There is an Alpha and Omega interplay. The Alpha of the illusion is that there is something wrong with you for taking on the costume. The Omega is that in order to get out of it, you have to pay a price. You have to suffer enough, you have to pay a penance. You have to balance your karma. In other words— you cannot just walk away from it. That is what the ego is trying to tell you.

The ego was created out of taking on the illusion, and it is going to die when you take off the costume and walk away. It does not want to die, so it is telling you: "You cannot just walk away from me! You have sinned. You have to pay back your sins, Jesus has to pay back your sins. You have to pay back your karma. You have to beat yourself up for three hundred and fifty-seven embodiments before you can be good enough to walk away from me."

That is the lie!

A new view of karma

Someone was asking me about karma and she said: "But maybe I have to be in the situation I am in because I have karma from a past life and I did something wrong." That is the old traditional teaching about karma, and I have recently received a higher teaching on it.

What is karma? It is like everything else in the material universe. Everything is an image that is projected onto the Ma-ter light. For example, in a past life you might have been a princess who abused your power and treated people badly. But what really happened was that you took on a self-image of yourself as a bad person. Now you think you have to beat yourself up and punish yourself, until you have punished yourself enough that you no longer need to feel you are a bad person. Now you have suffered ten times more than the people you made suffer, so you must be okay or fixed now. This projection from outside ourselves mirrors back our belief that we can't just walk away from our role.

In Mother Mary's *Eightfold Healing Invocation* it says that everything in the material universe is an image that is projected onto the Ma-ter light many times every second. Your karma is not some external force. Your karma is the image in your consciousness that you are projecting onto the Ma-ter light hundreds of times a second. You do not see it because you never *can* see the filmstrip or the individual picture, you just see it as a blur. You do not see that you are projecting this, and that is why you are susceptible to the illusion that this is a continuous movement, that it is something coming from outside of yourself.

5 | FIRST RAY: A NON-LINEAR VIEW OF KARMA

A dictation by Master MORE

MORE I AM. You should know that I come quickly and I leave quickly. When I have had my say, I do not care to observe the usual politeness of ending in a certain way. When enough is enough, then I move on.

That is a clue for all of you. When enough is enough—just move on. Throw off the shackles of whatever consciousness you have accepted. You have a right to any experience you desire, but you should know that when you have had enough of a given experience, you can indeed move on.

This is the master key to true healing. It is the key to the restoration of true healing. Take a look at how people seek healing on this planet. Take a look at the medical profession that you have today. What is it they promise you between the lines? They promise you that when your body manifests a disease, they can give you some mechanical way to heal it. You do not need to address the consciousness that precipitated the disease in the body. You do not need to look at the beam in your own eye.

This is what they promise you. Is that not what so many religions have been promising people throughout the ages? "If you will follow our outer religion, if you will observe the rules and regulations we give you, then you will one day enter the kingdom of God without looking at the beam in your own eye."

Ah, this is indeed the promise. How many people have believed it, only to find out – after that embodiment – that it was a false promise and they had to come back to earth? They are becoming increasingly suspicious of religion, seeing the hypocrisy of a religion where even the priests themselves believe that it is enough to follow the outer observances. They think they can do whatever they can get away with, hidden behind the facade of a given church, such as the Catholic one with its rampant child abuse that is surely a desecration of everything Jesus stood for. Did he not say that it was better to have a millstone put around your neck and be thrown into the sea than to hurt one of these little ones?

You see it in so many other churches where a pastor in a fundamentalist church recently was exposed as having said that: "You can be a man of God and have a little fun on the side." What hypocrisy to claim that you represent God and yet, you think that what you can hide from your fellow men is also hidden from God. God is not up in the sky looking down at you, but it is within you, waiting for when you will seek the Divine Lover who loves you as his beloved son or daughter.

Honesty is the foundation for true healing

In order to restore true healing, we must begin with a solid foundation. We must begin with the First Ray of the will of God. What, then, is the quality of the First Ray? You may think of it as the will of God, you may think of it as the power of God, but how about another quality: *honesty*.

5 | First Ray: A Non-Linear View of Karma

Honesty, my beloved, is that not a quality of the First Ray? Is it not an expression of the will of God and the power of God? What is the core of honesty? Is it not oneness with the will of God? Truly, God is the ultimate honest being—for God cannot hide anything from itself.

You may have heard the old question asked by the linear mind: "If God is almighty, can God create a rock so big that God cannot lift it?" God is One, so God cannot create anything that is hidden from itself—and thus the honesty. Consider the very core of dishonesty. It is the belief that something can be hidden, that it is possible to say or do certain things while thinking something different within. Indeed, the serpent, to Eve, portrayed itself as the liberator, come to set her free from the shackles of the command of the spiritual teacher in the garden. Right there is where the foundation of disease is laid—in the dishonesty, in the illusion that something can be hidden.

Consider honesty and the message of your free-will right to have any experience you want, to enter the theater of life and put on any costume that you desire to experience. There is nothing wrong, sinful – or whatever you want to call it – in trying on many different costumes on the stage of life. This is what God has given you a right to do.

When you begin to create the belief that you are trapped in a particular costume and that some external force is preventing you from moving on, dishonesty enters the picture. Why do I say dishonesty? Because when you consider this from a realistic perspective, you realize that God has given you complete freedom to try on any costume you like. God does not force you to try on any costume whatsoever, which means what? It means that you, yourself, *you* are choosing which costume to put on.

When you build the belief that you have not chosen your current situation – that your situation is not the result of your own choices, past and present – you put yourself in a situation where you are trapped in what we have called the catch-22.

When you imagine that some external force has put you in your current situation, who can set you free from that situation? Logically, it must also be an external force, must it not? That means you have given away your power to change your situation. You have put yourself in a passive mode of waiting for some external force to do it for you. You have done what you also have a right to do—you have given away your free will to an external power.

Again, God has given you *free* will. You have a right to do this. You have a right, as Maitreya explains in his book, to decide that you no longer want to decide. You can make the decision that you no longer want to make decisions. Therefore, you create the graven image that there is some external power that is ruling your life.

Beware the subtlety of free will

The serpent will whisper in your ear that you have a right to create that role, that costume, and to try on what it feels like to be disempowered. From the perspective of the linear intellectual mind, it will seem that the serpent is right. But the subtlety here is that when you do give away your power, then how can you step outside of the costume? How can you just leave it behind and walk away from it? Do you see the subtlety?

One cannot necessarily say from a linear, analytical perspective that the serpent is wrong. God has given you complete freedom and does not limit your choices. You may try on any costume, but no matter which costume you take on, God accepts you for the being that God created as an extension of itself. Any time you desire to put off the old man and put on the new man in Christ, the new man in Oneness, God will welcome you with open arms. God does not limit your freedom to take on a costume or to take it off again.

The serpentine logic does indeed limit your freedom. When you accept the lie, the illusion, that some external force – such as the angry God in the sky who has caused you to be born in sin – has precipitated your situation, you cannot simply believe that you can just take off the costume, put off the old man and be reborn and become a new being in Christ. While God has given you power and the freedom to exercise that power, the serpent and the serpentine consciousness aims to take away your power.

I, as the representative of the Will of God, will say that the overall will of God is that you exercise your free will and create any experience you want so that you have an opportunity to learn. That is why you have the potential to separate from oneness and to believe in the serpentine lie and to follow the false path, the downward path, of separating yourself further and further from oneness.

This is your right. I champion it. But my point here is that it is not in any way, shape, or form the will of God that you should suffer or be stuck in a limited sense of identity. It is not the will of God for you personally that you should become less, in the sense that you see yourself as less than the pure Being that God created.

The Alpha and the Omega of healing

There is an Alpha aspect of the will of God, which has given you complete freedom of choice. There is an Omega aspect of the will of God, which desires you to use your freedom of choice to become *more*, not *less*.

What is the lesson in terms of true healing? What is true healing? *It is self-healing!*

What is the purpose of life? It is the growth of the self, the growth of your self-awareness. This is the entire purpose for the world of form where you might start out with a very localized sense of identity, being identified with some material form, such as your physical body. No matter how limited that identity might be, you have the potential to grow in self-awareness until you reach the consciousness of the Being out of which Being you are. This growth is self-growth. It is not forced upon you by God, for self-growth cannot be forced.

The beginning of true healing is indeed when you recognize that you have chosen to separate from Oneness. The reason your physical body or your mind needs healing is that you have made choices that limited yourself, rather than expanding your sense of self. You became trapped in an illusion whereby you no longer see yourself as a spiritual being who has temporarily taken on a particular role and costume in the drama of the material universe. Instead, you think that you are trapped in this universe, trapped in a particular role. This is giving away your power to heal yourself.

How can you exercise that power? When you truly understand free will, you recognize that it is *free*, completely free, my beloved. God has given you a will that is completely *free*. This means that as you can choose to take on a particular costume – no matter what that costume may be like – you do, at any moment, have the complete freedom to separate yourself from the costume—to just take it off, to let it drop from you, to let the old man die and to be reborn in a new sense of self. This is recognizing the power that God has given you. It is the ego and the false teachers, those in the serpentine consciousness, who are seeking to take away your power by making you believe that you either *are* that costume or that you cannot just take it off.

Opening up to a new view of karma

When you look at humankind, there is indeed a dividing line that you might observe. Many are still completely identified with the physical body and their growing up in a particular circumstance of family, culture, nationality, religion, ethnicity, race or whatever division you have. The more spiritual people have started to awaken from that illusion and realize they are more than these outer identities and labels and divisions. Still, when you begin to awaken and realize you are more, you are faced with the lie that you cannot simply walk away from your old identity. You have made mistakes, you have sinned. Somehow your sins must be repaid, your karma must be balanced.

May I ask you to partake of a little thought experiment here. Let us take the old teaching given in the East – even a teaching that we have found it necessary to give in previous dispensations of the ascended masters – namely, the teaching that karma is some external force. You have committed errors in a past life and you owe some kind of debt to life and the scales must be balanced. The energy you have misqualified needs to be rebalanced.

Now, this is not necessarily incorrect. You have free will to do anything you want. But what is it that allows you to do anything in the material world? It is that you are receiving a portion of spiritual light from your own I AM Presence, which you then express through your four lower bodies. You are, of course, responsible for what you do with that energy. You cannot permanently leave the earth behind until you have at least raised up all energy that you have qualified with the vibration of non-love, thus limiting all life.

You must come to a point where your presence on this earth is at least a balance—you do not pull life down. Of course, you did not come here to pull life down, nor did you come here to struggle for hundreds of embodiments only to come back to a balance point and then leave. You came here to bring a positive gift, to shine your light in the darkness of the material universe and to ultimately raise up this sphere, as Maitreya explains, to where it can ascend and outpicture the kingdom of God. Let us consider that you are a co-creator who has experimented with free will over many lifetimes. You have taken on a certain role, identified yourself as a separate being, and you have used the energy given to you by your I AM Presence to seek to own and possess things for that separate self. Perhaps you have been seeking to raise it up in comparison to others, thereby attaining some prominent position in society that enabled you to put other people down so that you would seem more important.

There are, of course, many ways to make such karma, as we call it. Now look at this realistically and recognize that there is nothing that can be said with words that cannot be twisted and turned by the serpentine consciousness and the serpentine logic. This is the essence of the serpentine logic, namely that when you eat of the fruit, you become "wise as God," you become as God, "knowing good and evil." This means that you enter into the duality consciousness where you now think – your ego thinks – that it has the right to define good and evil in an ultimate sense.

This is why there are religions on this earth that define themselves as being the only true religion, thereby defining the absolute belief that all non-members will burn forever in hell. There are those who have espoused a particular political philosophy as superior to any other, therefore giving rise to the belief that it is justified that they seek to suppress any other philosophy, imposing their own system upon the rest of the world.

The serpentine consciousness entraps you in the belief that the forms you see in the material world have some ultimate reality. You cannot simply walk away from them. You are crucified by the form, by the image, by the consciousness. As was outpictured by Jesus, you enter into the drama of life, and they may indeed "crucify" you. It seems like there was, even for Jesus, nothing he could do but play that role.

Look at the stations of the cross outpictured through the Catholic tradition. Jesus is condemned to death. Jesus accepts his cross. However, even that is a passive act of accepting what others want to put upon him. Jesus falls, someone helps Jesus carry the cross, someone wipes his tears, someone attempts to tell him not to go through with this. He is nailed to the cross, he dies, he is taken down, he is put in the tomb. All passive things, my beloved.

What is missing from the steps of the cross, the stations of the cross? Well, many things, but for one, the reality that Jesus *chose* to enter Jerusalem, knowing full well what might happen. Most importantly, while hanging on the cross, he *chose* to give up the ghost, thereby in an instant putting off that sense of the separate self, showing the potential that all of you have to instantly let the old being, the old self die. Thereby you do not cease to exist, as the false teachers and the ego would have you believe, but indeed you are reborn into a greater sense of self, the self that you still are in the eyes of God.

A revolutionary view of karma

There is a deeper reality. Returning to the concept of karma, what is the illusion superimposed upon the concept by the serpentine mind? Understand that the serpentine mind is based on separation, and when you are separated from your source, what must you believe about the power of God? You must believe that it can only come from outside yourself.

When you see yourself as a separate being, you cannot accept that the power of God can come from inside yourself. You are susceptible to the belief that in one extreme you need an external savior. In the other extreme you need to do something down here on earth, as a separate self, in order to be redeemed of your sin or to balance your karma.

Be aware of what I am telling you. Be alert now, and perhaps even step back and see how your own outer, analytical mind will seek to play tricks on you so that you either do not hear my words or do not hear the true meaning. What was said earlier? You have come to accept that there is something wrong with you, something particular, some particular problem that blocks you from entering the kingdom of God. What is truly wrong with *you* is the concept that there is something wrong.

Where does that concept come from? From the illusion of separation, from the creation of the separate self! There is indeed, one might say, something wrong with the separate self, if one wants to think in dualistic terms. But there is nothing wrong with you, the being that you truly are.

From a greater perspective there is not even anything wrong with the separate self, for God does not think in terms of right or wrong. God only thinks in terms of what is real and what is unreal. Only that which is created in oneness, as an expression of oneness, only *that* is real. Anything created out of the consciousness of separation is not real and thus cannot affect that part of you which is real. It cannot limit it, cannot encage it in a particular role, or costume, or form, or sense of self.

Do you begin to see what karma truly is? You have been so accustomed to, so conditioned by the dualistic mind, that you have come to believe that there really are two opposites—and that one of those opposites is God and the other opposite is that which is anti-God. This is the arrogance of the fallen beings who in their spiritual pride believe that by rebelling against God they actually had an affect on God and the spiritual Beings who have not separated from oneness. God is not in the opposite polarity of separation. God is One, undivided, indivisible, unconditional. How can any condition oppose that which is unconditional?

Do you see that in oneness there can be no conditions? How do you separate from oneness? *By creating conditions!* But how can you create conditions? You must create two conditions, at least two, that oppose each other.

If there is not the opposition, then you still have oneness and so you have no separation.

I AM the master of the Will of God. I have my beloved friends on the other six rays. Am I in opposition to Saint Germain because I am on the first and he is on the seventh, thus on opposite ends of the linear scale? How could this be possible? How could the Will of God oppose the Freedom of God, when it is the will of God that all beings be free—and that you become free by being one with the will of God that raises all life?

You may think that in a past life you created bad karma and that in order to ascend, you must balance that karma by creating good karma. But good and bad are dualistic conditions. You cannot neutralize, balance or negate one dualistic condition by going into the opposite. You cannot overcome a problem with the same state of consciousness that created the problem.

What is karma? It is that you use your creative power through the filter of a separate, dualistic self. Anything you do through that filter creates karma that separates you from oneness. It was because you came to see yourself as a separate being that you became focused on the self, and therefore might have done something that was egotistical or selfish according to the standard definition—thus creating what most people see as negative karma. It was the illusion that you are a separate being that caused this.

Well, then, how can you counteract that by doing something else through the separate self? Do you see that the very concept that you have created negative karma as a separate self and that you have to balance it as a separate self is illogical, contradictory? As long as you are striving to balance the karma that you see as being made by the separate self, you are reinforcing the illusion that you are a separate self.

When balancing karma hinders your ascension

You may think I am saying the same thing over and over—and I am. But I am saying it with slightly different angles, for I am giving you a geometric thoughtform. If you do not see it from one perspective, perhaps you will see it from a slightly different one. The idea is this: Consider how the concept that you have to balance your karma reinforces the sense that you are a separate being. Does it not imply that you cannot ascend – meaning, in its essence, come back to oneness – until you have balanced the karma?

In your mind you are saying: "I am a separate being, and I must remain a separate being until, at some future time, I have balanced the karma made as a separate being and – poof – I will one day ascend without fully understanding how this is happening." Some of you have indeed, in previous ascended master dispensations, been given an image – or we might say you have accepted an image – that even the ascension is a somewhat passive process where you balance your karma and then the rest just happens automatically.

This is not so! How do you ascend? By taking back the power of your will! Do you think that I, Master MORE, am standing up here in heaven seeking to force people to ascend? What would be accomplished by that? They would enter heaven with the same state of consciousness they have right now. We do not want any long faces in heaven, nor do we want any other of the theatrical faces that you see on earth. We want you, as you are—in oneness.

We are not thereby saying that you return to heaven the same as you came out. You learn by being in these denser realms, you expand your sense of self beyond what it was created as. But as you come back into oneness, you recognize that you and we are not different. You are extensions of our very own Beings.

My proposition to you is simple. Consider that you, as a separate being, come to the conclusion that you are – after all – a spiritual being, that you came from heaven and that you want to return. In order to return you have to balance your karma, so you set about this with the same consciousness of separation.

Some progress can be made this way. You *can* balance energy. We have the Alpha of your state of consciousness that you superimpose upon the energy, the Ma-ter light. We have the Omega of the Ma-ter light taking on a lower vibration as a result of the images you superimpose upon it. You can actually, to some degree, fulfill that balancing act, for certainly a selfless act will balance karma, as you call it. But I must tell you that you cannot complete this process while you still see yourself as a separate self. It is not possible.

Why is it not possible? Because of what I have explained—you can only enter the kingdom of heaven by becoming one with the power of God within you. You can only become one with *that* by overcoming the separate self.

You must *choose* to ascend. It is not a matter of fulfilling outer requirements and then, "poof," you are in the ascended realm. It has to be a decision, a choice.

A faster way to rise above karma

While you *can* make some progress from the consciousness of the separate self, consider another route. Consider that instead of focusing on balancing karma, as some external force, you instead listen to the words of Christ. Did he not say: "Seek ye first the kingdom of God and his righteousness and all these things shall be added unto you."

What is the kingdom of God? It is indeed the Christ consciousness based on oneness where you have the righteousness – the right use – of your creative power. You use it to raise up the All instead of the separate self. Consider that instead of focusing on an outer, somewhat mechanical, act of balancing karma, you focus on switching your sense of identity, switching your self-image, switching your perspective. You are going through a seismic shift in identity where you no longer see separation but see oneness.

What will happen in the process? What will happen is that you take back your own power, you reconnect to the higher being you are and now you can say with Jesus: "I and my father are one. My father worketh hitherto and I work."

When you come into that state of oneness – at least some degree of oneness although not yet the full Christhood – and you see that you still have some karma left, how hard do you think it is to balance that karma when you have the power of God flowing through you to do it? It is much easier to walk the path by first seeking oneness than by seeking to fulfill an outer requirement of balancing karma, and then thinking that oneness will come automatically. Thereby, you are limiting yourself – perhaps for the rest of this embodiment – to only exercising the power that comes through your separate self, instead of the power of the greater being that you are.

Illusions, my beloved—illusions! How subtle is the logic of the serpentine mind? How subtle it is when you look at it from inside the separate self. How obvious it is when you reach for the Christ mind and gain that unconditional perspective where you do not see truth as expressed in a particular word or teaching. You have followed the call of Christ: "God is a Spirit, and they that worship him must worship him in Spirit and in truth."

When you know this Spirit of Truth, you know the vibration of truth, and you have the ultimate co-measurement, the ultimate guiding rod, the staff of Moses, that will part the waters of the dead sea—as a representation of the duality consciousness. You may then walk across safely and yet, when the hoards of death come behind you, the waters of their own dualistic consciousness close upon them. They are swept up in the turmoil, while you walk to the other side, to the land of Israel, that which *Is Real*.

A non-linear view of reincarnation

Consider that you have heard that El Morya, Master MORE, was embodied as Thomas More, as Thomas Beckett, as this or that Master, or this or that historical figure. Finally, if you go way back, I was embodied as Abraham. But you see, Thomas More is dead. Abraham is dead. Although you may think that I was embodied as Abraham, I tell you it is not so. For before Abraham was, I AM.

Am I thereby denying that there was a previous embodiment as Abraham? Am I denying the teaching given? No, I am not. I am asking you to step up higher and realize that as an ascended being, I have become one with a greater Being out of which the being came that embodied as Abraham. The sense of self that embodied as Abraham and as these other figures is no more. I AM MORE. I have risen beyond any earthly sense of self. I have taken off the costumes. I have stood naked before the pool of healing waters and I walked through it to the other side. I AM reborn, as you can indeed be reborn, my beloved.

Follow your bliss! Consider what gives you the greatest joy, for you will find that what gives you the greatest joy is the sense of oneness with your inner Being, with your God Flame, with the greater spiritual Being out of which you have come. Use that as the measuring rod for whether to do this or to do that here on this stage of life.

What gives you the greatest joy is what brings you closer to oneness with your greater Being. If something takes your energies down, takes your attention out, makes you feel that you have to live up to a certain image, that you have to step into a certain role, then step back and say: "This is not for me!"

The female representatives are currently more in tune with their spiritual beings and their divine plans than many men. You sense that when a man approaches you and may have the best of intentions – but in his mind he has a certain image of how you should be if you accept his proposal – you feel that he is taking you away from your bliss.

Step back and look for what is your bliss, and follow that—as many of you have already done. I am simply bringing to your conscious attention that you can become more aware of this, that you may more consciously sense in your heart what is your bliss, what expands your being, your sense of being, your sense of joy.

This can be done in many ways. You can indeed do it through devotion, as many people have done throughout the ages, being devoted to God, to Jesus, to Mother Mary, to the Buddha, to Krishna or to other true spiritual representatives. There are, as described in Hinduism, several ways to God, several forms of yoga. Follow the one that gives you the greatest joy, and do not see that other people are wrong for following *their* bliss.

I say to you, my beloved, I AM the representative of the Will of God because I AM unconditionally devoted to the Will of God. I love the Will of God. I love the Power of God, expressed with the unconditional love that raises all life.

How can you ultimately come into oneness with the will and the power of God? Can you take the power of God by force through the separate self? Nay, you can only love the will and the power—the will being to raise up all life. When you have no other motive, then the power of God will flow through you to raise all life.

Be sealed, my beloved, in my love—for the Will of God and for you. It is the will of God that you have free will, and you may think that if you make "wrong" choices I will not love you. But God gave you free will and thus – whatever choice you have made – I love you unconditionally.

This, of course, does not prevent me from being the stern master who is not seeking to rebuke you, but to give you that sense of co-measurement—that the serpentine mind cannot argue with, cannot twist and turn. It is immovable, like the Rock of Christ. When you are honest, you will seek that immovability of the Rock of Christ in order to be able to discern the real from the unreal.

My beloved, *I AM real*. Will you acknowledge that you, too, are real? Then be sealed in the Flame of Reality.

6 | SECOND RAY: WISDOM IS A VITAL FORCE OF HEALING

A dictation by Lord Lanto

Wisdom is the principal thing, and with all thy getting, get understanding. I come to give you wisdom. The name that I have used before is Lanto, but I AM MORE. For as my beloved brother, MORE, I too, have transcended any particular manifestation or form ever worn on earth.

I aim to begin by taking you on a meditation. As you might listen also to the music behind my words and flow with both the words and the music. Envision in how many societies wisdom has been written down in books, stored in dusty and musty libraries. People have thought that in order to acquire wisdom, they need to come to centers of learning where men have gathered together these books containing the wisdom. You have to then isolate and insulate yourself in these temples of learning, so to speak, and acquire that wisdom from without.

I would take you out of the dusty and musty libraries of the world. Come with me, flow with me, as I fling open the doors to the library and invite you to follow me into the bright sunshine where you suddenly realize that while you had your eyes glued to a book, spring has arrived.

The birds are singing, the flowers are blossoming—radiating their subtle fragrance that does not impose, but still draws the senses to a new sense of reverence for the miracle of life, repeated every year when the trees turn green and the birds sing. Not, as the "wise" ones say, that they sing to attract a mate or defend a territory. While they do sing to take care of these biological needs, what drives them to sing is the River of Life flowing through them—the joy that wants to be expressed. As we walk away from the library without looking back, we walk into a beautiful meadow with tall green grass, millions of wild flowers, butterflies, bees. The birds are singing, the meadowlark is hovering in the air, radiating his song of joy to all, whether they listen or not.

We will indeed listen, as we feel the soft earth under our bare feet and walk into this meadow, immersing ourselves in the sense and sounds and the sights of spring—the feeling, as we feel the earth, as we bend down to feel the softness of a flower petal. We go beyond the senses, and we sense that behind the outer sensory impressions there is a vibration of spring. A vitality of this unstoppable force, the Fountain of Youth that is welling up in the trees, in the birds and the flowers—in everything, including now, ourselves. We feel from the earth this fountain of youth flowing into our bodies, flowing up through our legs, into the torso, into the head and creating a golden ring of light around our heads.

Tune in to the vibration of this vital force that animates all life. Ask yourself: "How do the birds know what to sing?" How does the meadowlark know to sing in a different way than the robin? How does a particular flower know to be yellow and not blue or red? How do the trees know to sprout a certain kind of leaves so that the maple trees do not by accident bear acorns or the cherry trees grow apples?

There can be only one thing that makes all this possible and it is wisdom. It is not the kind of wisdom that you find in the dusty libraries. It is the vital, ever-flowing wisdom. Although cycles are repeated every year in nature, wisdom itself is forever transcending itself, becoming *more* in that flow. Because wisdom is one with the River of Life, my beloved.

Know wisdom as a living force

What is true wisdom? Is it the kind of wisdom that calls people to isolate and insulate themselves in a dusty library where they have their eyes glued to a book? Nay, my beloved. When they are so focused on this worldly wisdom, they separate themselves from the River of Life. You indeed see so many institutions of higher learning on this planet where the teachers and professors have isolated themselves, not only from society but from the River of Life. They think that because they have acquired such great wisdom, they are now self-sufficient, self-contained, and they know everything that they need to know.

If all the wise men stepped forward, could they indeed make one little plant grow a flower? Could they make the meadowlark sing? Nay, they could not.

The true wisdom is not what causes you to isolate yourself from the River of Life. The true wisdom is the vital force that magnetizes you to immerse yourself in the River of Life and flow with that wisdom—instead of using the worldly wisdom to build some kind of palace for the separate self where the separate self can feel important and enthroned. It feels that it has its surroundings, even the entire world, under control. As you indeed see some of the "wise" men in the world, and even some of the "wise" women in academic circles, who believe that they know so much that they feel confident in declaring that there is no God.

How do they explain that the meadowlark sings? They cannot come up with a mechanical cause for the miracle of spring. Do they really have wisdom? Do they have understanding? Or do they merely have a graven image that they reinforce and polish, feeling that if so many people around the world accept it, if so many researchers and scientists contribute to it, then it must be real.

Why people build temples

Where is the little boy who cries: "But the emperor has nothing on?" I, then, will play the role of that little boy. I look to many of you to also step into that role and, in various ways, cry out. Not with *those* words, but simply pointing out that there is something missing, that there is more to understand about the miracle of life, and that life cannot be reduced to a machine that follows mechanical laws.

I ask you to consider how human beings have built temples—temples of learning, temples of religion. You might go down in this place of Lourdes to make a few observations. What started the miracles of Lourdes, the miracles that the best doctors in the world cannot explain in terms of mechanical laws? What started it was an apparition of Mother Mary, a force beyond the material world. Although Mother Mary was revered by a human institution with huge temples, she did not appear to the Pope or in a basilica. She appeared to a humble girl walking through the meadows. She appeared in a humble grotto that none of the people who lived here had paid attention to, for that was where they had sent the swine to forage.

Is there not a message there that the "wise" ones have failed to see? Look at that humble grotto, and then step back

– mentally, so that you do not fall into the river behind it – step back mentally and look up and say: "Oh, but who built that elaborate cathedral up there on the rock?" Ask yourself, given that Mother Mary appeared to a humble girl in a humble place, did she really want such an elaborate structure to be built? Did she want something that takes the attention away from what is the center of this place of healing, namely that there is something flowing from outside the material universe, and *that* is why healing can occur. People accept that, even though it cannot be explained by the worldly wisdom.

See how the ego and those entrapped in it could not build a simple, humble chapel. They had to build something that actually demonstrates, by its size, the insecurity of their egos and the institution that they claim to be the only true church of Christ. Look how similar things have happened in the worldly institutions of universities where, again, you see the need to build elaborate structures, to accumulate massive amounts of information and research, yet they still cannot explain why a flower appears.

I am not thereby saying that there is necessarily anything wrong with having an institution – be it religious, or an institution of learning – for there can be value in having a focal point. What I am saying is simply that if the institution becomes a closed circle, becomes an end in itself – by shutting off the flow of wisdom – that institution no longer serves the purpose of setting people free by helping them immerse themselves in the River of Life. Indeed, it serves the opposite purpose of making them feel more and more trapped in a worldly sense of identity. Look at the Catholic priests and popes and cardinals, how trapped they are in a certain mindset. How alien it would feel to them to hear Mother Mary speak through a human being who is not part of their institution.

Then look at the popes and the priests and the cardinals of the scientific and intellectual world who claim to be so different from religion, but have built institutions that are so similar to religious institutions that one can only chuckle over the fact that they themselves cannot see it. They cannot see that they have created their own priesthood, their own doctrines, their own rituals. These intellectuals from the world of science would also feel it very alien if they were to even consider that perhaps there is a spiritual world beyond the material, and perhaps a spiritual being, such as myself, can speak through a physical mouthpiece that has become the open door.

What is true wisdom?

Certainly, those who are the spiritual people can see that something is missing from the worldly wisdom, from the religious wisdom that also seeks to accumulate in underground musty libraries. Look how the religious libraries of the ages release only what they think will reinforce the image they want to portray, keeping everything else under lock and key so that no one will see it and be able to question their doctrines.

Again, what is true wisdom? True wisdom is that which challenges your current perception, your current self-image, and magnetically draws you to look beyond it—to reconnect to that ever-flowing fount of wisdom that is always transcending. True wisdom can never be captured by a religious doctrine, by a scientific theory, by any amount of research, even a political philosophy. It can never be encaged in any man-made institution or book or computer file.

Wisdom is *alive*. Wisdom is a living, vital force that tells all life how to become more. If you want true healing, it is not enough to seek the wisdom of the world. You must tune in to the vibration, the flow, the fount of wisdom. You must immerse yourselves in the living waters of wisdom and realize that water wants to flow—it does not want to stand still. It is with wisdom as it is with any other vital force. Do you want to flow with it?

Well, then you can experience healing. You may indeed benefit from studying the worldly wisdom of anatomy and how the body works and body chemistry. You may indeed benefit from studying spiritual teachings, such as the ones we have released about the four lower bodies, so that you know that healing cannot take place in the physical alone.

But I come to show you – I come to radiate to you – that there is more to wisdom. You might think that you are spiritual students, that you have spent ten, twenty or thirty years studying spiritual teachings in this lifetime alone and perhaps in many embodiments. You might think that in order to reach whatever goal you have set for yourselves – be it healing, be it the ascension, be it the Christ consciousness – you may think that you are lacking some kind of knowledge, some kind of wisdom, some kind of secret formula. Once you acquire that from a source outside yourself – "poof" – you will be healed, you will be enlightened, you will ascend, you will be the Christ.

I tell you, it is not enough to think this way. It is beneficial for a time to think this way and to seek something from outside yourself, to seek enlightenment, to seek a greater understanding. Do not misunderstand my words. I am not telling you that you should not have studied. You were called to study and you have done so.

What I aim to show you is that there comes a point where one must go beyond studying. One must say: "It is not a matter of knowing something, it is a matter of experiencing something. It is not a matter of seeking knowledge from without, it is a matter of realizing that I have access to the kingdom of God within me. When I am willing to go within and connect to the fount of wisdom, then I will be enlightened, then my consciousness will be raised."

Not in the sense that my consciousness will be permanently raised. There are still many of you who think that once you attain the Christ consciousness, it is permanent. But the Christ consciousness is oneness with the River of Life that is constant self-transcendence. The Christ is constantly transcending itself, becoming *more*.

Stillstand is the cause of disease

There is no standing still in wisdom. The ego, the separate self, seeks to stop the clock, stop the flow. It seeks to stand still and posses a certain experience instead of flowing with the River of Life and transcending any previous experience. This is how you create the conditions that manifest as disease in the body and the mind and in the environment and in society. It is then that the closed circle must begin to break down.

Do you think that the second law of thermodynamics, that the wrath of Shiva, is a destructive, negative force? It is a very loving force that seeks to break down the very mental prisons that are keeping people trapped. If you came upon a prison where people have been locked up in a dark dungeon for nigh a lifetime, would your breaking down those walls be a destructive force? Well, only if you were attached to the prison and wanted to keep people there forever.

It is, indeed, a safety mechanism built into life itself. When you close your mind to the ever-flowing fount of wisdom that transcends itself constantly, then your mind becomes a closed system. Then, the second law of thermodynamics, the contracting force of the mother, the wrath of Shiva, will break down those mental images that are encasing your immortal spirit in an illusion of a mortal identity.

The intellect is a tool with limitations

Let us move into a more subtle way of looking at this. You might recognize that my beloved brother, MORE, gave you a very subtle, a very esoteric, discourse. You may indeed need to study it many times over to unlock the keys, and so it is with my release today.

So many of you have studied spiritual teachings for many years. So many have come to a point where you know there are things that are unreal, you have increased in understanding and discernment. You also sense that there is something in yourself that you do not see, some illusion that you have not yet uncovered. It is as if you understand something intellectually, but you cannot apply it to yourself. It is as if you see it, but you see it when it is portrayed as being outside yourself. You cannot truly stand in front of the mirror – mentally speaking – and see that particular aspect of duality in yourself. You cannot separate yourself from it.

I come to give you the concept that when wisdom is approached only from the point of the intellect, *that* is when it becomes a closed system. This is what many of us gave discourses on [See the book *How to Communicate From the Heart*.] where we talked about the database in the subconscious mind. Now you want reality, you want new ideas, you want wisdom to fit into some category in the database so that the ego can feel it still has control.

If you take the so-called "wise" people in the world – be they the intellectuals in the field of religion or the intellectuals in the field of academic science – you will see that for all of their intelligence, for all of their knowledge, they have not recognized a very simple truth, namely that any tool you use has certain limitations.

You all know that a car is a great tool for moving from place to place, but only when you have a firm road to drive upon. When it comes to crossing the ocean, the car is a somewhat limited device, and you will not get far by driving down to the beach and into the water. Yet, the intellectuals in the world of religion and science do not see that the intellect likewise is a great tool for a particular purpose, but it cannot take you beyond certain limits. As I started out by saying, the intellect cannot help you connect to the fount of wisdom. Where do you connect to the fount of wisdom? Well, of course, in the heart. Before we could give a teaching on the restoration of true healing, we had to give one on restoring the flow from the heart, the communication from the heart. It all goes together, yet we must take one step at a time. You cannot intellectually understand what it takes to transcend the separate self.

Even this messenger has for a long time been thinking that if only we, of the ascended masters, would give some kind of teaching through him, then that would awaken the people who are struggling, those who are so willing to change but cannot see what it is that is standing in their way. It is in compassion for these people that he has been asking us in his heart: "Isn't there some way to help them see, to help them understand?" Only recently has he come to see that it is not possible to give an outer teaching that is a magical formula that will mechanically unlock the understanding of anyone who reads it—not even if they study it in a more profound way than with the intellect alone.

Why do you seek a guru?

As my brother, MORE, was explaining to you, once you have taken on a role and identify yourself with that role, you believe that you cannot simply step out of it, you cannot simply walk away from it. Do you see – building on what my brother explained – that as long as you think you are missing some crucial piece of information, you are subconsciously affirming the image that you are separated from Christhood, from the kingdom of God, from enlightenment or whatever it may be?

What is the crucial piece of information that you have not yet found? It is the realization that what is wrong with you is the sense that there is something you do not know – something that you do not have access to within yourselves – and must find from an outer source. Again, this is subtle. As MORE was also explaining, you *do* need something from an outer source in the sense that you need something from outside the closed circle of your separate sense of identity. This is why we, of the ascended masters, have established a long tradition of the guru-chela, the teacher-student/disciple relationship. While you are trapped and identified with a particular role, you need the teacher, the guru, to come and simply demonstrate to you that there is a state of consciousness beyond your current state of consciousness.

So many spiritual students seek a guru or a teacher because they believe that the guru or teacher can give them the information they are lacking. In some cases people are lacking a certain understanding. As you grow in understanding, you can begin to detach yourself from the illusions. Yet there comes a point where you now have sufficient understanding, and it is no longer a matter of receiving that crucial piece of information, that secret formula, that philosopher's stone, that final initiation that you receive on the 33rd step or whatever secret initiatic process you think you have to go through.

No, my beloved, it is a matter of recognizing that after that point, you cannot progress by only listening to the outer teaching given by or through the teacher. You must go beyond the teaching and absorb the vibration that is coming through a true teacher. This is precisely why it is essential to practice your discernment and not follow the false teachers of this world.

What do I mean with the false teachers? Here is another subtlety. You may go into the world and see the many teachers out there, and you may look at the teaching they are giving forth and you may say: "That is true. That is very profound. This person must be a true teacher."

Listen to what I just said. It is not the outer teaching alone, for there are many teachers in the world, and even in the mental realm, who have attained great knowledge. You have the libraries of the world and the academics who have attained great material knowledge, or even great theological knowledge. The crucial distinction is: Have these teachers truly gone beyond the outer wisdom and recognized the underlying, superior, undivided, unconditional wisdom which boils down to one realization, namely that all life is one!

There is absolutely no point in seeking to become a teacher in order to be thought wise among men and raise up the separate self. There is only one true way to be a teacher, and that is to constantly strive for oneness and greater degrees of oneness, until the separate self melts away and you are not now concerned by anything. You are not seeking to raise yourself up, you are not feeling rejected, you are not concerned about other people's reactions. You are willing to be an open door for the fount of wisdom to flow through you.

Even though that fount is expressed in outer teachings, there is the underlying vibration that comes from the River of Life, which is truly the oneness of all those who have overcome the illusion of separation, the consciousness of duality. It is the flow of the Holy Spirit where we have all added our Being to that wind of the Holy Spirit that seeks to enlighten the people on earth.

You see, this is the key, my beloved. A false teacher may have great knowledge, may have great teachings, but is nevertheless seeking some advantage for the separate self, whatever that might be. Some have great knowledge but seek to attract female students for sexual exploitation. Some seek money. Some seek pride and a sense of superiority. Some need to be constantly admired. Regardless of whatever truth may be in their teachings – truth, when you evaluate it based on the intellect and the linear mind – they are not true teachers if they have not connected to the underlying oneness and therefore are simply seeing themselves as an open door.

They are not the ones who have the wisdom, the wisdom that is flowing like a living fount, like the living word that is not just a teaching that you can study with the intellect, but the sound. The words are cups of light that contain the vibration that is the final step that people must take in and accept in order to rise beyond the separate self.

Drink me while I am drinking thee

Master MORE talked about the path of adoration. What is it that can happen to those who truly follow that path? It is that they go beyond any outer expressions and lock in to, open their hearts to, receiving the vibration of a particular master. You have the saying: "Drink me, while I am drinking thee." As the student is willing to give up anything in this world – any part of the separate self to be closer to the master and come into oneness with the master – the master is drinking the impurities that the student is giving up. In return, he is radiating the vibration of the master as the student is drinking in.

This is the true process of the master-disciple relationship that Jesus came to demonstrate, and which you see that few of his disciples truly understood. Peter, of course, being the primary example of one who could not let go of his intellectual, outer image but constantly wanted Jesus to conform to it. He could not simply sit at the feet of the master and drink in the vibration of the Master Jesus. But the children could, which is why Jesus said: "Let them come to me and forbid them not, for of such is the kingdom of God."

I have no secret formula to offer you, for there is none. Not so long ago, Gautama himself – the Lord of the World – gave the image of a dark lord that was supposedly residing in a castle guarded by all these lower ranks of those who serve the dark lord out of fear. If you walked through the fear and actually walked into the castle, you saw that there was no dark lord.

Look at how many people in the world – in spiritual and New Age organizations, in traditional religions, in science and academic circles – have a similar image. Somewhere there must be the ultimate temple of wisdom, and when you walk in there, you see the secret formula that will enable you to know all things and master all things.

If you could go to this imaginary temple, penetrate to the very core, there would be no secret formula whatsoever. God hides his face from the profane. God hides the secret of life from those who are approaching it from the consciousness of separation. You only discover the secret of life by becoming one with something that is more than the separate self. Only that something must, of course, be part of the River of Life.

How can you fully receive the wisdom that I, Lanto, represent? By looking beyond outer words and teachings. By tuning in to my vibration and accepting that you are worthy to receive that unconditional love with a tint of the unconditional, infinite wisdom of God. The true wisdom that I AM – with which I have become one – cannot be reduced to words that can be spoken in the material world. It cannot be reduced to formulas or rituals or teachings. It is alive, it defies any structure whatsoever, my beloved.

Going beyond your own mind structure

Certainly, you need structure in the material universe. We are not trying to break down structure. We are seeking to raise up structure to outpicture the kingdom of God and the Golden Age of Saint Germain.

For you personally there must come a point where you are willing to go beyond the structure that you have built so far. That structure still serves to maintain the ego's sense of security and control. As long as you cling to the structure, cling to the sense of what you know, of what you think you know, you cannot receive the unconditional wisdom. It is only by absorbing that wisdom that you will fully transcend the sense of separation and come to see that which you cannot see right now.

There is no way to outsmart the intellect and the dualistic mind by using the intellect and the dualistic mind. For every dualistic argument there is a counter-argument that will negate it, which means that any form of dualistic wisdom is relative. It only exists within the dualistic framework; it must have an opposite. How can it be absolute wisdom, how can it be unconditional wisdom? It simply is not possible.

In order to be the wise ones, there comes a point where you have to say: "I have attempted to understand for a long time, but now I see that it is not by seeking an outer, structured wisdom that I will go further. I will not overcome the catch-22 I am in by attaining some understanding. I am in a catch-22 because I see myself as not having wisdom. How do I overcome the catch-22? Only by being willing to let go of all I think I know, to be like a little child, to have the childlike mind that is not asking but that simply observes."

Why did I have you enter the meditation of walking out of the closed library into the spring, the miracle of life? Because this is what you need to do. You need to walk away from all that the ego thinks it knows about the spiritual path and find some way to simply absorb your own higher being, a particular master, or even something from nature. You need to have your mind switch its focus so you now experience oneness with something beyond the separate self. Only in that oneness, in that experience of oneness, will you be whole. Only in that oneness will you be healed, my beloved.

True wisdom leads to true healing

Based on this teaching, let us tie this to personal healing. As you heard expressed before by a person who had a vision of sitting on the rock and her view was blocked by a big building. Instead of seeking to break down the building or run away from it, she allowed herself to become one with it. This is, indeed, an essential key to overcoming disease.

A disease is a projection of a mental image based on the illusion of separation. Your default reaction when realizing that your body has manifested a disease is usually one of two, or perhaps both in a mixture. One is denial where you want to run away from it and deny the reality of it. One is wanting to fight it and destroy that which is threatening to destroy your body.

Either reaction only reinforces the sense of separation, the illusion of the separate self. Whether you seek to deny and run away, or whether you seek to fight and destroy, you are seeking to solve the problem with the same state of consciousness that created the problem.

May I suggest you contemplate that instead of running away or seeking to destroy, you look at the disease as a message. You look for what kind of illusion is outpictured in the disease. Instead of running away from it, you walk right into it, you look at it. Instead of seeking to get further away from it, you seek oneness with it.

Do you see the psychological mechanism, my beloved? First you accept that you are a separate being, you accept an illusion that springs from separation. That illusion manifests a disease in your body, and now you seek to separate yourself from the disease. In seeking separation from the disease, you reinforce the image of separation, the illusion of separation. What is separation? It is running away from oneness! How can you come back to oneness by seeking to run away from that which is created out of separation? It cannot be done!

What is the only way to progress? It is to stop running away from any image, any imperfection—to walk right into it, to merge with it. Not in the sense that you let it pull you down, but that you, in merging with it, see beyond it and see that beyond this imperfect image and manifestation is the reality of the Ma-ter light, which is an expression of God. You see oneness behind the separate images, and in seeing oneness behind the separate image, you finally see that the separate image is unreal. This you cannot see as long as you are trying to run away from it or trying to destroy it, for that only reinforces that it has reality.

Do you see that beyond the words I am imparting to you is a vibration of victory? When you have wisdom, true wisdom, you can overcome any condition in the material world. They are all unreal, they are all projections of an unreal image. *You* are real, and when you stop running away from that which is unreal – but instead seek to merge with everything – you will also merge with that which is real. You will know that you are real, and you are more than the unreality.

You will, therefore, shift your sense of identity. As Mother Mary has said, those who are healed are those who can accept that they are healed. Those who know are those who can accept that they are one with the fount of wisdom. They are no longer students who need to know, they are masters who have attained gnosis, oneness, oneness with the fount of wisdom itself.

That is what I offer you, for that is the path I have followed. I have walked it; I know it works, I am living proof that it works. I am looking to some of you to also become the living proof that we may enlighten many others and have them see that this is the time, not to increase intellectual knowledge but to acquire true wisdom and therefore enlighten the world with wisdom's flame.

Are you with me in that oneness with the fount of wisdom? Then let us illumine the world—not by more intellectual knowledge but by Being who you truly are, by being expressions of your God Flame so that people may see that there is indeed *more.*

7 | THIRD RAY: YOU ARE ALWAYS WORTHY OF LOVE

A dictation by Archangel Charity with Paul the Venetian

"And though I speak with the voice of men and of angels and have not charity, I am nothing." Words to meditate upon, my beloved. You have heard a piece of music that conveys the grandeur of the vibration of the archangels. Charity, I AM. I come to give you a sense of what charity really is, my beloved.

Indeed, charity is not the entirely right word, but given the limitations of language there was no word that could adequately convey the vibration behind it. You, in your language and understanding, might come up with a better word and indeed, it is, "unconditionality." That is the vibration that is conveyed through the Third Ray, which you normally call the Third Ray of love.

Love, as so many other words, has received such a dualistic overlay over time that it is almost a useless word. Unconditional love, therefore, is, of course, a much better concept. But why not simply unconditionality?

What is the River of Life? It is the unconditional expression of any God quality. There is no way to progress beyond a certain point on the spiritual path without truly tuning in to the vibration of unconditionality—as you heard from Lanto, tuning in to the vibration of wisdom.

There are so many people in spiritual and religious movements who have come to understand the need to rise above selfishness, self-centeredness and the lower expressions. What they are seeking is to attune themselves with the vibration of love, but it is the dualistic love that is opposed to fear, anger, hatred. Love in the divine sense can, of course, have no opposite or it would not be divine.

As Master MORE has said, it is the grand illusion of the fallen beings that they actually oppose God. You can only oppose that which is in the realm of duality so what you oppose is a graven image of God. Many people are not opposing anything but they are seeking to come into love. But if you seek to come into attunement with a graven image, how can you ever reach true love? It is, as Lanto explained, impossible.

Consider unconditionality

Thus, the need to consider unconditionality. *Unconditionality.* This is, indeed, why we have given you the concept that at a certain point of the path, it is necessary to stop trying to change yourself. The only way to switch out of that last illusion of the separate self is to accept yourself – unconditionally – for who you are.

You have heard of the need to make that shift from the first two rays. I, along with Paul the Venetian, come to give it to you from the perspective of the Third Ray.

How can you progress to the Fourth Ray of purity unless you tune in to unconditionality? Is it not the conditions that manifest impurities in your minds and bodies—even in the physical body of the earth, seen as so many natural imbalances and disasters?

Again, there is no sacred or secret formula that will work automatically. The concept that you are not able or worthy of expressing a higher love, well, that concept, that conception, is the problem.

Love is an unconditional force that wants to be expressed. You do not have to *do* anything in order to be an open door for the expression of unconditionality. What condition could you possibly have to fulfill in order to express that which is unconditional—and thus flows and flows and transcends and grows and expresses, regardless of any conditions?

Do you see, again, the impossibility of this, how illogical it is and how only the separate self can believe this? You are more than the separate self. As long as you hold on to the concept that you need to move to a certain state of perfection – before you are able or worthy to have the love of God flowing through you – as long as you see yourself separated from the flow of love, the love cannot flow. It will not accept any conditions.

You have the right to accept conditions for yourself. But do not fall into the trap of the subtle consciousness of the beings who are completely identified with duality, and therefore in their arrogance believe that they can form an opposite polarity to God. You cannot limit God, you cannot limit love, you cannot limit the expression of love.

You either let it flow, or it flows around you. There is nothing in between. You may think there is something in between because human beings have for so long created the dualistic, relative image of love, as an opposition to hatred, anger, fear etc. Some people have become very good at putting on a facade of being loving and kind.

You may go and see this in many places, including in this center of healing where you have certain people who are very good at portraying an image, as representing an earthly institution. Or you may go to the humble ones who stand all day, helping people walk through the healing waters, and you may see that there you find an expression of love that has no pretense, no conditions. It is all washed away in the desire to help others.

Overcome your fear of rejection

Love does not seek to own. When it does not seek to own, it follows that it needs nothing in return. Consider the fear of expressing love out of fear of rejection. When there is fear of rejection, you have not yet tuned in to the vibration of unconditionality. When love is expressed unconditionally, how could there be fear of rejection?

How can unconditional love be rejected? Unconditional love is self-contained. It finds its joy simply in being expressed, in expressing itself, in flowing.

When you think that you have to express love only for one particular person – and that you want that love to be received by that person, perhaps even be received in a certain way – you are not in the flow of unconditional love. You have tuned in to the lower vibration of conditional love. You may still have love for a person, you may still desire to express that love, but you have not yet reached the highest potential. You fear rejection or you seek to own or posses or have something in return.

When you think that you need something from any human being or from any source in the material universe, you have a sense of lack. You have a deficit consciousness. You think you are missing something and that someone else must come in and fill it, fill that hole, so that you can be complete. This is all an illusion.

Even the concept of twin flames – that there is one human being who is your twin flame and therefore that twin flame is the perfect love who can complete you – even *that* is not the highest understanding. Your real spiritual twin flame is your higher self, your I AM Presence. Only by coming into oneness with *that* will you be complete, will you be whole.

Unconditionality and healing

What does this mean for the entire concept of healing? It means that you cannot heal yourself from the consciousness that you need healing. You cannot become whole from the consciousness that sees itself as unwhole.

The only way out of the catch-22 is to transcend the illusion that you are not whole. This, of course, sounds like another catch-22. How can you transcend the illusion that you are unwhole while you are feeling unwhole?

The reality is that you *can*—when you recognize the fact of who you are. You are a self-conscious being, and as Master MORE explained, you have been given complete free will. You have the freedom to create any experience that you desire to experience. How do you create an experience? By stepping into a costume, a role, and then thinking: "This is who I AM." As we have said, no matter how much you have identified yourself with that separate sense of identity, you still are who you are.

You have the potential to recognize and acknowledge who you are. You have the potential to say: "It was not some external force – be it a serpent or some other external force, even the external God wanting to punish me – that caused me to descend into the sense of unwholeness. It was choices I made."

When you recognize that *you* made the choices to descend into the sense of unwholeness, it follows logically that you also have the power to change those choices. You can replace them with choices that bring you into wholeness, or rather, choices that bring you out of the illusion that you are separated from wholeness. How can you, indeed, be separated from anything that is unconditional?

"Unconditional" means that it is everywhere present. You cannot find a place where the unconditional love of God is not present. It is impossible.

You are like a fish denying that it is wet. And I know that fish have not been generally seen as having a high intelligence, but nevertheless, clearly you can see that for a fish, *that* is pretty stupid.

You recognize, of course, that your ego is not all that smart—even though it thinks it is, even though other people may think it is. You can, indeed, as some have done, manipulate yourself into a position where most of the world thinks your ego is pretty smart or superior in some other way. Yet when you can begin to laugh at the ego, then you have already started to separate yourself from it.

Unconditionality in relationships

There is indeed a need to recognize that love is not that serious, romantic love that you see in the big dramatic pictures or operas or movies or books. My beloved, love is not to be taken seriously.

If you take love seriously, it can only be conditional love. When you are in tune with the unconditional love of God, you are simply flowing with the River of Life. Thus, you can only be joyful.

Consider that you find yourself thinking that you are in love with another person, yet you do not feel joyful about this. You feel tense, you feel afraid of being rejected, or you feel that the other person should return your love or should behave in a certain way. You are in a sense – if you are willing to be honest with yourself – seeking to restrict the other person rather than setting that person free. Do you not see that unconditional love can never seek to restrict anyone, but only wants everyone to be MORE and to be free to flow with the River of Life? How can you, then, create the image in the mind that there is only one person on this earth who is worthy of your love, and you absolutely need to have that love returned? If not, you will go into this dramatic sense that you see in the operas of being willing to die rather than have your love rejected. Can you not see how comical this is? Indeed, it is the divine comedy, although it is not truly divine, but only the man-made image of the divine.

Laugh at your own seriousness when it comes to love. Step out of that operatic costume of the serious lover. *Just step out of it!* Become the joyful lover who realizes that you are the beloved of an even greater lover, namely the Divine Lover who loves you as its beloved.

Indeed, your higher being, your I AM Presence, is your personal Divine Lover who loves you as its only beloved son or daughter. If you want that personal love for you, do not seek it from another human being who cannot give it to you. Seek it from your own higher being. Be full in that love.

Then you can, when you fully embrace and accept that fullness, move on to merge into oneness with that flow of love. Thereby, you become one with the Divine Lover and now you *become* the Divine Lover in embodiment—who is the open door for the flow of love. You are the open door for the force that loves all life and seeks to raise up all life. How can you then fall prey to the illusion that your love should be focused on one particular person?

Am I thereby saying you cannot have a love relationship between man and woman? No, I am not. I am only saying that you will never have a successful relationship, a relationship that lives up to its highest potential, unless you set yourself free from this overlay of conditionality—and thereby you set your partner free. Your relationship becomes a playful, joyful, flowing relationship that is not hemmed in by boundaries and conditions and expectations and blaming and feeling that your love is not returned.

Why do you want to go to heaven?

As Master MORE has said, if your approach to spirituality is not driven by joy, then what is the point? Why do you want to get to heaven if you think it will make you miserable? Why do you want to have a love relationship if you think it will make you miserable?

Switch your perception. Step out of the conditionality and embrace unconditionality. Do you feel that you cannot let go of your love for this particular person? That is a condition. As long as you hold on to it, it will make you miserable and perhaps make the other person miserable as well.

Now, of course, I am an expression of the unconditional love of God and I love you unconditionally—even if you choose to make yourself miserable. I have no conditions in my love and thus, you can receive that love no matter how you see yourself right now. No matter that you think that because of something you have done – or something you have *not* done – you are unworthy to receive love, it is not so.

If you cannot switch out of your sense of being unworthy – if you have studied, if you have given rosaries or other forms of meditations and practices and you find that you are still stuck in a certain condition – you only have one last option. And that is to stop trying to get out of the condition, but to embrace it.

What is it that happens when you enter into a state of lower vibration, when you accept some kind of condition? You accept that, because of this or that condition, you cannot let love flow freely and unconditionally. It must be expressed or not expressed according to certain criteria. This is what makes you feel incomplete. You shut off the flow from your higher being, the flow of the unconditionality that flows through your I AM Presence and seeks to raise up all life. That is why you begin to feel miserable. You feel that because of this or that condition, you cannot love.

Therefore, love the condition that makes you think you cannot love. Love the feeling of being miserable. If you can love that which so many people deem not lovable, then you are no longer separated from the flow of love. Certainly, one day, you will wake up and say: "Hallelujah, I am no longer miserable." Thus, indeed, follow your bliss.

Consider the power of music

May we, as the representatives of the Third Ray, call your attention to the power of music. Most of you realize that you have, throughout your life, had certain pieces of music that lifted your spirit and helped you tune in. You may not have recognized this with the outer mind, nevertheless the music helped you tune in to a vibration beyond your normal state of consciousness, thereby helping you tune in to a vibration beyond your conditions. If you feel any upliftment through music, *use music.* Find the kind of music that uplifts you because it expresses the flow, the flow of the River of Life.

Do not simply listen to it while you are driving your car or washing the dishes or doing other mundane things. Once in a while, go into a room where you can be alone and undisturbed. Start the music, turn off the light, lay down on your bed so that you feel the least amount of gravitational pull on your body. Then allow the music to carry you with its flow until you find yourself in that sacred space of unconditionality. You suddenly hear that beyond the music is that chime that is the sound of life itself. When you hear that chime, my beloved, that cosmic hum, you have, again, a sense of co-measurement of what love really is when it is unconditional.

You can use that to gain a different perspective on your life and how the conditionality takes away that sense of floating where there is nothing that pulls you into a particular condition, into a particular role and costume in the drama outplayed in the material universe. This is not escapism—when you use it to not simply run away from your problems. You use it to get a different perspective on your problems so that you can recognize that you *are* not the problems. You are *more*, for you have experienced that you are *more*.

Do you think that the theatrical lover that I was talking about can float in a space sublime? Nay, for he is too wrapped up in himself and his own conditions, and he cannot let go. But *you can!* The real you *can* experience unconditionality. Only by experiencing *that*, will you truly know that there is something beyond the conditional world. Only when you know it, can you move to the next level of merging with it. You now see first yourself as the object of the Divine Lover's love, and then merge with the Divine Lover so that you see – that you are the open door for – the love that wants to be expressed to all life. That is the key to overcoming the false sense of love, the conditional sense of love.

The body is not your enemy

You cannot simply force yourself to love everyone or to love your disease or to in any other way force love to be expressed. You can only tune in to the state of unconditionality and let it flow—*let it flow*.

What does that mean, my beloved? When you think about this honestly, you will see that there are so many things in this world that you do not wish to see, that you recoil from, that you withdraw from, that you would rather not know are in existence. Certainly, this is understandable, given the condition of the world.

Nevertheless, the reality is that when there is something you do not want to look at, then you think, you feel, you sense, that you cannot express love to that something. You, in a sense, feel that *that* something could not be worthy of love. You must be the judge and must withhold it so that love cannot flow through you to that particular condition or that particular person or these people of a different race or religion or whatever divides people.

When you begin to shut off that flow of love, what must inevitably happen? Your being, your lower being, becomes a closed system. When this has filtered through the four lower bodies and reaches the physical, there is disease.

Now you think that your body is working against you. You are afraid to take a look at the condition, you would rather not see it, you want to run away from it, as Lanto explained. You think you could not possibly love that which is destroying your body.

What are you doing in that process? You are saying that the cells that have cancer, I cannot love those cells. But what are the cells doing? They are out-picturing a state of consciousness that has caused you to shut off the flow of love. When you then say that you cannot love the cells that are out-picturing that consciousness, how can the cells free themselves from that condition?

The cells – you must recognize – do not have the sense of self-awareness that you have. They can only outpicture what is projected upon them. When you have first projected an unloving image that caused them to take on a disease – be it cancer or something else – and then you reinforce that by projecting another image that these cells should be destroyed and ripped out of your body – for you do not love them, perhaps you are angry at them and you hate them – well then how can the cells free themselves from that double indemnity, that double burden you put upon them?

You are the only one who can break that vicious circle. You can do it only by realizing that it was the lack of love that caused your cells to outpicture the disease. The only key to true healing is to restore the flow of love—and *you* must be the one who restores it. You do not have to love the disease, my beloved. But you have to love the cells so that you love them free of the disease—free to outpicture the higher pattern of oneness, of perfect health.

As Lanto explained, there is wisdom everywhere. There is wisdom in your cells. There is not self-awareness, but there is the wisdom of the Divine Mother that knows how to express perfect health—if it is only allowed to outpicture what is within it. Has not God written his law in your inward parts? When you love the cells free, they will know how to shake off the cancer or any other disease and outpicture their natural state of perfect health.

My love is always there

I am pausing to take in the return current of your consciousness—of your fears and your doubts about what we are saying to you in this and the previous releases. I am absorbing the consciousness. The fact that you doubt my words, that you are afraid to implement them, does not mean that I do not love you. I love you regardless of how you respond or do not respond to my words and my vibration. My love is unconditional; it is timeless. If you cannot accept it now, be not dismayed. You do not need to beat yourself up over the fact that you cannot instantly accept what you are hearing.

I want you to know that I am always there. My love is always there. If you cannot accept it now, then at whatever time you *can*, do not fall prey to the illusion that because you could not accept me that time in the past, you cannot accept me now either, for you are not worthy. Do not build layers and layers of illusions.

Remember my words: My love is unconditional. You do not have to fulfill a condition in order to be worthy of it. You have only two options: You can *accept* or you can *reject*. My love is unconditional so if you reject my love, I am not affected by that rejection.

I still love you unconditionally. No matter how violently you might reject it at this present moment, at any moment in the future when you desire to throw off that costume, my love is there for you to accept. Your ego may want you to think that this cannot be so. *Yet it is so.*

It has always been so.

It will always be so.

This is the truth about love. This is true love. If you desire to feel separated from my love, if you desire to reject it, I love you for rejecting me. Whatever you feel, whatever you think, I love you.

Feelings and thoughts are fleeting images that pass through the mind. Turn off the film projector and you will see that the screen of life is still white, no matter what images were projected upon it. Your core being, your Conscious You, is a blank screen, in the sense that although you were created with individuality, you were not created with *conditionality*. You were not created with any dualistic conditions, my beloved.

You were created with unconditional individual characteristics. I know full well that your linear mind cannot comprehend this concept. But there must be some expression of words that you can ponder, until you come to the point of switching your perception. You recognize the reality of unconditionality and the unreality of the conditions set up to obscure the white screen by making you focus on the fleeting images that can never satisfy your true being, your true longing for love.

How can any love coming from this material realm satisfy your built-in longing for love? Your built-in longing for love is the longing for oneness with who you are, your own higher being. It is your longing to be in the flow of the River of Life by fulfilling the role for which you were created by your higher being—to be a co-creator and to bring the kingdom of God into manifestation in the material universe.

Tune in to love

My words are coming to you through a person in embodiment who, as is inevitable when you are in embodiment, has a limited capacity for love. Certainly, one cannot be in embodiment and at the same time be in the fullness of the ascended consciousness—which is in the fullness of unconditionality. Do not focus on the outer messenger. Go beyond the outer form, go beyond the sound of the voice, go beyond the words.

Follow the words, follow them as a stream of consciousness that reaches to the very being that I AM. I am one with the hierarchy of God Love, of unconditional love and with all of the beings who are expressions of that unconditionality. Follow that stream of consciousness and recognize that my capacity for love is indeed unlimited. I can take in and consume any condition that you desire to surrender to me. I give you, as the conclusion of this release, an opportunity to release into the stream of my consciousness any condition that you desire to let go of. You have said, with Master MORE: "Enough is enough." Thus, I will have this messenger recite while you surrender.

[Messenger recites as the words come from within:]

Love is a flowing stream, a fount of unconditionality, like the water that moves, moving over the rock – even the hardest of rock – wearing it down, little by little. It is so much softer than the rock that it is unfathomable to the linear mind how it could ever wear down the rock. Yet, love is like that. It flows unconditionally and if it seems like it gets nowhere, if it seems like people do not receive it, do not change, it just keeps flowing.

Over the span of millennia, it eventually wears down that solid rock of the separate self.

Truly, the Divine Lover will never leave his beloved alone, will never stop flowing, will never stop giving. Eventually, even the hardest of conditions will be worn down by the flow of love, the eternal unstoppable, unconditional flow of love. Is it not so that any condition is made of smaller units, as you know the rock is made from molecules and atoms, and even beyond, from the tiniest particles that make up the atom. The love flowing may only manage to dislodge one elementary particle from the rock, but yet, *that* is still a change.

The flowing love is not *discouraged* but is *encouraged* and therefore flows even more and dislodges an atom, and another one, and another, and another. Soon, the River of Life begins to carve a gorge into the bedrock of the human consciousness. Flowing, flowing, ever-flowing. See how even the mightiest of mountains can be worn down over time by the gentle rain descending from heaven, like the gentle rain of love that falls upon the just and the unjust, upon the evil and the good.

To love, there is none just or unjust, none evil or good. There are no conditions in that flowing love, there are no conditions whatsoever. To love, the conditions are unreal, impermanent. Love knows that if it keeps flowing, it will wear down even the hardest of conditions. Even the most hardened heart will be worn down by the unstoppable flow of love.

One day, that heart will look at itself and say: "Why do I keep separating myself from the flow of love? I have had enough of the experience of being separated. Now I am curious as to how it would feel to be in the flow of love." Suddenly, it surrenders into the flow like a dam bursting—and suddenly the River of Life that has been held back for so many lifetimes is released in an outburst that no conditions, that no ego – even the strongest ego – can hold back. The real you flows with it and finds such joy, such freedom, in the release from conditions. The total unconditional release.

[Archangel Charity continues:]

Thus, breathe in [audience inhales]. Become aware of the condition and then release it as you breathe out [audience exhales].

Now breathe in and hold, and as you breathe out I breathe in. Breathe out [audience exhales while messenger inhales].

As I release my unconditional love, you breathe in and breathe in that love [messenger exhales, audience inhales].

Now release, as I breathe in the conditions [audience exhales while messenger inhales].

Inhale the love [messenger exhales, audience inhales].

Release [audience exhales while messenger inhales].

Inhale [messenger exhales, audience inhales].

You have now experienced the in-breath and the out-breath of love. Yet, I AM not limited to time and space, and you may repeat this exercise any time, perhaps after listening to a piece of music that reawakens your sense of flow.

We, the representatives of the Third Ray, congratulate you for being willing to come into our Presence and thereby, perhaps without realizing it, having separated yourself, to some degree, from your fear. You cannot be in the Presence of Unconditional Love if you are fully identified with your fear. The very fact that you are here demonstrates that you are no longer fully identified with the separate self. I admonish you to embrace that new sense of self where you know you are *more*, where you have experienced oneness with the More.

Be sealed, even though it is, again, the limitations of words. How can you be sealed in that which is unconditional? My beloved, go beyond the sense of needing to be sealed and just *be* in the flow of unconditional love.

8 | FOURTH RAY: ACCELERATION IS THE KEY TO WHOLENESS

A dictation by Serapis Bey

Serapis Bey is the name I have been known under as an ascended master. I, of course, AM MORE than this. I am more than the hierarch of Luxor. I am not limited to a particular place on earth, or a particular pile of rocks.

I say this so that you can see that there is nothing on earth that is inherently sacred, in the sense of human beings calling things sacred. The pyramids and the temples of Egypt are just that—stacks of stone, my beloved. Unless they become the lively stones of the heart, by being endowed from within, they have no special vibration, no significance as such. It is not necessary or beneficial on the spiritual path to revere any outer symbol. It is necessary to go beyond the outer appearances and symbols and tune in, as has now been said from different perspectives, to the true vibration behind it all.

I come to give you the opportunity – if you will be healed – to tune in to the Fourth Ray. In order to be completely healed, to be completely whole, you must, of course, walk the path of initiation on the seven rays, going beyond to the secret rays as well. But even if you walk the path of the seven rays, you can attain wholeness, healing.

You can accelerate beyond any earthly condition

You have heard from the master of the First Ray how it is necessary to use your will power to consciously take back your power. You have heard from the Second Ray of how it is necessary to go beyond outer wisdom and study and to come into gnosis with the Spirit of Wisdom. You have heard from the Third Ray of how it is necessary to come into oneness with the flowing fount of love, the River of Life. Once you have passed the initiations on these three rays, it is necessary to take another step that many have not understood.

In order to be able to receive this release from my heart, this messenger had to pass a test himself. It has been a long several days for his physical body and even his emotional and mental body. Before he took this dictation, he went to his room, feeling his energies were low and thus, as is natural, thinking: "I need to rest for a few minutes." He laid down to rest, and suddenly he was open to receiving the thought from my heart: "You do not need to rest, you need to accelerate your being."

This is the essence of the initiation of the Fourth Ray of purity. You may walk through the initiations on the first three rays. You may have a sense of accomplishment. You may even feel so enveloped in love that you think you do not need to go beyond it. But I tell you, it is necessary to go beyond in order to reach the fullness of wholeness. In order to go beyond that level of the Third Ray, you need to accelerate, to step up.

This is one of the major blocks to healing. What do people naturally feel when their physical body breaks down? They are tired, they are in pain, they feel drained of energy. They feel, do they not: "I cannot possibly accelerate. I am too tired, too sick, feeling too bad." But you see, *this is unreality.*

You are not tired, sick, or feeling bad unless you choose to step into one of the roles that the other masters have talked about and identify yourself with that role. You identify yourself as feeling bad, feeling tired, feeling drained, feeling sick, therefore by the very focus of your mind on that image making it a manifest reality, albeit a temporary one, in your physical temple.

Transmuting or removing energy

As the other masters have attempted to explain to you, there is the illusion created by the ego – and the dualistic mind and the entire mass consciousness on earth – that because of this or that condition you are experiencing, you cannot accelerate. You need rest, you need restoration.

There is no such thing as rest. You will not become whole by resting. This is not to say that you do not need rest. But I am saying that there comes a point where you need to recognize that it is not rest that you need at this particular stage in the healing process—*it is acceleration.*

Now, you can, of course, not say to an ill person: "Get out of your bed and accelerate." The person needs to be taken through the steps of the first three rays. First, realizing what Master MORE explained so carefully, namely that you need to take back your power to make decisions. Then, having the wisdom to know what is real and unreal and that all these conditions and mental images are ultimately unreal. Then, locking in to the flow of love, knowing that no matter what mistakes you have made in the past, you can just walk away from it.

Let us go beyond that expression of walking away from something, for in reality, of course, you cannot walk away from anything. You cannot, as other masters have attempted to explain, rise above the duality consciousness by using the duality consciousness. Let us look again at the concept of purity and the need for purification. It is very easy with the linear, analytical mind to step into the image that you have a container – your aura, your physical body – that has taken in impurities from the world. Therefore, it needs to be cleansed, it needs to be purified by removing those impurities, by taking them out and putting them somewhere else.

This is logical to the linear mind. I understand that some of you will even use previous teachings to say: "But have we not talked about this very process, is that not the idea of the violet flame, to transmute the misqualified energy?" There is, again, a subtlety that the more mature students need to contemplate. The act of transmuting energy is not the same as removing energy.

As has been explained, you receive spiritual light from your higher being. You choose how to focus your consciousness, your awareness. You color the light with a higher or a lower vibration. The light that is colored with the lower vibration will eventually work its way down through the four levels of the material universe, until it reaches the level of your physical body. When it accumulates to a certain concentration, it will begin to burden the cells so they cannot function properly, and thus disease will manifest.

What is it that has caused the coloring of the light? It is the illusion of a separate self, the focus on you being separate from other people. This is the belief that you have a right to do what is best for you, even if it harms other forms of life—or other such beliefs that justify self-centered, egotistical behavior.

Now you recognize that you are ill, your body is ill, and it may kill you. Your first instinctive response is: Get rid of the disease, which means getting rid of the impure energies. Even though you sometimes take on energies from the world, you cannot take anything into your system unless there is already the state of consciousness that corresponds to the energies you are taking in.

If you simply say: "I want to take this energy that is making my body ill, remove it from my body, and dump it on the world," then you have not truly come to a higher spiritual understanding. You are seeking to overcome a problem from the same state of consciousness that created the problem—namely the illusion of separation.

You see that many people, when they become ill, become very self-focused, very self-centered. They just want to be healed, no matter what. This, of course, cannot lead to true healing. It may lead to a suppression of the symptoms of the physical body but that, of course, is not the same as true healing.

Accelerating imperfect energy

What will it take to be truly healed? It will take that you use the insights that you have gained on the first three rays so that you take responsibility for the energy that is truly a reflection of your consciousness. You say: "I will stop the process of coloring light with a lower vibration. I will first look at the beam in my own eye, I will consider whether it is imperfect beliefs – illusions – in my own consciousness that has added to the accumulation of misqualified energy in my four lower bodies and in the four lower bodies of Mother Earth."

"Then, I will change that consciousness so I can stop misqualifying light. I will look at the message in the disease manifest in my physical body, look at the consciousness and come to see and surrender that consciousness. But when I have then stopped the continued process of misqualification, I will take the next step. I want to purify the energy that I have already misqualified so that I do not burden other forms of life."

In making that decision, you are switching out of the separate self, you are switching out of the self-centered perspective. Now is where you need to reach the ultimate clarity of recognizing that the only way that you can purify the energy is not by somehow destroying that energy, or removing it to some remote location, some cosmic garbage dump somewhere. The only way is to *accelerate* it so that it shakes off the imperfect vibration and is again raised to the level of love, the level of purity.

What is purity? It is, of course, unconditionality. Again, there is a dualistic concept of purity, as the opposite of impurity. When you are in the dualistic mind, you think, of course, that in order to attain purity, you have to overcome, destroy, or seek to run away from and cover over the impurities. You do not want to look at the impurities. You go into the state of mind that you do not want God to see your impurities, you do not want other people to see them, you do not want your spiritual master to see them.

You seek to hide, and in seeking to hide them from your God, and your master, and other people, you of course first of all hide it from yourself. You cannot then look at it yourself, and yet, if you cannot look at the impurities, you cannot do the one thing that is needed to overcome them, namely to accelerate them out of the impurity, to raise the vibration.

Again, you see the catch-22 created by the mind, the dualistic mind. What is purity? It is not the absence of impurity. It is a particular vibration, a frequency, a living stream of consciousness. I am one with that stream, and I am radiating it through the words that you hear. You have an opportunity, when you hear or read this release, to tune in to and absorb that purity so that at the end of this release, you will not simply feel that I have given you theoretical concepts. I have given you more, a sense of co-measurement and oneness with the vibration of purity.

The extreme realism of purity

The linear mind will seek to tell you that before you can become pure, you must get rid of the impurities. When you have emptied yourself of impurities, *then* you might be worthy to receive some grant of light from above. Again, this is the illusion and the lie of the duality consciousness.

Consider who I am. I represent the Fourth Ray of purity. What are we assigned to accomplish by God? We are assigned to help all life attain purity. Is it logical that I would stand here saying: "You are impure, and when you raise yourself to a level of purity, *then* I will work with you?" How would I ever accomplish my job and my assignment from God if that was my approach? It is not logical, yet the dualistic mind and the false teachers want you to believe in this so-called logic.

It is my joy, my honor, my profound, deepest love to help you become pure. I am willing to work with you at any level of consciousness where you are at. How can this be so? The linear mind struggles to see this, and the linear mind, the analytical mind, the dualistic mind will never see it. But *you,* as the extension of God's own Being, can see and experience this.

Indeed, to me, no impurity is real. This means that I can see beyond all impurity and see what you often cannot or dare not see in yourselves: the pure being that was created out of the mind of a Being that is in oneness with God. I see that you are *real*. Therefore, why would I condemn you? Why would I look down upon you in any way, shape, or form because of some illusory impurities that you have chosen to take on as you take on a costume?

I know the reality that you can overcome any impurity that you have taken on in the material universe, or even in other realms. Any impurity can be overcome, *that* is what I know because I have proven it in myself. I have seen it proven in many others. In coming into oneness with the vibration of purity, I know that it is so high that there is nothing of the lower vibrations of the material universe that it cannot accelerate back into purity. This is the extreme realism that I come to bring you.

You may believe that when you are ill – when you are tired, or even just on your spiritual path (even if you have no particular physical illness) – there are certain things you cannot overcome. You may think that there are certain problems you have where you must remove or destroy the problem. You may think there are certain illusions and you need a certain insight to overcome the illusion.

You come to a point on the path where you do not need love, you do not need wisdom, you do not need power—for you have gone through the initiations of the first three rays and they have brought you to a particular point. Those vibrations of the first three rays will not bring you beyond that point. Only the Fourth Ray will bring you beyond, and the Fourth Ray is the ray of acceleration. That is why I AM the master of the ascension, for what is the ascension but an acceleration?

What is acceleration? It is that you do not let any condition on earth hold you back. Acceleration must begin with a shift of self-image where you realize that you are a spiritual being— not a material being. You are more than these material conditions, and therefore you have the potential to simply raise your vibration, and thereby raise the vibration of any condition that you have outpictured through the energy that has been flowing through your four-lower bodies.

Become like a rocket

You, as the spiritual being, can raise that vibration. You can accelerate it. You are like a rocket that is sitting on the launchpad. The engines have been started, they have been revved up, they have smoke and flames coming out. Yet, you do not quite dare to push the button that lifts you off from the earth. For many of you, *that* is the only thing holding you back. You have not come to that point where you are willing to recognize your full potential and to truly accelerate yourself out of the problems, out of the wounds, out of the setbacks, out of the diseases, out of any condition that you think is holding you back.

Your ego desperately wants you to keep thinking that it can hold you back.

A rocket, if it had self-awareness, would see itself as a rocket and would know that when it is put on the launch-pad, when it is fueled, it is just a matter of pushing the button and then it will accelerate out of the force of gravity, until it escapes the gravity of earth and goes into orbit. This is simply a matter of the laws of physics. Of course, when you are talking about self-aware beings, it is not just a matter of laws. You have, when you have passed the initiations of the first three rays, followed the laws to where you are ready, you are on the launch-pad.

We still have, of course – as is the case any time you deal with self-aware beings, – a decision that must be made. It is the decision to push the start button so that the full force of the rocket can be released. A rocket that has not left the ground is not a rocket. It is a pile of scrap metal. Yet, it has the potential to take flight and move beyond the gravitational pull of the earth.

You are like rockets, sitting on the launch-pad. You are still waiting for someone to come and push the start button. That "someone" will never come, for the someone that must push *your* start button – instead of pushing your ego buttons – is *you*.

You are the only one who can make the decision to accelerate, to take off, to not let anything stop you, to not let anything hold you back. This, again, is an essential ingredient in true healing. What is it that the mass consciousness, the consciousness of duality, wants you to believe when your body gets ill? It is that you cannot simply accelerate away from the illness. You cannot escape it—it is permanent, it is unavoidable and this and that and the next thing. It wants you to believe that the disease is ultimately real and thus has power over you.

Of course, it *is* unreal—but how do you escape it? Only by looking at the reality that no matter how you feel, no matter how burdened you feel, you are more than these burdens.

You have the potential to decide to unleash the full power of the rocket of your I AM Presence and accelerate your being, accelerate your cells, accelerate your very atoms, and rise above the vibration—even raising the vibration of the burdened cells and atoms.

Deciding to go global

This is the decision that needs to be made, and what is it you are actually deciding? You are deciding to shift away from confirming the reality of the separate self. How can you do it? You must find some cause outside of the separate self that you are willing to serve.

In order to push the start button and start the acceleration there must be something that makes you say: "This is not about me and how bad and burdened I feel. This is about why I actually came to this earth, to serve in a greater cause of serving the ascended masters, serving God, serving other people, serving to bring forth the Golden Age of Saint Germain," or some other goal that reaches beyond the separate self.

This messenger was directed some time ago to read the autobiography of Lance Armstrong, who was told he had terminal cancer and was given a 50-50 percent chance to survive, even though the doctors thought he had only a 3 percent chance to survive. The book describes how he first went through anger and the focus on self, and then one day shifted to a focus beyond the self, of how can we help overcome the disease of cancer for other people.

This is the essential switch in awareness where you go from the local awareness of the separate self to the global awareness of seeking to raise all life. That is the decision that will start the acceleration. Now you are saying: "I cannot let any conditions stand in the way of my service to God. I love this MORE. I am willing to look my separate self straight in the eye and say, 'You are not right when you tell me I cannot. For my God within me tells me that I *can,* for with God, all things are possible."'

Purity is unconditionality. What is it you are purified from? It is the conditions, the conditions that you have come to accept as being real, as having power over you. When you make the decision to accelerate beyond the limitations, then you will begin to tune in to the vibration of purity. You will begin, by absorbing that vibration, to experience and know the reality of what I am saying. There is never a condition that is so bad that you cannot accelerate and therefore take a positive attitude, a positive approach—and still have awareness enough left over to help other people.

One person among you can testify to this, of going through severe illness but still having people come to her at the hospital, still having that positive approach—and therefore, in that very focus beyond the self, receiving the healing. You cannot heal a problem created through the separate self as long as your self-awareness is focused inside that theatrical role of the separate self.

Accelerate, my beloved. Accelerate your way out of trouble. Instead of going into the dualistic reaction of either trying to flee, to take flight from the trouble, or to fight and destroy the trouble.

Overcoming perfectionism

There is no substitute for purity. There is, I am tempted to say, no greater joy than purity. But, of course, my beloved brothers and sisters on the other rays might say: "Serapis, you are getting a bit ahead of yourself here. You are being a bit excited about your own ray, but do not forget that we are equally excited about *ours.*" Of course, I bow to the realization that comes from my oneness with the other chohans on the other rays. Truly, we see each other as facets of the diamond, as we see you as facets of the diamond—the diamond heart of God, out of which all has sprung.

The Third Ray has the potential of having you go through the process described so beautifully in the gospel of John [messenger pauses and says "Excuse me."] — described so beautifully in the New Testament, of "being made perfect in love." [The expression is in the Letter of John]

You see, I deliberately caused this messenger to make a mistake, to give him another test of whether he could accelerate out of it and continue to stay with my vibration instead of going into a lower reaction. There are indeed many who feel that in order to be worthy to be a messenger of the ascended masters, you have to reach some state of perfection.

What is perfection? When you rise to the Fourth Ray and go through the initiations, I can assure you that one of the greatest tests for the students that come to my retreat is to overcome perfectionism. Perfectionism is a curse put upon humankind. It is a concept that has been perverted by the duality consciousness. Many people believe that perfection means that you live up to certain conditions. Any condition can exist only in the mind of duality. Any condition in the mind of duality has an opposite polarity, or it would not exist.

Love is in opposition to hatred or fear. If love has an opposite, it cannot be perfect love. Perfection cannot have an opposite—even though you may talk of imperfection. When you realize the reality, you realize that imperfection is not the opposite of true perfection, for perfection is simply *beyond* imperfection.

What has been done by the mind of duality is to create a dualistic concept of perfection that can, indeed, be in opposition to imperfection. You think that what makes you imperfect is a certain condition, and in order to become perfect, you have to take on another condition. Whether it is an "imperfect" condition or a "perfect" condition, any condition that you take on only affirms the reality of the separate self.

It is your ego that makes you feel unworthy. It is the ego that struts of spiritual pride—feeling better than others by having taken on the condition that it has defined as perfect. Either way – whether you are conditionally imperfect or conditionally perfect – you are trapped in the conditions of the separate self. How do you overcome it? You overcome it by seeing the illogical nature of this concept and realizing that you cannot set up any condition that defines perfection. In fact, if you were to truly look at the worldly concepts of perfection, you will see that they are in all cases not clearly defined.

When you start to define what perfection is, you immediately run into a dualistic argument—is it *this* or is it the opposite? Maybe one could argue that the opposite of that particular condition also has some merit. Maybe that should really be part of perfection, or should it be another one, or a third one, or a fourth one? Before you know it, you are so confused that you do not know what is up and down, and so how can you reach perfection?

You need to come to the point where you recognize that it is not possible to define perfection by setting up any condition whatsoever. Perfection means unconditionality. Unconditionality does not mean the loss of individuality. You do not become nothing by becoming unconditional. You become *no thing*, meaning, no condition in the dualistic realm, no thing in this universe. You become free of being tied to anything – any "thing" – any sense of identity in the dualistic realm.

The initiations of the Fourth Ray

The pyramid at Giza was originally designed for spiritual initiates on the Fourth Ray of purity. The king's chamber – or so it is called – was meant to represent that state of the death of the conditioned self. Those who had been prepared – through a very long, gradual and difficult process of initiation – would be led into that chamber, would be put in the sarcophagus and would then be left alone for 24, 36, or 48 hours—being left in complete darkness, complete silence, complete sensory deprivation.

As you will know from those who have been exposed to this as a form of torture, this is the extreme fear of the separate self. It does not know what it is when it has no sensory input. If you were to be exposed to this initiation before you were prepared for it, there is a high likelihood that people would go insane immediately upon experiencing that sensory deprivation.

An initiate that is prepared can use it to simply accelerate its sense of self out of the body and go to a higher realm, as you all do at night—perhaps without being consciously aware of it. This is the process that you are all going through, that you have been going through in a more difficult way than the initiates who came to a mystery school and isolated themselves from the world. You are going through it while still being immersed in an active life in the world. The process is much the same, although more gradual. You are coming closer and closer to the point where you can let the separate self die and surrender to unconditionality, the unconditionality of your higher self, your true identity.

The fear, of course, is: "But if I give up the ego and the separate self, what will I have left?" Do you think, my beloved, that this sense of fear is alien to me? How do you think I qualified for my ascension, unless I experienced that fear myself, faced it, and overcame it? How do you overcome that fear? By knowing you are *more* than the separate self. Then making the decision that you will not simply let the separate self die and be nothing. You will be reborn in the process by accelerating your entire being.

The Alpha and Omega of transcendence

You may think that all that happened to Jesus on the cross was that he hung there, going through the sense of separation of being left by God and then gave up the ghost, as we have talked about earlier. The deeper reality is that giving up the ghost was the Omega side of the equation. The Alpha side was that at the same time as he gave up the ghost of the separate self, he deliberately and willfully accelerated his sense of self to that higher vibration of the purity of who he really is—as that spiritual being that was never confined to the lower sense of self.

The giving up is the Omega, the acceleration is the Alpha. There is a point where you have given up enough that you are capable of making that final push away from the gravitational pull of whatever separate self is left, even the gravitational pull of the mass consciousness. At that point, there is only one thing that is necessary. It is the Alpha thrust of accelerating your sense of self whereby you accept that you have shifted your identity.

You may say: "But I cannot, in one step, accept that I am the full Christed being." This is not what I am asking you to do. I am asking you to acknowledge that you have followed the spiritual path, that you have gone through the necessary steps and that you have indeed reached a point of attainment whereby you are able to accelerate your service. You have gone through enough in your own being that you are now ready to bear witness and help other people. You are able to step up, my beloved. You are able to step up your service and your sense of self. Many of you have reached that level of attainment.

The only thing that is left is the acceptance of this fact. The acceptance of this fact is not a passive thing. Acceptance might seem passive—you accept something given to you from without. But acceptance also has an active quality of deliberately and consciously making the decision to choose to accelerate your sense of self. In accelerating it, you experience it, and in experiencing it, you accept it even more fully. This is the key to healing.

Acceptance is the key to healing

As Mother Mary said in the beginning, why are some people coming to Lourdes and they are not healed, and some people come, go through the same water, and they are healed? The difference is in the acceptance, but more than the passive acceptance. Those who are healed accelerate – even if they would not be able to use these terms – their sense of self and accept that they are no longer the ill person that walked into the pool. They are the healed person that is walking out of it.

You, of course, do not need a pool of water to come to this acceptance—for then you might have ascended after taking swimming lessons as children. You do need to recognize that there comes that nexus point where you have done enough in the Omega. But it is necessary to go into the nexus, accelerate your sense of identity, come into oneness with the Alpha of your being, and then let that Alpha flow through you for the raising up of all life. *That* is the decision you face on the Fourth Ray.

I ask you, as you retire each night, to make a call to be taken to the etheric retreat of Serapis Bey, centered over Luxor, Egypt, so that you may receive personal instructions for how you, personally, need to accelerate beyond that last illusion that is holding you back. Be willing to see it, and I will help you see, it in the days, perhaps weeks and months, ahead. You are capable, my beloved. You are a rocket sitting on the launch pad. Your engines are fully fueled and ignited, but you do not yet have liftoff.

The movement created by spiritual seekers is ready to take off and accelerate beyond what most of you can even dare to envision right now. When you accelerate your sense of self, you will not grow your movement by your own power, but by the power of God and the Holy Spirit through you. This is precisely how the Christian movement grew 2,000 years ago—by the disciples being willing to step out of the separate sense of self and lock in to a cause. The cause was that of going out into all the world and making all people the disciples of Christ and the true Way of Christ—not to be confused with the Christian churches.

Contemplate this. Contemplate this shift of self. I hope you will, indeed, listen to or read this release over and over again, until you feel you have truly absorbed not just the words and the concepts and the ideas, but the very vibration of the hierarch of the Fourth Ray of purity.

Receive the blazing Sun of the Fourth Ray of purity, radiating into your Heart Chakra. If you receive it, you then become, as Mother Mary so beautifully put it, a crystal in the chain. The light will radiate through you to all life, and to the many thousands and millions of people on this earth who are also ready to break through, to accelerate into a new level of consciousness. Thereby, they will accelerate their society to an entirely new level where in a decade, or a little more, people will look back at the present time and say: "My goodness how the world has changed. How could we ever have believed that such an acceleration was possible. Where did it all come from?"

The writers of history will look back at the many thousands of years previously and be in bewilderment as to how such an acceleration could take place. At least they will be bewildered unless they understand the spiritual equation that all life is one. When a critical mass of people accelerate their consciousness, it will pull up all life on this blessed planet.

My release is complete. With unconditional gratitude, I leave you bathed in the light of purity. The unconditional purity that *I AM*.

9 | FIFTH RAY: CLOSING THE GAP ON THE SPIRITUAL PATH

A dictation by Mother Mary

Mary is my name. The Divine Mother is my office. Yet, I, am MORE. What is the desire of the Divine Mother for her children? It is to have them awaken to the reality that they, too, are *more*. You were created out of the More of God, the desire of God, to be *more*.

How can an almighty, self-sufficient, self-contained, all-pervading, omnipresent being become more? Only by creating self-aware extensions of itself that start from a particular location in cosmic space and then grow in self-awareness so that they become more, giving your Creator the experience of becoming more through you.

It is inevitable – when you see this journey – that you start out feeling small, but it is not inevitable that you feel alone. The sense of aloneness comes from separation, but the message we are bringing you – again and again from different perspectives – is that separation is not real, separation is an illusion.

Why separation is an untruth

This messenger once said to another person: "If God is omnipresent, how can one find a place where God is not?" The person was shocked, for having grown up in a traditional Christian culture, he had been so indoctrinated with the image of the external, remote God in the sky that his mind could not comprehend what he was told. Yet, it is reality.

You cannot, my beloved, separate from God. It is, again, the illusion, the spiritual pride and the arrogance of those who have decided to rebel against God that they believe they can set themselves up in opposition to God and turn the earth into a place where God is not present. Or they think they can create a hell where God is not present. God is present everywhere and in everything, through the office of his Son, the Word, or rather the Logos—for without him was not any thing made that was made.

You may look at yourself right now and see that you are at a certain state of consciousness, at a certain state of being somewhat enveloped in material circumstances. Yet, I tell you, with the pure love of my Mother's heart, that no matter how you may look at yourself right now, no matter how you may look at your past and the mistakes you think you have made, you could not possibly do anything that would make God or the Divine Mother turn away from you.

You can, of course, use your free will to turn away from God. This is your right that God has given you. But know that even when you do turn away from God, God is still experiencing everything you experience through you.

My point is simply that if you desire, my beloved, to have the experience of being alone, being left by God, feeling rejected by God, then, as Master MORE explained, you have the right to have that experience for as long as you want. If you come to a point where you desire to no longer have that experience, then I submit to you that it is possible to instantly switch your perspective on life and recognize that God is here with you, the Divine Mother is here with you. Therefore, you do not need to feel alone. You are never alone, for all life is one.

The only way to be free is to stop running away

I assure you that when you give up the sense of aloneness, you will find it so much easier to deal with whatever circumstance you may be facing, be it external circumstances or the internal circumstances of your mind. What have the masters that have spoken before me been saying? They have been saying that when you accept the illusion of separation, out of that illusion springs an image that is projected upon the Ma-ter light and that will eventually manifest as some kind of condition in your physical body. The illusion of separation is an act of running away, running away from God. Trying to run away from the condition in your body or the consciousness behind it will not set you free. The only way to be free is to stop running away, my beloved.

As has been said before by us, if you keep doing the same thing and expect different results, well, you are not likely to get different results, are you now. There comes a point of truth, a point of realism, where one must ask oneself: "If I keep doing what I have always done, is it likely that my life will change?"

Ask yourself: "Am I happy in my present state of consciousness and in my present circumstances?" My beloved, listen carefully. Many of you will instinctively say: "No I am not happy." But I ask you to step back and ask this question at a deeper level.

What we have explained in the previous releases in this series of discourses is that you have free will. Everything that you are facing in your life is a result of choices you made. Because of that, you have the potential to take back your power and change the choices of the past by making choices that are not based on separation and duality but choices based on oneness. You can, indeed, have the power, the wisdom, the love—and the acceleration of the three of them coming together in that intensity of the white light that propels you beyond your present state of consciousness, any state of consciousness.

You, who are the spiritual people, must come to that point where you say to yourself: "Am I happy in my present state of mind?" Meaning, if I have not taken back my power to change my present state of mind, is it because I actually enjoy torturing or putting myself down? Is there something in this experience of seeing myself unworthy or feeling alone that I have not had enough of? If you honestly recognize that you have not had enough of that experience, then know that neither I, nor any other being in heaven, will condemn you for it. We respect free will absolutely and unconditionally.

You have a right to any experience you desire for as long as you desire it—within certain boundaries of time and space, of course. Nothing in time and space can be permanent or last forever, but within very wide boundaries, you have the right to any experience you desire. If you honestly recognize that you desire to continue with the experience that you have through your present state of consciousness, then embrace it, my beloved. Embrace your misery, your sense of unworthiness, your sense of aloneness, your fear. Embrace it and enjoy it, for this is what you have chosen to manifest right now.

The gap between you and your goals

If you find, with your self-examination, that "I am not happy in my present state of mind," then you have another consideration to make. It is possible – because you have not been given the correct understanding of who you are and of free will – to be in a twilight zone, in a no-man's land, and this is what other masters have attempted to explain before me. This is the catch-22 where there is a part of you that wants to change, but yet you cannot change. There is something holding you back, something that prevents you from fully changing. You might look at spiritual movements and see so many people who have been walking a spiritual path for many years. They have studied teachings, they have practiced techniques, they have sought healing. They have attempted in many different ways to change their life experience, their state of consciousness.

Many people have gone through the first three rays, to some degree taking back their power, for you cannot be in a spiritual movement or on the spiritual path without realizing that you have to do something. They have also spent countless hours studying spiritual teachings, and thereby they have increased their understanding. They have even had so-called peak experiences of experiencing a higher state of consciousness, perhaps even unconditional love in glimpses. They might even have put the three together and accelerated themselves beyond the level of consciousness they had 1, 10, 20 or 30 years ago. Yet there is still a gap between where they are and where they want to be.

They are not happy, they are not at peace in their present state of consciousness. They are not, as the saying goes, walking their talk. They can talk a good game of spiritual theory, but when it comes to applying it in their practical, everyday life, there is a gap. What I endeavor to start with this release is the Omega aspect of this crash course in the restoration of true healing.

The figure-eight flow

I ask you to visualize a figure-eight and realize that the lower figure represents the material world whereas the upper figure represents the spiritual. In personal terms the upper figure is your I AM Presence and higher being, even the higher beings out of which you came, reaching all the way to the Creator, which we might represent as a point at the very top of the figure-eight. Although, of course, the Creator needs no real representation, for by creating a representation, we might cause some to reinforce the image of the external creator. Nevertheless, for the purpose of this linear illustration, let us simply make it so.

Look at the opposite point at the very bottom of the figure-eight. That is where you are in consciousness when you awaken and begin your spiritual path. This may not have happened in this lifetime, or it may have happened by you having an experience in this lifetime where you felt that your life had turned around and you realized that you had to change something in your life. For some it may come as a hit-rock-bottom experience where they feel they cannot possibly go any lower, they cannot possibly continue doing what they have been doing.

For many of you, you have already had that experience in past lives, and you came into this lifetime knowing that there was something you had to find. You were looking and searching for what it was, and there came a point where you became consciously aware of the spiritual side of life and the potential to actively raise your consciousness by your own efforts, so to speak, of being willing to go through the initiations of the first four rays, as described previously.

Now visualize that you start at that very bottom point, of the lower point of the figure-eight flow. That is the point where you consciously start walking the path. At that point, you start with the initiations of the First Ray because it is not enough to realize that you can take a step—you have to summon the will to take a step. You have already summoned some of that will, or you would not be where you are today where you can even find and receive this message. You go through the initiations of the First Ray of power and will, and you climb up the left side of the figure-eight, the lower figure of the figure-eight, going in a clockwise direction, as if the lower figure was a circle.

You come to a certain point of having passed enough of the initiations of the First Ray that you can move on and begin to internalize more knowledge, more understanding, more wisdom. You study, and you study, and you study. After you have internalized and climbed to a higher point on that circle, you come to the Third Ray of love and you receive some experience of something beyond your normal state of consciousness. It may not be the full unconditional love of God – although it is certainly possible to have that experience – but there is *some* love. You have climbed to the point where you are now approaching the nexus of the figure-eight.

The nexus, of course, is the point of the Christ. For the purpose of this discussion of personal healing, what is that point of Christhood? It is the point that Serapis spoke about where you decide that you can take what you have gained through the first three rays, put the blue, the yellow and the pink together – having attained some measure of that balance of what has been called the threefold flame of the heart – and blend the three together to the intensity and the purity of the white light. You then use that white light to consciously and deliberately accelerate your state of consciousness to a certain level.

You are crucified in matter

In a sense, what did Jesus demonstrate by coming into embodiment and letting himself be crucified? What did Jesus mean when he said: "Before Abraham was, I AM?" Certainly, the physical body of Jesus could not be older than Abraham—that makes no logical sense whatsoever. There must be a hidden meaning, which of course, you cannot divine by taking the Bible literally—as it was never meant to be taken literally. The reality is that many of the statements made by Jesus were not made by a particular individual being embodied at a particular point in time and space. It was made by the Logos, by the

Word, by the universal, cosmic Christ consciousness speaking through him. What was meant to be illustrated here is that the Christ has been crucified in matter by allowing people to project whatever images upon that Logos so that they could be outpictured by the Ma-ter light as physical form. Even though I have said earlier that everything is made out of the Ma-ter light, there is a deeper understanding that the Ma-ter light springs from the Logos of the Christ consciousness. That is why the Christ consciousness, of course, is everywhere. Everything that is made out of the Christ consciousness has the Christ consciousness embedded within it.

The Christ consciousness is not necessarily expressed in form. It lies dormant, for it has been crucified by the lower images, the images projected by those who have decided to leave the oneness of the Christ consciousness, go into the illusion of separation and duality, create images from that state of consciousness and project them onto matter—which then is why the Christ is crucified. This is why Jesus came to demonstrate that even though the Christ will allow itself to be crucified, you cannot limit or confine the Christ. Even though the Christ is crucified in matter, the Christ knows that it is *more,* that it is *One,* that it has the potential to be resurrected and ascend.

How do you personally come up higher? By following the example of Jesus, the embodied man who was crucified, who fulfilled a mission and who gave up the ghost. What is the message for humankind as a whole? It is that Jesus, as you see outpictured in the outer stations of the cross, was condemned to death by the consciousness of death, the consciousness of separation and duality. Jesus accepted that cross and then Jesus was nailed to the cross, gave up the ghost, moved on.

Then comes the significance of Jesus being taken down from the cross. It is the choices of self-aware beings – humankind – that have nailed the Christ to the cross of matter. The Christ cannot take itself down, for the Christ is only hanging on the cross in the minds of people in duality. You see the message here? You may think, my beloved, that human beings had the power to nail Jesus to the cross, and they did have the power to nail the outer person. But they could not nail the Christ consciousness to the cross in the sense that the Christ consciousness is the same yesterday, today and forever—and is therefore not changed in its self-awareness, self-image, by anything that happens or is done to it. It is only in the minds of the people, and therefore – in reality – when they nail Christ to the cross, they are nailing themselves to the cross.

Do you see? Do onto others what you want others to do to you. The deeper meaning being that what you do onto others, you have already done to yourself. In order to be able to nail Jesus to the cross, humankind must first have nailed themselves to the cross. The Mother and her children are indeed nailed to the cross, but only in the minds of the children, for the Mother always knows who she is.

Why can't people close the gap?

Why is it that so many people in spiritual and religious movements have the will to change yet there is still a gap? They have the wisdom of spiritual concepts and may even see how they need to change. They have had an experience of unconditional love, of a higher state of consciousness. They may even have gone through the acceleration of raising their consciousness. Yet there is still a gap that they cannot close. They cannot come to that sense of inner peace, for they cannot embrace whatever situation they face and stop running away, stop seeing that gap, and fully *be* in the moment, whatever the moment might bring. Why is that, my beloved? Well, it is because after you pass the initiations of the first four rays, you have entered that point of the nexus of the figure-eight. Now you face an entirely new kind of initiation that very few people have understood.

So listen, attentively. Look at the mindset when you realize you are at the bottom of the figure-eight and you want to rise higher. You gradually expand your vision that there is a spiritual realm beyond the material. You build your desire to come into oneness with that Spirit, to reach up. Because you have had the images of the external God in the sky, you might build the subtle sense that you have to raise your consciousness into the spiritual realm.

You might take on the subtle lie that the material world is an enemy of your spiritual growth and that you need to escape the material world and ascend into the spiritual realm. You might think that as you climb that lower figure of the figure-eight and reach the nexus, that is the point where you are free. Now you can go into the upper figure of the figure-eight and continue the initiations there.

Many people think that what they have done on the spiritual path on the first four rays, they simply need to continue that mindset and that thrust, and *that* will carry them on to the Fifth, the Sixth and the Seventh Ray and beyond. They think they have to continue in that direction, to continue to do what they have been doing.

This, my beloved, is a fundamental error, a fundamental misunderstanding. I use strong words because I want to shock you into realizing that if you truly want to close the gap between where you are and where you want to be, you need to change your mindset. It is the mindset that sustains the gap, irregardless of the fact that you have made much progress on the path so far. You cannot go beyond the Fourth Ray by using the mindset that helped you climb the lower figure of the figure-eight to the nexus point. This is what Jesus describes in his *Course in Christhood*. I desire to give you a different perspective as well.

Surrender is the only way

What will it take to experience true healing? You cannot become whole, you cannot become healed, by will power alone, by wisdom alone, by love alone, or by purity alone. Why not? Because as you climb that lower figure of the figure-eight, you are carrying with you the separate self. As some of you have come to realize and see clearly outpictured in your own minds, it is inevitable that as you increase your understanding of spiritual concepts, your ego will not simply die. It will morph itself into a form that for a time will make you believe that the ego can actually be perfected and become acceptable to God.

It is possible to use a spiritual teaching and spiritual practices to "perfect" the separate self so that it seemingly lives up to some condition that will make it acceptable in the eyes of God and therefore give it entry into the kingdom. This is what Jesus illustrated in his parable about the wedding feast where all are invited, but if you come in without a wedding garment, then you cannot stay.

You will not actually be cast into outer darkness by any external force. The reality is that there is still a remnant of the separate self, and it will pull you out of the wedding feast—and that is what creates the gap that you seemingly cannot cross. You are trying to fit the square peg of the separate self into the round hole that leads to heaven. You are trying to carry that luggage with you through the narrow door into the train that simply will not fit. You have to decide that if you want to get on the train, you have to leave your luggage behind and give up the ghost. How do you, then, give up the ghost? This is the question you need to ponder. You cannot give up the ghost by seeking to perfect the ghost.

The only way is the path of surrender. Surrender, my beloved, may sound like a strange concept. You have grown up in a culture on this planet that is infused with the consciousness of competition and war. What does the word surrender mean in war? Well, it means that you give up and you are defeated. What does surrender mean in competition? That you give up winning and therefore you lose.

The concept of win or lose is dualistic indeed. One must lose in order for another to win. Where is the true victory in that? Surrender in a spiritual sense is not a passive act of giving up. It is an active process of giving up the ghost. Giving *up*, not giving up. You give *up* the ghost to a higher vision, for you are willing to give *up* the separate self in order to become more whole.

You are willing to give *up* a part of that separate self in order to experience more wholeness. You are willing to give up one dollar to receive a million in return. There is no loss in true surrender. There is only freedom. This is what many of you have not fully locked in to in your minds.

Being right among men or right with God

What I desire to give you here is one illustration of where you have not understood this, and it is in your personal relationships with other people. When souls come to the retreat of Serapis Bey, they are put into groups with other souls with whom they have clashing astrology, personality, karma and so on. Those who have the greatest potential to clash are put together, and they will stay together until they come to the point where they begin to recognize that something is more important than being right.

What did Master MORE say? What have other masters said? The world is a drama—you can play any role you want for as long as you want. When you come to the spiritual path, and when you desire to ascend beyond a certain level, then you must come to the realization that you no longer want to play the dualistic game where you win or lose, or where you are right or wrong compared to others. Instead of seeking to be right, to be understood, to be heard, to be validated by others, you realize that it is more important to find wholeness within yourself than to be thought of a certain way by other people.

Do you see what Jesus demonstrated by letting himself be crucified? There are those who will say that Jesus lost, that they did to him whatever they wanted and thus *they* won. But do you see that they did not win? Had they won, Jesus would have fought the forces of anti-christ, which is precisely what they want. When you, as a spiritual person, think you have to fight and destroy the forces of anti-christ, they are successful in pulling you into the dualistic struggle. Do you see the reality here?

Think about your situations where you have conflicts or tussles with other people. Think about how easy it is to be pulled into this dualistic sense that you have to be right, that they are wrong, that you have to be heard, that they do not hear you, that you have to be validated, but no one cares about you.

What do you do? You go into the mode of wanting to force others to change. You can have passed the initiations of the first four rays, but yet you cannot pass the initiations of the Fifth Ray until you realize what I am talking about here. You must be willing to be non-attached to what happens on earth. You must come to the point where you have the full understanding of free will and the absolute respect for free will. You recognize that without free will there would be no growth possible, there would be, in fact, no self-awareness. The very purpose that God has for creating the world of form could not be fulfilled without free will because God desires you to become *more* through your own free-will choices.

When you recognize *that,* you recognize that your reaction to any situation on earth is not something that is forced upon you by outer circumstances or other people. You must come to the point of truth where you take responsibility for your state of consciousness and you say: "The concept that *you* made me feel this way must go. It must get out of this consciousness, for I recognize that no one makes me feel a certain way. I am responsible for my state of mind, for my thoughts, my feelings, for my sense of identity."

You are not responsible for other people

So many people have risen on the spiritual path to where they have enough mastery over the physical aspect, over their actions, that they would never do anything they deem as non-spiritual. But they have not yet attained mastery over the inner state of mind, their thoughts, their feelings. They can stop their thoughts and feelings from being expressed in actions, or at least, certain types of actions, but they cannot stop their thoughts and feelings, for they have not taken that full responsibility.

The Omega aspect of taking full responsibility is that you also realize that other people have free will, and *they* are responsible for *their* reactions towards you. You cannot hurt another human being, just as another human being cannot hurt you. You can use what another person does to you as a justification for going into a lower state of vibration where you feel hurt. The other person can do the same by letting one of your actions or words be a justification for descending in consciousness.

You have a right to make that choice. The other person has a right to make that choice. Therefore, you must come to that point of the sense of truth where you realize that the Law of Free Will makes you one hundred percent responsible for your own actions, your own feelings, your own thoughts, your own sense of identity. But the Law of Free Will also says that you are one hundred percent *not* responsible for the actions, feelings, thoughts and sense of identity of any other human being. You are not responsible for other people.

So many of you on the spiritual path feel a sense of responsibility towards others. What happens when you feel that false sense of responsibility, my beloved? Well, what happens is precisely that you cannot have full mastery of your own state of mind, for subconsciously you believe that because you are responsible for other people, you should allow *your* state of mind to be dependent on *their* state of mind. You are thinking you have to allow your state of mind, your life experience, to be dependent on the choices made by other people.

You will never close the gap, my beloved, as long as you hold on to this false sense of responsibility. You will never be in a situation where all other people on this planet will be in total agreement with you. They are individuals, they are different. What you are essentially thinking – at a subconscious level, not consciously – is that you can only attain happiness and inner peace when all of the people behave in such a way that they do not pull you out of the centeredness of happiness and inner peace. Thereby, you think that for this to happen, all of the people must become like you. If they are different, how could they not disturb your sense of peace? It, of course, is the ego who has this feeling.

As long as you have not seen that this is an aspect of ego, you can identify yourself with it. You must ponder this until it clicks, so to speak, and you literally experience the reality of free will. You literally experience the surrender of that false responsibility, the sense that your state of mind depends on other people's state of mind, that your state of mind depends on material conditions in this universe. My beloved, would you breathe in with me, and then breathe out that false sense of responsibility?

Do you feel lighter? Do you feel a release? Some of you do. All of you *can*, if you keep pondering this until you can come to have enough understanding that you can make a conscious decision to actively surrender this sense of responsibility.

Many of you on the spiritual path have descended into embodiment on earth a long time ago for the purpose of helping to raise this planet and raise the consciousness of humankind. Some of you descended because a member of your spiritual bands – perhaps one that was very close to you – chose to enter into duality and fall into a lower state of consciousness, and you came to save that one.

Those are the ones who might find it most difficult to release the sense of responsibility for others—if you descended to save one person. Many of you descended to save humankind as a whole. You will find it slightly easier to let go, for your sense of responsibility for others is not quite as personal, and thus you can separate yourself from it more easily.

When you recognize the reality of free will, you recognize that no one can save anyone else. Jesus has been called the Savior, but it is, again, because they want to project a graven image upon him to obscure his true mission. He did not come to save anyone but to show everyone how they can attain salvation within themselves by walking through the initiations of the seven rays and releasing the illusion that they need salvation, that they are separated from their source and from the kingdom of God.

Completing the circle of initiation

When one starts at the bottom of the figure-eight, one clearly sees that there is a gap between where I am, and where the kingdom of God is. You have to create a thrust in order to rise above the gravitational pull of the mass consciousness, as Serapis illustrated with his analogy of the rocket. There has to be momentum, you have to create a force, and you have to do it partly with the state of consciousness you are in at the time, meaning

9 | Fifth Ray: Closing the Gap on the Spiritual Path

that your separate self, your ego, will be involved. The ego will color your efforts to some degree by its desire for self-elevation and for feeling important. That is why you respond to spiritual teachings that tell you that you have an important mission to save the world for Saint Germain, and bring the Golden Age and do all of these outer things. You think that you actively have to be part of this, you have to create some kind of force or thrust that makes it manifest. This is correct—through the initiations of the first four rays. But you will not get beyond that point until you realize that what has carried you to this point will not carry you further; it will weigh you down.

Look at a rocket that has several stages. First it has a very large booster that is meant only to accelerate it to a certain point, and then the fuel in that booster is burned out. It must now be separated from the rocket and it falls away and the rocket starts another engine that takes it beyond to orbit. If you insist on holding on to the mindset that boosted you through the first four rays, you cannot progress, you are stuck in a no-man's land. You are feeling that you *want* to change, that you *have* to change, you see a glimpse of what has to change, but you cannot internalize it, you cannot bring it into your consciousness.

The illustration that I want to give you here is that when you come to the nexus point of the figure-eight, you have the potential to attain a new perspective, the perspective of the Christ mind, the mind of oneness rather than the mind of separation. When you attain that perspective of the Christ mind, you see clearly that the path forward does not go into the upper figure of the figure-eight. No, it goes out from the nexus point and down on the right side of the figure-eight where you now begin to descend again. Why does it seem like – in order to rise higher on the spiritual path – you have to start descending? Well, it is because what you have done so far is to take a part of your consciousness and thrust it beyond the mass consciousness. There is still a part of you left, and that is why you feel a gap, that is why you are not quite there, you are not quite together, you are not quite whole.

You must use the higher thrust and insight and perspective you have gained with a part of your mind to go down again and rescue, so to speak, all other parts of your being, all other fragments of your soul, if you want to call them that. Even beyond that, you must come to recognize that you are one cell in the Body of God and that your job is not just to resurrect that one cell that you are, but to resurrect the entire body.

In order to rise higher personally, you must begin to share and give out what you have gained by seeking to go out into the marketplace and reach other people. This Jesus demonstrated by going into the marketplace of life, giving people what they needed, whether it was a higher spiritual teaching, whether it was healing, whether it was a cup of cold water in Christ's name, a listening ear. You all have qualities that you are aware of, or can quickly become aware of, that can help other people. Some of you have expressed it, all of you have it. All of you have already used those qualities, but you need to come to the point where you are willing to use them more consciously. Not for your own personal growth, but for the selfless service of raising other parts of life, for it is in that service that you are healed.

Your potential to give service

Many of you have already done this throughout your lives, but I tell you, again, there are levels of awareness where you become more and more aware of your potential to give service—not by using your own internal qualities alone but by being the open door. Do you see that while you are reaching up on the one side of the figure-eight, the lower figure, you are reaching up for the Spirit?

In the nexus you connect to it, and then comes the Omega thrust of bringing it down to serve all life. Then you become, as Jesus said: "I AM the open door, which no man can shut." Do you see how this ties together with my teaching about being non-attached to the reactions of other people?

You must come to that point where you know that you are the open door which no man can shut. Neither the man of your own ego can shut your door and cause you to withhold your light and your love and your service, nor the reactions of other people—whether they reject you or ridicule you or whether they feel that they have put you down and won some petty victory of the dualistic self over you.

Do you see that you are not here to battle and engage them? You are here to simply stand and *be* and radiate your light and demonstrate that whatever they throw at you cannot touch you, cannot change your self-image.

Do you see that this is what Jesus did to the scribes and Pharisees and others? He demonstrated that whatever they threw at him, they could not engage him in the dualistic battle. He would simply be who he was—state the truth. You are not here to state it – all of you – the same way that you saw Jesus state it. You are here to state and to radiate the light that you are, and to not allow any lower force to cause you to shut it off. That is the initiation that begins on the Fifth Ray. That is the initiation, the mindset that will bring you closer to healing. You will only heal your lower being by reaching beyond the lower being and seeking to heal others, seeking to bring the light.

The Divine Mother and her children

The painting you heard described – of the soldier's body that was shattered on the battlefield and the mother going in and assembling the parts of the body – that was an image that was inspired by me upon that particular artist to illustrate what has happened to the Divine Mother. The body of her children has been scattered on the battlefield of life, the battlefield of duality.

The Mother calls and sings to bring her children together, but they cannot hear her song. What does the Mother look for? She looks for those who are the more mature of her children – who have come into some degree of oneness with her, realizing that they *are* the Divine Mother in expression – who will then go down and sing to people in a way that they can hear, and that they, thus, cannot as easily ignore.

Again, you are not here to change their minds, my beloved. You are just here to show them that it is possible to change your mind—that you have done it and that they cannot force you to descend to their state of consciousness.

You have heard us talk about the closed circle. What is the closed circle, what is the closed system? It is the mindset of the ego and the separate self. What is – if you strip away all of the outer camouflage of the separate self – the one question asked by the ego and the separate self—the constant question that the ego is projecting out from itself? It is this: "Validate me. Tell me I am real. Tell me that the illusion I have created – the image I have created of what life is, what God is, what I am – tell me it is real. Affirm it. Affirm me. Affirm me. Affirm me."

How can you help people who are so trapped in this consciousness that they are not willing to rethink it, to reconsider it, to consider that it might be wrong? Do you help them by affirming their illusion? Of course not! How can you help them? By demonstrating that you are not trapped in that illusion, by standing there firm and letting them attack you, letting them ridicule you, letting them ask questions—but you remain who you are. You demonstrate that whatever they throw at you, they cannot pull you into their state of consciousness.

You are not affirming the reality of their state of consciousness, you are demonstrating the non-reality of it. That is why you need to work on your attachment to the reactions of other people. You cannot stand firm in who you are if you have a sense of responsibility for others, if you are attached to their reactions, or if you are still so identified with your separate self that you want validation from others.

You are a spiritual being, my beloved. You are here to help those who are trapped in duality. Do not expect that you can open your mouth and they are instantly going to say: "Oh, he is right." They cannot see it. Do you not see that?

Do you not understand that for you to help a person, you must demonstrate repeatedly that you will not affirm the person's state of mind? You must sometimes – as some of you have experienced with your friends or even family – you must let them question or attack or seemingly reject you many times. If you can stay centered and non-attached, one of two things will happen. Either the person will have a breakthrough and see that they can follow your example and reach a higher state of consciousness—and thus, they will come with you up. Or they will come to the point where the Law of Free Will mandates that they have had enough opportunity, and therefore they reach what we have called the judgment. This does not necessarily mean that they are condemned to hell, but it means that they have had enough opportunities from you, and therefore, you can now move on and seek to help others. You do not need to encounter that person or even that state of consciousness anymore.

You need to come to that point where you are non-attached to whatever state of consciousness you encounter. This, of course, is difficult, I understand. Do you know why I understand? Because I see that the consciousness that you will encounter, the consciousness you will encounter in other people, is exactly the consciousness that you have not yet raised in yourself.

Whatever wounds you have left, whatever unresolved substance you have in your own being, *that* is what you will encounter from others. The unresolved stuff in your own being will act as a magnet that magnetizes these other people to you. It is, of course, the most difficult for you to depersonalize your relationship with these people and remain non-attached. The unresolved substance in your own mind, the beam in your own eye, holds you into an attachment and a dualistic reaction.

My beloved, you are, indeed, mature on the path. You can come to understand this, you can come to realize it. You can come to very quickly apply it and feel that release: "I do not have to react the way I have always reacted. I do not have to affirm the reality of a lower reaction." I have an option to step outside of my previous reactionary pattern of that costume, see it as a costume and say: "I have had enough of playing that role in the drama of life. This role no longer reflects who I AM."

This is something we will talk more about in the coming releases. I want to give you a glimpse of what is ahead, as I have attempted to reach to what has come before, bringing it together. I hope that you have now gained a new vision of the spiritual path and what the spiritual path is all about so that you can change direction instead of seeking to always reach up.

Be willing to go from the nexus out. Bring back all the parts of yourself. Bring back all the parts of your larger self, the Body of the Divine Mother so that we may all come into wholeness, into oneness. Thereby, we can be the chalice that can receive the vision for the kingdom of God and the Golden Age of Saint Germain.

I thank you for being who you are—whomever you think you are. I love you unconditionally. I love both who you really are and who you think you are. I hope I have shattered the illusion that you are not loved by the Divine Mother. Whatever you feel towards me, however you respond or not respond to my words, I love you for that response.

I AM love, and you cannot come up with any response that will force me to no longer love you. I choose to be One with the River of Life.

10 | SIXTH RAY: THE UNCONDITIONAL JOY OF SERVICE

A dictation by Lady Master Nada

Nada is the name I have given. It is a name that has been associated with the Sixth Ray of service and ministration. But, of course, as you might have noticed with all of those who have spoken before me, I AM MORE. Why do we say this? You will see that we have given you our past lives in order to signify to you that because we have been embodied and have ascended, you too can ascend.

We also know that the human mind, the dualistic mind, will take anything and turn it into a graven image, and therefore say: "Ah, yes, Nada. I have a little box in my database where I can put her." If you put me in a box in the database, you will not tune in to the fullness of who I AM, for I will not fit in any database on earth. I AM beyond conditions, and service, true service, is beyond conditions. Why, my beloved, is this so?

You volunteered to descend into the denser realms of this material universe. Perhaps you were previously in a higher sphere. At some point you volunteered to serve in raising all life. How do you raise all life, my beloved? Why do you need to raise all life? Because, as Maitreya explains in his book, God creates a sphere that has a basic structure but is not yet completely filled with light. Then God sends extensions of itself into the sphere to be the open doors for bringing more light. In serving in that process, they grow in self-awareness.

You came here to bring light

You came into form in order to serve by bringing the light, out of which you came, into this world, raising it up, spreading the light, filling the world with light, so to speak. What is the light of which I speak? It is *spiritual* light.

If you want a visual illustration, consider the planetary model of the atom with a nucleus and electrons orbiting around it. Consider how much empty space there is. If you look at the proportions of the atom, compared to the proportions of your solar system, there is actually more space between the electrons and the nucleus than there is between the Sun and even the most remote planet.

In the structure of matter, at the current level of this material universe, there is much empty space. There is much room to be filled with light.

You came here to share your light. For many of you, when you came here there were already beings who had descended into the duality consciousness. When you came, you experienced that your light was not received. Not only was it not received, it was rejected, or you received the message that only if your light lived up to certain conditions would people receive it.

Gradually, you came to accept the idea that you should either color your light or suppress the flow of light through you. The reality of disease of any kind in the physical body is that it began in the higher bodies as a suppression of the light that you are. When you suppress the light, then you are not in the River of Life. You do not feel fulfilled, happy, at peace, joyous. You do not feel alive.

Suddenly, you have people who come to the realization that they have a disease in the physical body that might actually kill the body. What do they try to do? They try to suppress even more. But it was suppression that started the chain reaction that led to the physical disease. How can more suppression help you overcome the physical condition?

When people come into a spiritual movement, their ego morphs into a so-called spiritual ego, or spiritual persona, that takes on the characteristics that it thinks it needs to take on. In many cases that means people accept that you should behave a certain way. There are certain things you should not say, certain things you should not express. Many people grew up in an environment where everyone suppressed their emotions. Some have overcome this to the point of feeling comfortable expressing positive emotions, but not feeling equally comfortable expressing so-called negative emotions.

Many of you will recognize the same pattern. You realize that in a spiritual movement, certain things are appropriate and certain things are not. Why do you have *four* lower bodies? Because the material universe is at such a low vibration that you cannot express light here from the etheric level directly. You need lower bodies, gradually stepping down the light, eventually reaching that level of the material universe with its density.

You have four lower bodies that are designed to be vessels for transferring the light. If you are to express your light in the material universe, you must express it by letting it flow from your higher being into your identity body, into your mental body, into your emotional body, and then into the physical where you express it in different ways. One example is certainly through speaking the word, but also by a smile, by a look, by expressing that emotion that is genuine and sincere, thus uplifting another person.

Suppressed emotions block the flow of light

What I want to bring to your attention here is that what stops the light is the decision to suppress something. When things are suppressed, they cannot flow. When they cannot flow, well they must accumulate. You have many people who accept a certain sense of identity that sets limitations. They accept mental limitations of what is proper to think or believe. They accept other limitations for what emotions are proper, and you see the suppression in the emotional body. The suppressed emotions will naturally begin to accumulate. As the emotional body fills up, there is no longer the flow of light that can penetrate through the suppressed emotions.

The light cannot reach your physical body and renew the cells. The cells begin to outpicture that they cannot flow, that they cannot bring forth new life and so they bring forth lower manifestations. As a spiritual person, can you see that when you realize you need some kind of healing in the physical body, your spiritual imagery, your spiritual persona, your spiritual culture can be a direct block to that healing? You are not willing to acknowledge that in order for you to be healed, you have to re-establish the flow of light through the emotional body. The only way to do this, my beloved, is to go into the emotions that have accumulated and get them flowing again.

In many cases this means that you must stop suppressing the negative emotions and give expression to them for a time— no matter how wrong or shallow they might seem. Some people have gone through several years of journaling, expressing whatever came to them. If you do not express it, you cannot re-establish the flow and thus you can continue, for the rest of your life, being stuck at a certain level of consciousness. You think – with the outer ego that has taken on this aura of spirituality – that in order to reinforce the image that you are a spiritual person, you cannot express any negative emotions. If you do, you may indeed get a negative reaction and have others think negatively of you.

You want to continue to suppress these emotions, but in suppressing them, what are you doing? You are continuing to block the flow. You cannot break through – in your conscious awareness – to your conscious acceptance of who you really are. You remain trapped in a lower sense of identity. Certainly, the negative emotions are not pleasant. Certainly, they should not necessarily be expressed in a group setting. But you, individually, need to express the emotions so that you can work through them and not only theoretically understand, but directly experience, that you are more than the emotions.

What will happen is that as you give expression to them, and as you look at them, at some point, you will have that Aha-experience of realizing: "But this is not who I am. I am more than this. This is just energy that has taken on a certain vibration, a certain condition. But this is not the fullness of who I am. I am *feeling* this way, but that does not mean that I *am* this way."

Unless you look at the emotions, you cannot come to see that you are *more*. When you run away – do not want to acknowledge that you even have negative emotions, and do not want to give them expression – you are continuing to reinforce the gap, as Mother Mary spoke about, between where you are and where you want to be.

You cannot cross that gap, as we have given the illustration earlier, that you cannot move from point A to point B by first moving to the halfway point, and then to the halfway point of the remaining distance, and continuing to break the distance into smaller and smaller segments. You can continue this indefinitely because there will always be a gap.

The flow must be re-established, my beloved. When a river has frozen over in winter, the flow can be re-established only by the ice becoming liquid again. Before it can become liquid, heat must be applied to it. The heat is applied to your pent-up emotions by your conscious awareness, by your willingness to look at them, even the willingness to acknowledge that you had those negative emotions at some point.

I am not thereby saying that you need to acknowledge or accept the emotions as real or permanent. You need to come to the point where you can accept yourself for having those emotions, or for having had them in the past. You can look at yourself and realize that you had or have certain emotions because you are in a certain state of consciousness. Then you come to realize – as has been said previously, most clearly by Mother Mary – that God loves you unconditionally regardless of the state of consciousness you are in. If God loves you unconditionally, can you not then accept yourself unconditionally? Well, you *can,* if you are willing to simply shift your awareness.

You can instantly change your self-image

This is what I desire you to see: You can instantly make a choice away from non-acceptance and into acceptance. Why did you begin to suppress your light? Because you did not feel that your light was acceptable to others. You began to think that the light was not acceptable in a general sense. How can you re-establish the flow? By coming to the point where you recognize and truly decide that your light is acceptable because it is acceptable to God, it is an expression of God. It is acceptable that you express that light in this world, regardless of how it is received or rejected by those who are in a state of consciousness where they too feel unworthy to receive that light—and therefore do not want to be disturbed by the light.

The Law of Free Will gives you the perfect right to shine your light even if others have used their free will to reject it. They have free will about what they do inside the sphere of their individual consciousness. They do not have a right to impose their will on anyone outside their own sphere of consciousness.

They do not have a right to tell you to shut off your light. You have a right to shine it regardless of how it affects others, for it is *their* choice how they will let it affect them.

There are some among you who have such a momentum on suppressing your emotions that you cannot fully accept your worthiness to come up higher, to be the open door for the light and the wisdom and the love and other qualities of God to stream through you. I must tell you that there are some among you who simply cannot make progress from your current level until you start being willing to express whatever emotions you have. I am not thereby giving you carte blanche, my beloved, to express your emotions to other people and thereby perhaps abuse them.

I am saying that it is possible to find certain environments with a therapist or a therapy group where the people know that expression of emotions is a healing process. Therefore, they will not take your expression of emotions personally—as it might be the case with your spouse or children or other people who are closely affiliated with you. Don't go home and yell at your wife—yell at your therapist, for he is paid to listen.

The problem is that the flow of light has been suppressed. You cannot solve the problem by continuing to suppress, or by suppressing even more and saying: "Now I am a spiritual person; I should not be feeling this way." If you are feeling this way, you are *feeling this way*. Look at the emotions, allow them to flow. Then, as you feel that release of having re-established a flow in the emotional body, follow the flow into the mental realm and see what is the belief that makes you think that in a particular situation, you have to respond with a negative emotion.

Only when you bring that belief into your conscious awareness, can you come to the realization that there is no natural law that says that in a particular situation you have to respond with a negative emotion. It is a choice you have made to accept the belief that if people reject you, you can only respond by feeling hurt. If they direct anger at you, you can only respond with anger. This is a choice you made to accept this belief, and the belief is created out of the entire illusion of separation and duality.

Understanding the concept of being

You can then realize that you are more than this belief. You can separate yourself from it and look at it and say: "Do I really want to continue to respond this way, going into negative emotions?" You can realize that you are more than the belief. You can go on to the identity body and say: "But what is the identity that caused me to accept the limiting belief about myself that I was a powerless being who was forced to respond a certain way to certain outer stimuli?"

When you go to that level of the identity body and begin to tune in to the reality that you are a spiritual being, then you see that you are *real* and everything created out of the duality consciousness is *unreal*. Therefore, you have no obligation to let unreality affect the real you. Nor is there a natural law that says that the real you has to respond a certain way to that which is unreal. You can begin to choose – making enlightened choices – because now you see who you are, why you are here. You see what the problem is on earth and how to overcome it—by ceasing to set up conditions for the flow of the light through you.

One cannot be the open door, one cannot be a messenger, if one sets up conditions for how the Word, or the light, the flow of life, should be expressed through one's self. What is the essence of the concept of Being, that many of you have not truly understood?

Well, it goes back to Moses being on the mount and asking the God that spoke to him about his name. You know the traditional translation, I AM THAT I AM. You know the real translation, I WILL BE WHO I WILL BE. At any moment in time, I will be who I will be—regardless of who I was one moment ago. Right now, I will be who I will be. Regardless of what anyone thinks I should be in the future. When the future comes as the now, I will be who I will be.

When you are Being, you are expressing whatever comes to you at the moment. Whatever you expressed in a past moment, you do not create a mental image that says: "Because I did this in the past, I have to be bound by that in the future. Because of what was expressed a moment ago, I now have to limit my expression in the future." When you are in Being, you are in the flow of the River of Life. You are expressing, at the moment, whatever life wants to express through you. You do not need to judge, evaluate and analyze this with your outer mind. You are just letting it flow.

Do you see that this is Being in the NOW, whereas many people are either in the future or the past? They think back at the past and the mistakes they have made and they believe – when the devil whispers in their ear – that the mistakes they have made in the past have set a pattern for how they should be in the now and the future. Or they have come to a spiritual awareness where they realize that they need to be more than they are right now. They create the image of what they want to be, always seeking to force themselves to fit that mold, thereby creating the spiritual persona of the false self. They are condemning themselves to forever remaining some distance away from being the Christ in action.

Being and Christhood are very synonymous terms. What is the Christ? He is one that flows with the River of Life, she is one that flows with the River of Life. There are no rules in Christhood. There are no rules for what you should *be*, how you should express your Being. You are flowing with the River of Life. What does the River of Life want, what is its purpose for flowing? It is to raise all life. When you are Being, you are not putting up any conditions for how you should behave in a given situation. You are not saying: "Because I have received certain insights about how to behave from my spiritual teachers, this is how I have to respond to any and all similar situations." You are flowing with it.

Transcending the "mistake consciousness"

Even if you do something that other people might consider a mistake, you do not go into that state of consciousness of letting it be a mistake. Why not, my beloved? Because you know that whatever you were a moment ago, in this present moment, you have the perfect freedom and right to *be* who you will Be. Even if you were less a moment ago, you can now choose to *be more*.

Why analyze and grumble about the past? Why reinforce the image of separation that you are not where you should be? You do one thing that was an expression of Being. Perhaps you come to the experience that this was not all that you wanted to be—but then you just *be more*. You flow, you shift.

You do not stand still and analyze and say: "Why did I make that mistake? How can I avoid making that mistake in the future?" In going into this analysis, you have separated yourself from the flow instead of just *being more*. When you are in the flow, there are no mistakes. Why is this so? Because you are in the flow of service to life, and what does the River of Life seek? It seeks to raise up all life. Imagine yourself going out in the streets and you meet a particular person and that person is in a particular state of consciousness. That person may not be ready to receive the fullness of the spiritual understanding that you have acquired. The person may need a cup of cold water in Christ's name, some kind of expression, some kind of word, whatever it may be. The person needs a particular key in order to take the next step on that person's path.

You are not seeking to save the person in one step. You are seeking to raise that person higher, as can be done given the person's state of consciousness. When the analytical mind comes into play, you want to create the database that says: "This person, this type of person, should be helped this way." Now you have the analytical mind, the ego, evaluating every person you meet and saying: "Which file folder does that person belong to? Which label can I put on that person, for now I know how to always behave towards that kind of person."

Each person is a unique individual

It is not possible to create types of persons, kinds of persons, for everyone is a unique individual, which you know very well in yourself. You look at yourself and realize that if there is something you haven't yet gotten – in order to break through to being who you are – well, it must be because you cannot make that breakthrough the same way others have done so. You need a particular individual key and insight to unlock your being. Though you might receive help and inspiration from others, there comes that point where you need to see the beam in your eye, the particular individual block that you have that stands in the way of you fully accepting yourself.

So it is with every other person on earth, my beloved. That is why you cannot give full service to life as long as you are trapped in the analytical mind. You can only give full service by Being in the River of Life, by flowing with it. When you meet a person, you spontaneously express exactly what that person needed to take the next step. Then, you don't build a habit of saying: "Oh this is how I should be always, for that really helped that person. I must be able to help all other people the same way." You fall into the trap expressed in the popular saying that: "If the only tool you have in your toolbox is a hammer, you think every problem is a nail." You have to hammer at it like you always have been doing. Yet life is not something that can be categorized, my beloved.

Life is not a mechanical device

Take a look at your scientists, the materialistic scientists who have been studying and studying and studying—trying to penetrate into deeper levels. First there was the organs inside the body when they started preforming autopsies and cutting into the body to see what was inside. At the level of the visible organs and bones and structures, you cannot fully explain disease. With the advancement of science – or so-called advancement of science – they realized that there were smaller units inside the organs, namely the cells.

For a time they thought: "Now we have discovered the ultimate unit where we can discover all of the problems that will lead us to solve the riddle of health and life." Then they realized there are smaller structures inside the cells, be it DNA or something else. But the cells are made from molecules. The molecules are made from atoms. The atoms are made from subatomic particles, and this is where they have stopped. They actually believe that when they understand the building blocks that build your physical body, they can do what Dr. Frankenstein attempted to do: put together a mechanical replica of the body and then it will magically come to life.

This is what they believe – some of them – that life is a mechanical thing, a machine. If only you can create the right gears and levers and pulleys, then the machine will start turning, and you will have created a living form. But it is not so. You know that quantum physics has gone beyond the level of subatomic particles and recognized that subatomic particles are somehow connected with consciousness. This is the missing link in current science where they come to the realization that everything is an expression of consciousness.

Therefore, life is an expression of consciousness. Life is alive because it is not predictable, it is not mechanical, it cannot be categorized. It cannot be reduced to pulleys and levers and this and that aspect of a machine. Life is spontaneous. Life is creative.

When you are in the flow of Being, you will *be*, to every person you meet, exactly what that person needs. One person might need the gentle encouragement and nourishment of the mother. Another person might need to be shocked out of their state of perfectionism, of superiority. Another person might be so trapped in a particular mental image that you need to do something that seems like a mistake—from the viewpoint of that mental image, and then demonstrate that you can move on, that you are not bound by that mistake.

This is Being, my beloved. How does this relate to healing? Well, true healing is when you go into that flow of Being, the flow of the River of Life, so that the light can now flow. In most cases, of course, you have blocks in all of the four lower bodies, but it is especially the emotional body that prevents the light from your higher being from breaking through to the physical. The emotional body is vibrating just above the physical body. When the light cannot penetrate the emotional body, you can understand something intellectually, you can even affirm over and over again that "I am a spiritual being," but if the light cannot go through the emotional body, it cannot heal the physical. It cannot provide that acceleration that allows the cells to start vibrating faster, literally throwing off the impurities.

Your emotions are not your enemies

You need to dare to come to the point where you are not suppressing your emotions, where you recognize that your emotions are not your enemies. Your emotions are one expression that is needed to bring the fullness of life, to bring the higher vision you have into physical manifestation. You may have a good mental vision of what perfect health should be like. You may focus on that vision, you may even give outer affirmations of the vision. But if you cannot truly feel the vision, feel perfect health, feel wholeness, then the wholeness cannot break through to your physical body and nourish it.

What gives nourishment to the physical body? There is an Alpha and an Omega. There is the Omega aspect of what you take in through food, heat, sunlight, and so on, which gives physical nourishment. As I have just explained, your body is more than a machine. It can only function by also receiving spiritual nourishment. As the food that you eat is just a vehicle for getting the nourishment, the vitamins and minerals, into your body – where the physical body can absorb it – your emotions are also a vehicle to bring the spiritual light into the physical realm where your cells can absorb that spiritual light and therefore be accelerated and nourished by it.

If your emotions are blocked, how can the light descend? The body is left, so to speak, to its own devices, to the material world alone, and this cannot bring the fullness of healing. Be willing to make the shift where you do not seek to squash, deny or run away from what you actually feel. Listen to your feelings. Acknowledge them. Give them expression if you feel you need to, and get the flow to go through the emotional body.

Now, Mother Mary talked about the need to surrender. You need to surrender the need to suppress the emotions, to surrender the entire idea that you need to analyze and categorize your emotions. Emotion means energy in motion. When you try to put it in a category and put a label on it, you stop the flow. You cannot overcome negative emotions by categorizing them as negative and seeking to hold them back. You can overcome them by overcoming the belief that created them, by accelerating the belief, and thereby accelerating the emotional energy that has been misqualified by a lower vibration.

You do this by re-establishing the flow, not by thinking that when you destroy the negative emotions or deny them, then the flow will somehow happen. It is, again, so common that the duality consciousness, the ego, puts the cart before the horse, thinking that if only I get rid of all the negative emotions, then the flow will come through my emotional body. The reality is that the only way to get rid of the negative emotions is to re-establish the flow. It is only by re-establishing the flow of higher frequency energy that you can transmute or accelerate the lower frequency energy accumulated in the emotional body.

If you have blocked your emotions and built a habit of not acknowledging them, you are in a catch-22. You must, then, do something to change the equation. It can be therapy, it can be spiritual exercises. I can assure you that Mother Mary's rosaries and invocations [See *www.transcendencetoolbox.com.*] are designed specifically to get the flow re-established through your four lower bodies by challenging your illusions. I must tell you also that it is necessary to engage in activities that raise your focus to something positive, so that you feel a positive feeling flowing through you.

This can be a spiritual activity, or it can be music, as talked about earlier. But may I make a suggestion that I know will seem radical to many people. While listening to music can indeed attune you to a higher vibration, it is, as Mother Mary attempted to explain, not enough to attune to the spiritual realm. You must – in order to take the next step – bring it down and start bringing it into the material realm and anchoring it there.

This can be done in many different ways. You have all experienced that when you have positive conversations where you inspire each other, then you have that flow. Many of you have already re-established a great degree of the flow. Many other people in the world have not started that process and are so blocked that they need something else. Of course, therapy is a valid option. It is also valid to express those emotions.

I suggest that you might find a place where you can be alone and not be worried about disturbing other people, and then you go out – be it in nature or in a somewhat insulated room, or perhaps driving in your car – and you just verbalize whatever emotions are there. You tune in to your emotions and you start verbalizing it, speaking it out: "This is what I feel." Give expression to the feeling itself whether it be anger, hatred or whatever. Give expression to it so that you can look at it. You can, of course, always go back later and invoke the light through a rosary or decrees to transform and transmute the energy.

Expressing emotions and misqualifying energy

Realize one thing, my beloved. Many of you think that if you give expression to negative emotions, you are misqualifying energy by giving it expression. But what are you doing? You are expressing something that is already there in your emotional body so the energy is already misqualified—only it cannot move.

By giving expression to it, you break the stalemate so that the energy starts moving. When there is movement, the light from Above can begin to flow. There is now room in the emotional body for it to flow in. You break the catch-22 and give expression to it.

By doing this, you will feel a release. If you cannot yet speak it, then write it. Write a journal, as many people have done throughout the ages—writing down their thoughts and feelings. In writing them down, they are able to look at them from the outside instead of looking at them from the inside, thereby beginning to separate themselves from them.

Finally, I suggest that you, again, find a place where you can be undisturbed by the feeling of disturbing others, and then you begin singing the song that raises your awareness to the spiritual realm. As you start singing, allow the flow to accelerate and accelerate, for there is great value in flowing with this and allowing this flow to come through the song.

All of you can do this, for instead of listening to music, you now become a performer of music. I know very well that many of you do not have it in your Divine Plan to become public performers who are good enough to stand in front of an audience and sing or play. But those of you who do sing or play will know that there is great release in it, there is flow.

I am telling all of you to re-establish the flow, for you will notice how there is a certain part of your being that says: "Oh no, I am not going to do *that*. I am not going to sing at the top of my voice. That is a silly suggestion. How can an ascended master even suggest such a thing." That particular experience is an example of how you have suppressed the flow of light by imposing conditions upon it: "Oh the light could not possibly express *this* through me."

This is just one example among many of how these subtle beliefs – these subtle feelings of being shy or feeling inferior or what is appropriate and not appropriate – how these are the conditions that block the flow of life through your being. Why is it, as Mother Mary said, that so many people have studied spiritual teachings for many years but they do not walk their talk, they cannot bring it into practice, they cannot truly change? Well, it is because they are holding on to certain conditions that block the flow.

The initiations of the Sixth Ray

This is why – after you have passed the initiations of the five first rays – you come to the Sixth Ray of Service. As Mother Mary explained, you are not beginning to bring spirituality into the material realm until you go full circle, back to the point where you started. Now you have integrated spirituality instead of having it as a theoretical concept. Instead of having it as a goal "out there," you have come full circle to where you can accept who you are. You accept yourself as the spiritual being who is expressing its being in the material realm. In order to get to that full acceptance, you must practice. How do you practice? You practice by serving other forms of life, my beloved.

What is true service? It is that you come to the realization that service is not something you do out of your own needs, out of your ego's need to feel validated, to feel useful, to feel secure, to feel superior, to feel good. Your ego can create this spiritual persona that attempts to get you to serve in order to reinforce the ego's needs.

True service is when you say: "This person has a particular need, and I cannot let my own idiosyncrasies stand in the way of my being the open door for that need to be fulfilled." Or you can reach the other way and say: "The ascended masters have a need for something to be expressed, and I cannot let my outer personality stand in the way of this happening." This is what this messenger said to himself when he realized that Jesus wanted to use him as an open door for bringing forth a new awareness of his true teachings. He had to say to his own sense of insecurity: "I cannot let that stand in Jesus' way—I need to step outside of it."

It is when you begin to serve a higher cause or serve other people that you truly begin the process of separating yourself from the needs of the separate self. You may think that you have given service to life, and many of you truly *have* given service to life. But I want to bring to your attention that some of you – and many people in the world – have done outer acts of service that many will deem as being service, but they have done it in order to fulfill a need of the separate self. Therefore, in giving that service, they reinforced the "reality" of the separate self.

Take an honest look at many people in religious movements who have dedicated their lives to serving God in a particular church, perhaps by doing a humanitarian mission. They have done it with a subtle overlay of wanting to demonstrate the superiority of their Christian faith or their particular church—as even Mother Theresa was tainted by her uncritical acceptance of the Catholic Church. [For more teachings on Mother Teresa's crisis of faith, see *www.ascendedmasteranswers.com*.] Even though these people perform outer acts that are good, the more good acts they perform, the more they reinforce the illusion of the ego—that it is good. The ego thinks that by continuing to perform good acts, it will eventually reach a state of ultimate goodness where it will be acceptable in the eyes of God.

This will never happen, as Mother Mary explained with the parable of the wedding feast. You can fool the entire world, but you cannot fool God. God knows the difference between true service and self-centered so-called service. God knows your heart, the heart of all people.

You have free will. You can continue for as long as you want to have the experience of pursuing the quest for perfecting the separate self. This is your right, my beloved. I am not here to tell you what to choose. I am simply here to explain to you the reality of the choices you have. So many people have come to think that they have no alternative, that the only way to enter heaven is to perfect the separate self. They do not see that there is more to their identity than the separate self. How can they make a free choice when they do not know their options?

If you are standing in front of two doors, and you know what is behind the one door, and it feels safe, but you do not know what is behind the other, how can you make a free choice as to which door to enter? We of the ascended masters have a right – and it is our joy – to illumine people to the fact that they have other choices. They have an alternative to remaining stuck in the false sense of service created by the separate self in order to validate itself.

The illusion that you are not free

If you look at your life honestly, you might come to the realization that you have had certain relationships with other people where you think you have to serve them or take care of them. This is because you have created a certain image, a certain illusion, and when you think you have to take care of someone else you are subconsciously saying: "I am not free to choose who and what I want to be. I have to perform this outer service, and therefore I have to squash the free expression of my being."

So many people in the world are performing acts of service but they are not doing it from the state of consciousness of true service. They think that in order to serve others, you have to fulfill their needs or act a certain way. Think back to what I said just a little while ago. You are walking in the streets and you meet a person. That person has a particular need, and in order to serve that person fully, you must give that person exactly what they need in order to come up higher.

The outer analytical mind will tell you that you need to establish some kind of image of how you are supposed to serve, what you are supposed to give to other people. If you will re-read, or re-listen to my entire discourse, you will see that what I said about Being is the key to unlocking your understanding.

When you meet a particular person, it is not just a matter of what that person needs, for there is an Alpha and Omega aspect. The person's needs is the Omega. The Alpha is who you are, and therefore what can be expressed through you. I am not asking you to decide with the outer mind what kind of service to give and how to give it. I am asking you to re-establish the flow through your being so that your own being spontaneously expresses what the other person needs. What does the other person need, other than an example and a demonstration that there is a higher state of consciousness than the state in which the person is trapped?

You cannot demonstrate this with the outer mind, with the separate self. You can demonstrate it only by being in the flow of life. When you are in that flow – and when you see how spontaneously your higher being gives another person exactly what that person needs – you will not feel that this will restrict you and your expression. You will feel it as the most natural and joyful expression of your true Being.

Do you see the difference between trying to force yourself to give service and just walking into the flow, thereby allowing your true Being to shine through and spontaneously and creatively bring forth exactly what can help another person? This is the true joy of service. You have heard the expression by Master MORE: "The reward for service is more service." It is because when you give true service, you feel such joy that you want to experience more of that joy. You immerse yourself fully in that flow of service where everything becomes a joy.

Your entire life becomes a joy. You are always serving in one capacity or another. Even if you are sitting alone in quiet unity and oneness with your higher being – simply feeling the light of your higher being flowing through your four-lower bodies, being radiated out into the world of form – this is also service. There are no set rules or restrictions or conditions for how to truly serve in Being. It is multi-faceted, each one of you having a unique crystalline structure in your I AM Presence. When the light streams through it, you bring forth a unique expression of God's being that no other being can bring forth.

When you allow that expression to come through you, God is experiencing its fullness through you. You experience the joy that is the Creator's own joy of being expressed. You can follow that joy, merge with it, until you see that everything is joy. The underlying reality behind all form is unconditional, never-ending, ever-flowing, ever-creative, ever-self-transcending joy. Joy is the motor of life. Life is bliss. Meaningless statements to the separate self, but once you experience being in the flow of joy, they take on ultimate meaning. I extend my gratitude for your patience. I hope you have chosen to gain some measure of joy from my sharing and your receiving. Have you chosen to have a different experience, I love and accept you unconditionally. You can, at any moment in the future, choose to tune in to the joy that I AM. As Jesus came on the Sixth Ray of service to bring joy to the world, so I AM one with the flow of joy. Be in that flow, and *be* the joy to the world.

11 | SEVENTH RAY: BALANCING THE SCALES OF LIFE

A dictation by Lady Master Portia with Saint Germain

Portia is my name and you associate it with the title of the Goddess of Justice. Yet, as with all those who have spoken before me, I AM MORE. Indeed, my beloved, you may think that justice is a serious matter, and you may not associate any joy with justice. But I can assure you that there is much joy in the office of the Goddess of Justice. In reality, I truly am not the Goddess of Justice—I would like to give you the image that I am the Goddess of Balance.

What is the universal symbol for justice? Is it not the scales? I come to give you a new perspective on what it means to manifest true healing. It is absolutely – and I deliberately say *absolutely* – necessary to come to a higher understanding of the concept of justice. Only when one fully understands justice, can one be free.

Is it not so that the earthly concept of justice is extremely dualistic? Does it not contain the concept that when you have made an error or some kind of crime, you need to be punished, perhaps by being put in jail. Only when you have

– according to some measure that few understand – been punished "enough," can you be let out and, so-to-speak, be free.

It might seem that for every wrong, a punishment must be meted out in order for the soul to be free. You do, indeed, see so many people on earth who think that if they get ill, they must have done something to deserve it. Therefore, their illness is somehow God's punishment.

The real God does not judge you

People easily condemn others, feeling they must somehow be bad people and that God is punishing them. The underlying belief is that people have created a false image of God. They think that God is the ultimate judge who sits up in heaven, looking down upon you with a stern expression on his face, scratching his long beard, ready to condemn you for any mistake you make—especially the blasphemy, so-called, of disobeying the earthly church that claims to represent that remote God in the sky.

Despite the fact that you have been brought up to fear God – so that through that outer fear you obey the earthly institution and its hierarchy – they also want you to believe that this God is good. A good God, then, could not possibly cause people to be sick. It will only make sense that people are sick as a punishment for some wrong they have done. They must have done something wrong, for God could not have made the mistake of creating a world where there is sickness, disease, illness and death.

The concept of justice, as it is commonly seen on earth, is intricately linked to this false concept of the external, judgmental God. Did not Jesus say that his father judges no man, for he has left all judgment to the Son? The Son is the Christ consciousness. The Christ consciousness is One, it is Oneness. It is meant to enable all self-aware beings with free will to experiment with their free will freely. No matter how far they might descend into a lower state of consciousness, they can, at any moment, reach for the Christ. The Christ will then help them free themselves from that limiting state of consciousness. *That* is the true meaning of Christ the Redeemer.

The Christ does not judge the way human beings judge. The Christ is simply that immovable rock, the same yesterday, today and forever in the sense that the Christ consciousness is always in oneness with its source, with the Divine Father, with its Creator.

The judgment of the Christ consciousness is to separate oneness from division, to separate those who are committed to oneness and the consciousness of oneness from those who are still attached to and not willing to give up the illusion of separation.

Crime and punishment spring from duality

In terms of the concept of crime, it is only possible to commit any kind of crime or atrocity when one is identified with a separate self. What is a crime? It is doing something that benefits one's self while hurting others. Obviously, it cannot be based on oneness that seeks to raise up all life. Crime can only spring from the duality consciousness. What you see on earth is that the concept of how to deal with crime also springs from the duality consciousness.

The human concept of justice is indeed a perversion of Divine Justice, which, as I said, should really be conceived of as balance—the balanced scales that are not pulled in either direction. Which directions am I talking about? The two extremes of duality where if one side of the scales is heavier, you are pulled towards one extreme. If the other side is heavier, you are pulled towards the other extreme. For example, some might be heavier on the scale of so-called selfishness, and they are therefore weighted down towards the extreme that people will call evil. As Nada just explained, many have taken on an outer appearance of service, but they do it in order to serve the separate self and seem good. They would then put weight on the opposite side of the scale.

Many people think that if you have committed evil in the past, even in a past life, and your scale is pulled down to one side, if you commit good in this life, you will put weight on the opposite side of the scale and you will gradually balance them. You may commit many good acts and raise up the other side of the scale, but you cannot hold it in balance. You cannot hold the balance, the scale will immediately begin to move down on the other side until you have another unbalanced situation. You are now moving from the extreme of relative evil to the opposite extreme of relative good, which is not God-good because it is not unconditional good.

There is, of course, no unconditional evil. That is why, in order to balance the scales, you must empty both cups so that you have no conditions on either side—neither the side of relative evil, nor the side of relative good.

God does not want you to be punished

In order to experience the fullness of healing in your four lower bodies, you must look this consciousness straight in the eye and see it for the illusion that it is. It is a complete illusion that God wants you to be punished for having made a mistake. It is a complete illusion that by suffering, you can somehow compensate for your own sins, or the sins of others, even the sins of humankind. It is a complete illusion that the spilling of the blood of Christ on the cross compensated for the sins of all of humankind.

God is – as has now been explained from six different perspectives – unconditional. An unconditional God does not require you to be punished in order to be free of a past mistake. The unconditional God knows that any mistake you have made is made because the real you, the Conscious You, has come to identify itself with or as one of the roles that have been created on earth out of the duality consciousness. Whatever mistake you made was an expression of the state of consciousness you were in at the time.

God knows you are *more*, for you are an extension of God's own Being. What is God's only desire? It is that you come back into oneness with who you are, re-establish your true sense of identity and therefore can say: "*I* did not make that error in the past. I was a different person back then. The person I was when I made the error, I have allowed that sense of self to die. I have been reborn and I am now a new being in Christ." This, of course, cannot be faked.

I am not hereby saying that people do not need to take responsibility. They need to see that the reason they were in a certain state of consciousness was that they made certain choices. They can only be free from that state of consciousness by neutralizing – by going beyond, by transcending – those past choices.

When you are willing to go beyond, when you are willing to let the old man die and put on the new man, then you must come to that point of recognizing that you are reborn, you are a new person. Therefore, *you* did not make the mistake, or the sin, or the error, or the crime or whatever it may be of the past. What sense does it make that if you did not commit the crime, you should still bear the punishment?

The only way to be free of a certain state of consciousness is to let the old sense of self die and be reborn into a new sense of self. Then you do become a new being—your identity has shifted, you are reborn. The concept of sin – the concept of karma that you must carry with you for a certain amount of time, until you have suffered enough or given enough violet flame, or done whatever else you might deem as some kind of compensation – that concept can only spring from the duality consciousness.

The more you strive, the harder you strive, to compensate for the past error, the more you confirm the reality of the separate self, the more you prolong the life of that separate self. It can only exist as long as you give it life energy through your sense of identity of being a person who deserves to be punished, perhaps by bearing a physical illness.

There is no external God who is punishing you through karma, sin, illness or whatever it might be. We have explained it before, but I will explain it again. Any condition you face in the material universe is the outpicturing of a mental image that you are projecting on the white screen of the Ma-ter light. That image exists only in your consciousness. It is like the filmstrip in the movie projector, and the light is the light of your I AM Presence, streaming through the filmstrip in your four lower bodies. When you truly change your consciousness, you change the filmstrip, and thus you change the image that the light is passing through. If you change the filmstrip in a movie projector, do you not then also change the image on the screen? Please answer, that I know you have seen the point. [Audience answers: YES.]

Change your mind in order to change your body

Should you not, then, begin to at least contemplate that if you truly change your consciousness, you will also change your physical body and any condition in it? That condition can only be a projection upon the Ma-ter light of a mental image. As the movie screen itself is not changed by the movie being projected upon it, neither is the Ma-ter light. You can instantly change the image on the screen by changing the filmstrip in the projector, and you can instantly change the manifestation in your physical body by changing the image in your mind.

This is an absolute truth, my beloved, but it is extremely difficult for human beings to accept it. They are so used to looking at the material world through the filter of the separate self, which believes that matter is solid, unchangeable and permanent.

Why does the separate self believe this? Because the separate self is created out of the same frequencies as the material universe, and thus, to the separate self, to the ego, matter *is* unchangeable. You have heard of the concept of mind over matter. Well, the ego can never have power to change matter. That which is of the same vibration cannot change something else in the same frequency spectrum. A lower vibration cannot be changed by a lower vibration. A lower vibration can be changed only by being accelerated by a higher vibration. Where is the higher vibration to come from? Well, from your I AM Presence, but how is it going to descend into the physical body? It must descend through your four lower bodies, including what represents the physical body, which is your conscious mind.

Why do some people come to Lourdes and are healed, while others are not healed? As Mother Mary said, those who are healed can make the shift in the conscious mind of coming to accept that the disease can instantly disappear. It does not matter that they see this as a miracle from God. What matters is that they believe in it to the point where they can shift their perception and accept the changeability of matter.

Matter is infinitely changeable, but only when you are willing to change the cause behind the effect of matter—namely the mental image, the condition of the mind. If you have the subtle belief that your illness is a punishment for some error committed – that you deserve the punishment and that you need to suffer for a time in order to be saved and go to heaven – how can you accept that you can instantly be free of the illness?

How can you accept healing? How can you accept wholeness, my beloved?

This is, indeed, a test that all must face. It is a test that Jesus had to face in order to attain that level of mastery where he could be the open door for the light of such a high vibration that it could instantly change matter and therefore manifest what people have called the miracles of Christ. They are not miracles in the traditional sense, they are simply the out-picturing of a higher law. As I said, it is not possible to change the vibration of matter through the dualistic consciousness. As Jesus expressed it: "With Man, this is impossible." With the manly, the human, the dualistic, the separate, the mortal state of consciousness, it is not possible to change matter through the power of mind.

It is only possible to change matter through the force that can be exercised through the physical realm. That is why you indeed see medical technology seeking to increase its power to change disease by force, by destroying the disease, even destroying the body in the process. You need to come to the true realization that Jesus came to, towards the end of his training period, the true realization that it – truly, honestly, absolutely, realistically – *is* possible to change any condition in matter in an instant—when you switch the mind.

Overcoming the consciousness of death

What is it that pulls you away from that knowing, that acceptance? It is the consciousness that has been called "death." Death has been called the last enemy, for death is the sense that matter is permanent, difficult to change. Behind that is the sense that matter is real, that it has some independent existence.

This, of course, is based on the illusion of the fallen beings who have rebelled against God and who have created the illusion that separated themselves from God and God's kingdom, creating a world where God is not. Therefore, they seek to spread that death consciousness to all people so that they reinforce it. Through their acceptance of death as inevitable, the acceptance of matter as real and separated from God, they give their light to the fallen beings who have no light, for they cannot receive it from within. Why? Because they have chosen to go into the ultimate state of separation.

There are degrees of separation, and until you reach that ultimate state, you still receive some light from your I AM Presence that sustains you. When you come to that ultimate state of separation, then you can no longer receive the light for you are not willing to accept it. It is not that the light is not there, that God withholds his light. I tell you that even the darkest being that you can possibly imagine, be it Lucifer, Satan or whomever, God is not withholding light from them. God still only desires to see them come back to oneness, but you can come to a point where you absolutely reject that you have the ability to receive light, or the willingness, or the worthiness or whatever it might be.

From that point you can sustain any form of self, any form of awareness, only by taking light from others—who are still receiving it from Above but who are misqualifying it through fear, anger or whatever lower feelings that are not of love. You will indeed see that this world is enveloped in a black cloud of the death consciousness. That is why death is the last enemy because it is so difficult to overcome the illusion that matter is real.

Your five senses are telling you that matter is real. Even your outer, analytical mind is telling you that matter is real. Therefore, it cannot simply be changed in an instant. You cannot see with the outer mind and the senses that behind the matter that seems so solid, there is only light—consciousness, and consciousness *can* change in an instant.

This you have all experienced—how you can change your mind in an instant, from a state of sorrow to a state of joy, or the other way around. Consider how simple it is to change your mind in an instant. Consider how women are often accused of changing their minds a thousand times. The reality here is that women are more in tune with the reality that you have a perfect right to change your mind at any time. God has given you free will. Who says that because you have chosen to be in a certain state of mind – for a day, or a decade, or ten thousand embodiments – you have to continue to be in that state of mind indefinitely?

This is the death consciousness, my beloved. The death consciousness says that once you have made the mistake of eating the forbidden fruit, of partaking of the duality consciousness, you can never overcome that duality consciousness. The Church of Satan says that once you have accepted membership, you can never renounce it for you have given your soul to the devil and you can never take it back. The reality is, of course, that there is no such thing as any permanence in the material realm. That which is unreal cannot permanently affect that which is real.

When you see that *you* are real, you know that no promise made, no curse put upon you, no illusion can ever hold you any longer than the moment when you decide that you are no longer the person who made the promise or made the mistake or accepted the death consciousness. You have been reborn, and thus you are free. You are free to *be* what you want to be. God within you will say: "I will be who I will be. And now I choose to be *more* than I was before." In that choosing, you are reborn, you are free.

Freedom is not found by running away

We have told you several times now that you cannot overcome a condition as long as you run away from it. You cannot overcome a fear as long as you are not willing to face it. How, then, do you overcome death?

Look at how many people in the world are seeking to run away from death, either by not thinking about it, by denying it or by using all kinds of means to prolong life, as they call it. Yet, it is truly the life of the physical body, or rather the life of the separate self, which thinks it needs that physical body. A part of the separate self is born to follow that particular physical body and will die when the body dies—even though part of your ego moves with you until you let it die by giving up the ghost.

How do you overcome death? By being willing to face your fear of death. Only when you face the fear of death, can you see that even death is an illusion. You will not die when your physical body dies. You will go on. Read the many near-death experiences and see how – when people let go of their attachment to the physical body – the transition out of the body was smooth, effortless, painless. Suddenly, people, or rather their beings, can find themselves in a higher space with a much expanded awareness.

What is there to fear in expanding your awareness beyond the narrow outlook on life that you have in the physical body? It is like a prisoner who has been imprisoned for so long that he clings to his bunk. When the guards come to open the door and say: "You have served your time, get out," he says: "I don't want to leave! I can't leave! I won't know who I am once I leave this cell!"

Ah, my beloved, perhaps here we are touching upon the real issue of the death consciousness, the consciousness of punishment in order to balance the scales. As Maitreya has explained so carefully in his book, there comes a point in the spiritual sanctuary of the mystery school where the spiritual teacher has taken you to a point where you need to become self-sufficient. So far, the teacher has given you a safe environment in which to experiment with your free will. He has taken upon himself the karma that you might have made from experimenting. You have been free of any sense of burden, but there comes a point where you must take responsibility for experiencing the conditions that you create in the mind.

This is truly the point where you, hopefully, have attained enough oneness with the Alpha aspect of your being, your I AM Presence, that you are able and willing to fulfill the Omega aspect of deciding how you will express your higher being in the material realm. As Maitreya explains, the role of your conscious self is to decide who you are, who you want to be, in expression in the matter realm.

Even though you have a crystalline structure in your I AM Presence, even though you have a God Flame that gives you individual characteristics, you still have total freedom as to how you will express that in the material realm. As we have said, you have the right to have any experience you desire. The reality is that there comes a point on the spiritual path where the teacher will step back and no longer tell you who you are, who you are supposed to be, how you are supposed to use your free will and express your creativity. At that moment, you can either move closer, move into oneness with your higher being and express what Nada explained as the spontaneous flow of Being. Or you can choose to go into a vibration of fear, for you are afraid of the total freedom, so you go into the state of duality and create the ego.

What the ego does for you

What does the ego do for you, my beloved? It gives you the illusion that you, the conscious self, you no longer have to make choices for the ego will do it for you. How does the ego make choices? The ego is not a self-aware being so the ego must look for some way that it can seemingly make choices, and how does it do this? It goes into the theater of life and looks for a predefined role and it says: "Ah, this is who I am supposed to be." It takes it on, and you must then go with it. Now you think you are a limited, mortal human being who cannot be creative, who is supposed to be a certain way. You have accepted a set of conditions, my beloved, and you think this is who you are.

Your former sense of self as a spiritual being has died, as Maitreya explains. You are now reborn into a limited being, or rather a being who thinks it is limited. This is spiritual death. The ego creates the illusion that you should never look at how you came to be where you are. The fallen beings have created the false sense that you can never escape from that choice to go into duality, you can never escape from the choice not to make decisions. They want you to permanently stay in that state of separation. The reality is that you have a right – at any moment – to undo the choice and take back your power, your willingness to make choices as to who you are, who you want to be in this material realm, how you want to express yourself, what you want to experience.

This is why we have said that if you desire to experience being miserable, embrace the experience and recognize that it is a result of your own choosing. You are doing it because you are seeking some kind of fulfillment from that experience. I guarantee you that the moment you fully embrace a limited experience, at that moment of fully accepting it, you will pass right through it.

You may think that by accepting death, you will move into death and die. You will not, for by accepting death you will move into it and see that it is an illusion. You will emerge on the other side, seeing that what seems so real – from the viewpoint of the separate self – is completely unreal—when you know that you are an extension of the infinite Creator who can never die.

How do you switch your perspective? Not by running away from that which you think limits you but by running right into it, by looking at it, by not seeking to hide anything from God, thereby hiding it from yourself. This is the value of the concept of confession, which, of course, has been perverted by the outer institution. The concept is that you honestly confess to yourself, to God, that you have accepted a limited state of consciousness. Then you accept the very reality that by confessing it, by acknowledging it, you have already started separating yourself from it.

When you are inside a dualistic role, a dualistic sense of self, you cannot see it for what it is. You are looking at the world from inside of it. It is like being inside a building where there is only a small opening to the outside world. Even though you can see out, you are only seeing a very small segment of the total view that is outside. When you step outside of the building, you see the entire view. You also see the building, and thus you see how limiting it was to your view when you were inside of it. Of course, once you begin to see how a particular, conditioned sense of identity limits you, you are no longer completely trapped within it.

You can continue that process of separation step by step, until you get to that final point where you realize that you have been crucified by that condition. You cannot take yourself down from the cross by using the same state of consciousness that is nailing you to the cross. You must give up the ghost in that final act of total, unconditional surrender that so few people on earth have experienced, even though it was demonstrated by Jesus on the cross, by Mother Mary when the archangel appeared to her, and by other people throughout the ages.

It is such a release, such a freedom, such a joy to go through that unconditional surrender where you surrender any condition, any illusion. Instead of running away from that which you fear, including physical death, you embrace it. You experience a sense that if you died at that moment, you could leave the earth with no regrets, no pulls, no sense of unfulfilled work.

11 | Seventh Ray: Balancing the Scales of Life

At that moment you can be reborn as a Bodhisattva who is now serving in true service to raise up all life and help them see the fruitlessness of trying to balance the scales by raising up one side of the scale or by putting other dualistic conditions on the other side. Instead, you are helping them see that it is possible to transcend the entire consciousness represented by the scales. You can transcend duality, move out of it and into the total freedom expressed by God to Moses: "I will be who I will be."

It has been the great joy of all of us to be with you. And thus, I, Portia, will step back and let my beloved consort, Saint Germain, step forward to seal you.

Saint Germain:

So, my beloved, you feel you have a need to be sealed by the God of Freedom? What, indeed, could I possibly do to seal you without recognizing the reality of the forces of anti-freedom? When you see their complete unreality, how could you possibly need to be sealed from them? How could you need to be protected? You see that they are unreal because they are made out of conditions that are unreal, that are illusions of the mind.

Yet, *you* are real, and how can that which is unreal affect that which is real? In that realization, you are ultimately free. You are beyond death, for how can death – unreality – affect life, and thus death has lost its sting. Death where is thy victory in freedom, the total freedom to *be*—whereas death is the subtle sense that you cannot be, and thus, you limit yourself and God's Being through you.

How, my beloved, do you ultimately become free? By realizing that freedom is not freedom *from* any condition, for freedom is not relative to any condition. Freedom is a vibration that is beyond conditions—it is unconditional freedom. It is a state of consciousness; it is a stream of consciousness that is constantly transcending itself. In that transcendence, it can never be pinned down or held back in any limited expression, for it is always *more*, it is free to express that more and become more at any moment.

How do you become free? By becoming one with that flow, that Spirit of consciousness, that conscious being that *is* freedom and that I AM one with and represent to the earth. I offer you my assistance in becoming one with me, if you desire to be truly free. I can do nothing else. I cannot give you an outer teaching, I cannot even give you light that you perceive as coming from outside yourself. I can only offer you this: my total Being, my Spirit of Freedom. If you merge with it, you will be one with freedom, and you will know that no conditions can limit you whatsoever.

Let freedom become contagious through you

You can be here on earth, here in physical embodiment, what Jesus demonstrated, what the Buddha demonstrated: a being who is not limited by death or the fear of death. You are not limited by conditions, you are free to express whatever God desires to express through you. By demonstrating this – so that others might experience your freedom – you are awakening them to their potential to be free. This is how freedom becomes contagious and how the consciousness of humankind is raised, and people see that what was limiting them yesterday was unreal.

You have seen the growth in freedom over the ages. You have seen that some people have become free of one condition only to create another. Nevertheless, you see that overall there is a growth of freedom. I tell you, this is the age of Saint Germain, this is the Age of Freedom where all can be free who are willing to be free.

Be willing, my beloved, to experience that ultimate healing, that ultimate wholeness, of giving up even the fear of death, giving up any condition. Be willing to stand here on earth and declare that you are a free being and that you do not accept any condition that limits your Spirit and the Spirit's expression through you in seeking to raise up all life by setting them free from the illusions that they think have power over their unlimited beings.

This is my offer. Contemplate it. But go beyond contemplating, and tune in to my vibration. I AM free, and thus not bound by time and space. This means I am with you every minute of the day wherever you go. I AM everywhere in the consciousness of God. I AM everywhere in time and space, but also everywhere beyond time and space. Although there is no meaning in saying "everywhere beyond time and space" because only in space can there be a sense of here, and only in time can there be a sense of past, present and future.

I AM in the unlimited, unconditional Being of God. You came out of that Being, and you can return to that freedom, even while you are still choosing to express that freedom through the seeming limitations of a physical body and an outer mind.

You came here to work with Christ to set the captives free. You do not set them free by seeking to change them. You set them free by changing yourself so that you are free and therefore can be that torch of freedom that burns even in the darkest prison and shows them that there is light outside the prison of their minds.

Thus, I do not seal you, I set you free in the Spirit of Freedom that I AM.

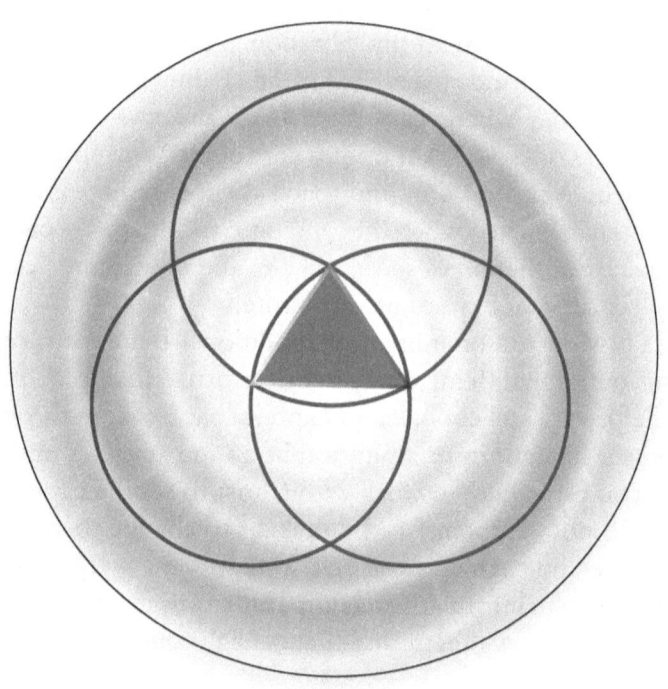

12 | CLEARING THE SECRET HEART CHAKRA

[*NOTE*: Study the dictation from the Third Ray.]

In the name I AM THAT I AM, Jesus Christ, I call to my I AM Presence to flow through the I Will Be Presence that I AM and give this invocation with full power. I call to beloved Omega, Archangel Uzziel and Venus to help me overcome all impurities in my Secret Chamber of the Heart Chakra. Help me be free from all patterns or forces within or without that oppose the free flow of love from my I AM Presence, including …

[Make personal calls]

1. I accept myself unconditionally

1. I accept that love in the divine sense can have no opposite, or it would not be divine.

> O Venus, show me how to serve,
> your cosmic beauty I observe.
> What love from Venus you now bring,
> our planets do in tandem sing.
>
> **O Venus, service so divine,**
> **you are for earth a cosmic sign.**
> **Your selfless service is now mine,**
> **a life in service I define.**

2. I accept the need to stop trying to change myself. I switch out of the last illusion of the separate self by accepting myself – unconditionally – for who I AM.

> O Venus, your love is the key,
> the hardened hearts on earth are free.
> Embracing future bright and bold,
> our planet's story is retold.
>
> **O Venus, service so divine,**
> **you are for earth a cosmic sign.**
> **Your selfless service is now mine,**
> **a life in service I define.**

3. I accept that there is no condition I could possibly have to fulfill in order to express that which is unconditional. Love flows and flows and transcends and grows and expresses, regardless of any conditions.

> O Venus, loving Mother mine,
> my heart your love does now refine.
> I am the open door for love,
> descending like a Holy Dove.
>
> **O Venus, service so divine,
> you are for earth a cosmic sign.
> Your selfless service is now mine,
> a life in service I define.**

4. I surrender the concept that I need to move to a certain state of perfection before I am able and worthy to have the love of God flowing through me.

> O Venus, play the secret note,
> that is for hatred antidote.
> All poisoned hearts you gently heal,
> as love's true story you reveal.
>
> **O Venus, service so divine,
> you are for earth a cosmic sign.
> Your selfless service is now mine,
> a life in service I define.**

5. I see that love will not accept any conditions. I cannot limit God, I cannot limit love, I cannot limit the expression of love. I now see myself one with the flow of love.

> O Venus, love fills every need,
> for truly, love is God's first seed.
> O let it blossom, let it grow,
> sweep earth into your loving flow.

> O Venus, service so divine,
> you are for earth a cosmic sign.
> Your selfless service is now mine,
> a life in service I define.

6. I surrender the dualistic, relative image of love as the opposite of hatred, anger or fear. I surrender the need to put on a facade of being loving and kind.

> O Venus, music of the spheres,
> heard by those who God reveres.
> Our voices now as one we raise,
> singing in adoring praise.

> O Venus, service so divine,
> you are for earth a cosmic sign.
> Your selfless service is now mine,
> a life in service I define.

7. I accept that I cannot heal myself from the consciousness that I need healing. I cannot become whole from the consciousness that sees itself as unwhole.

> O Venus, we are joining ranks,
> Sanat Kumara we give thanks.
> Our planet has received new life,
> to lift her out of war and strife.

> O Venus, service so divine,
> you are for earth a cosmic sign.
> Your selfless service is now mine,
> a life in service I define.

8. I surrender the illusion that I am not whole. I accept that I am a self-conscious being with completely free will. I have the freedom to create any experience I desire.

> O Venus, your sweet melody,
> consumes veil of duality.
> Absorbed in tones of Cosmic Love,
> all conflict we now rise above.

> **O Venus, service so divine,**
> **you are for earth a cosmic sign.**
> **Your selfless service is now mine,**
> **a life in service I define.**

9. I accept that no matter how much I have identified myself with a separate sense of identity, I still am who I AM. I now surrender the role of being separated from the flow of love.

> O Venus, shining Morning Star,
> a cosmic herald, that you are.
> The earth set free by sacred sound,
> our planet is now heaven-bound.

> **O Venus, service so divine,**
> **you are for earth a cosmic sign.**
> **Your selfless service is now mine,**
> **a life in service I define.**

2. I embrace my power to change

1. I accept that it was not some external force that caused me to descend into the sense of unwholeness. It was choices I made.

> Omega, I now meditate,
> upon your throne in cosmic gate.
> I'm born out of the figure-eight,
> that Alpha and you co-create.
>
> **O Song of Life, you vitalize,**
> **all hearts you truly synchronize.**
> **O Sacred Sound, you alchemize,**
> **turn earth into a paradise.**

2. I accept that I have the power to change all choices, to replace them with choices that bring me into wholeness, that bring me out of the illusion that I am separated from what is unconditional.

> Omega, in your sacred space,
> my cosmic parents I embrace.
> I see that it is such a grace,
> that I take part in cosmic race.
>
> **O Song of Life, you vitalize,**
> **all hearts you truly synchronize.**
> **O Sacred Sound, you alchemize,**
> **turn earth into a paradise.**

3. I consciously stop trying to get out of my sense of being unworthy—I embrace it, I love it.

Omega in the Central Sun,
you show me life is cosmic fun.
And thus a victory is won,
my homeward journey has begun.

O Song of Life, you vitalize,
all hearts you truly synchronize.
O Sacred Sound, you alchemize,
turn earth into a paradise.

4. I consciously love the condition that makes me think I cannot love. I love that which so many people deem not lovable, and thus I am no longer separated from the flow of love.

Omega, femininity
is doorway to infinity.
With you I have affinity,
to know my own divinity.

O Song of Life, you vitalize,
all hearts you truly synchronize.
O Sacred Sound, you alchemize,
turn earth into a paradise.

5. I do not seek to run away from my problems. I love the problems in order to get a different perspective on my problems. I recognize that I am not the problems. I am *more*, for I experience that *I am more*.

Omega, in your cosmic flow,
my plan divine I clearly know.
My heart is now a lamp aglow,
as love on all I do bestow.

**O Song of Life, you vitalize,
all hearts you truly synchronize.
O Sacred Sound, you alchemize,
turn earth into a paradise.**

6. I surrender the conditionality that takes away my freedom. I am willing to be in a state of floating where there is nothing that pulls me into a particular condition, into a particular role in the drama outplayed in the material universe.

Omega, cosmic Mother Flame,
this is the light from which I came.
As I take part in cosmic game,
Christ victory I do proclaim.

**O Song of Life, you vitalize,
all hearts you truly synchronize.
O Sacred Sound, you alchemize,
turn earth into a paradise.**

7. I experience unconditionality. I know there is something beyond the conditional world. I move to the next level of merging with it, and I surrender the false sense of love, the conditional sense of love.

Omega, I now comprehend,
why I did to earth descend.
And thus I fully do intend,
to help this planet to ascend.

**O Song of Life, you vitalize,
all hearts you truly synchronize.
O Sacred Sound, you alchemize,
turn earth into a paradise.**

8. From the state of unconditionality I am willing to look at any condition in this world. I now accept that I am free to express love to any condition. I set love free to flow through me into any condition.

> Omega, I do now aspire,
> to join the ranks of cosmic choir.
> My heart burns with a Christic fire,
> that is this planet's sanctifier.

> **O Song of Life, you vitalize,**
> **all hearts you truly synchronize.**
> **O Sacred Sound, you alchemize,**
> **turn earth into a paradise.**

9. I accept myself as the object of the Divine Lover's love. I merge with the Divine Lover, and I see that I am the open door for the love that wants to be expressed to all life. I am free to follow my bliss.

> Omega, my heart is ablaze,
> my life is in an upward phase.
> Come teach me now the secret phrase,
> so that I can this planet raise.

> **O Song of Life, you vitalize,**
> **all hearts you truly synchronize.**
> **O Sacred Sound, you alchemize,**
> **turn earth into a paradise.**

3. I am an unconditional being

1. I accept that the core of my being, my conscious self, is a blank screen. Although I was created with individuality, I was not created with conditionality.

> O Venus, show me how to serve,
> your cosmic beauty I observe.
> What love from Venus you now bring,
> our planets do in tandem sing.
>
> **O Venus, service so divine,**
> **you are for earth a cosmic sign.**
> **Your selfless service is now mine,**
> **a life in service I define.**

2. I accept that I was not created with any dualistic conditions. I was created with unconditional individual characteristics.

> O Venus, your love is the key,
> the hardened hearts on earth are free.
> Embracing future bright and bold,
> our planet's story is retold.
>
> **O Venus, service so divine,**
> **you are for earth a cosmic sign.**
> **Your selfless service is now mine,**
> **a life in service I define.**

3. I accept that no love coming from this material realm can satisfy my built-in longing for love. My longing for love is the longing for oneness with who I AM, my I AM Presence.

12 | Clearing the Secret Heart Chakra

> O Venus, loving Mother mine,
> my heart your love does now refine.
> I am the open door for love,
> descending like a Holy Dove.
>
> **O Venus, service so divine,**
> **you are for earth a cosmic sign.**
> **Your selfless service is now mine,**
> **a life in service I define.**

4. I accept my longing to be in the flow of the River of Life by fulfilling the potential for which I was created by my I AM Presence. I am a co-creator and I want to bring the kingdom of God into manifestation in the material universe.

> O Venus, play the secret note,
> that is for hatred antidote.
> All poisoned hearts you gently heal,
> as love's true story you reveal.
>
> **O Venus, service so divine,**
> **you are for earth a cosmic sign.**
> **Your selfless service is now mine,**
> **a life in service I define.**

5. I follow the stream of consciousness that is one with the hierarchy of God Love, of unconditional love, and with all of the beings who are expressions of that unconditionality.

> O Venus, love fills every need,
> for truly, love is God's first seed.
> O let it blossom, let it grow,
> sweep earth into your loving flow.

> **O Venus, service so divine,**
> **you are for earth a cosmic sign.**
> **Your selfless service is now mine,**
> **a life in service I define.**

6. I follow that stream of God's consciousness and recognize that God's capacity for love is indeed unlimited. God can take in and consume any condition that I desire to surrender.

> O Venus, music of the spheres,
> heard by those who God reveres.
> Our voices now as one we raise,
> singing in adoring praise.

> **O Venus, service so divine,**
> **you are for earth a cosmic sign.**
> **Your selfless service is now mine,**
> **a life in service I define.**

7. I release into the stream of God's consciousness all my conditions. In oneness with Master MORE, I say: "Enough is enough."

> O Venus, we are joining ranks,
> Sanat Kumara we give thanks.
> Our planet has received new life,
> to lift her out of war and strife.

> **O Venus, service so divine,**
> **you are for earth a cosmic sign.**
> **Your selfless service is now mine,**
> **a life in service I define.**

8. Love is a flowing stream, a fount of unconditionality, like the water that moves, moving over the rock – even the hardest of rocks – wearing it down, little by little.

> O Venus, your sweet melody,
> consumes veil of duality.
> Absorbed in tones of Cosmic Love,
> all conflict we now rise above.
>
> **O Venus, service so divine,**
> **you are for earth a cosmic sign.**
> **Your selfless service is now mine,**
> **a life in service I define.**

9. Love flows unconditionally and if it seems like it gets nowhere, if it seems like people do not receive it and do not change, it just keeps flowing. Over the span of millennia, it eventually wears down that solid rock of the separate self.

> O Venus, shining Morning Star,
> a cosmic herald, that you are.
> The earth set free by sacred sound,
> our planet is now heaven-bound.
>
> **O Venus, service so divine,**
> **you are for earth a cosmic sign.**
> **Your selfless service is now mine,**
> **a life in service I define.**

4. I am in the flow of love

1. The Divine Lover will never leave his beloved alone, will never stop flowing, will never stop giving. Eventually, even the hardest of conditions will be worn down by the flow of love, the eternal unstoppable, unconditional flow of love.

> Omega, I now meditate,
> upon your throne in cosmic gate.
> I'm born out of the figure-eight,
> that Alpha and you co-create.
>
> **O Song of Life, you vitalize,**
> **all hearts you truly synchronize.**
> **O Sacred Sound, you alchemize,**
> **turn earth into a paradise.**

2. The flowing love is not discouraged but is encouraged and therefore flows even more and dislodges an atom, and another one, and another, and another. Soon, the River of Life begins to carve a gorge into the bedrock of the human consciousness. Flowing, flowing, ever-flowing.

> Omega, in your sacred space,
> my cosmic parents I embrace.
> I see that it is such a grace,
> that I take part in cosmic race.
>
> **O Song of Life, you vitalize,**
> **all hearts you truly synchronize.**
> **O Sacred Sound, you alchemize,**
> **turn earth into a paradise.**

3. Even the mightiest of mountains can be worn down over time by the gentle rain descending from heaven, like the gentle rain of love that falls upon the just and the unjust, upon the evil and the good.

> Omega in the Central Sun,
> you show me life is cosmic fun.
> And thus a victory is won,
> my homeward journey has begun.
>
> **O Song of Life, you vitalize,**
> **all hearts you truly synchronize.**
> **O Sacred Sound, you alchemize,**
> **turn earth into a paradise.**

4. To love, there is none just or unjust, none evil or good. There are no conditions in that flowing love, there are no conditions whatsoever. To love, the conditions are unreal and impermanent.

> Omega, femininity
> is doorway to infinity.
> With you I have affinity,
> to know my own divinity.
>
> **O Song of Life, you vitalize,**
> **all hearts you truly synchronize.**
> **O Sacred Sound, you alchemize,**
> **turn earth into a paradise.**

5. Love knows that if it keeps flowing, it will wear down even the hardest of conditions. Even the most hardened heart will be worn down by the unstoppable flow of love.

Omega, in your cosmic flow,
my plan divine I clearly know.
My heart is now a lamp aglow,
as love on all I do bestow.

**O Song of Life, you vitalize,
all hearts you truly synchronize.
O Sacred Sound, you alchemize,
turn earth into a paradise.**

6. My heart looks at itself and says: "Why do I keep separating myself from the flow of love? I have had enough of the experience of being separated. Now I am curious as to how it would feel to be *in* the flow of love."

Omega, cosmic Mother Flame,
this is the light from which I came.
As I take part in cosmic game,
Christ victory I do proclaim.

**O Song of Life, you vitalize,
all hearts you truly synchronize.
O Sacred Sound, you alchemize,
turn earth into a paradise.**

7. I surrender into the flow like a dam bursting—and suddenly the River of Life that has been held back for so many lifetimes is released in an outburst that no conditions, that no ego, can hold back.

Omega, I now comprehend,
why I did to earth descend.
And thus I fully do intend,
to help this planet to ascend.

> O Song of Life, you vitalize,
> all hearts you truly synchronize.
> O Sacred Sound, you alchemize,
> turn earth into a paradise.

8. The real me flows with love and finds such joy, such freedom, in the release from conditions—the total, unconditional release.

> Omega, I do now aspire,
> to join the ranks of cosmic choir.
> My heart burns with a Christic fire,
> that is this planet's sanctifier.

> O Song of Life, you vitalize,
> all hearts you truly synchronize.
> O Sacred Sound, you alchemize,
> turn earth into a paradise.

9. I embrace a new sense of self. I know I am *more*, for I have experienced oneness with the *more*.

> Omega, my heart is ablaze,
> my life is in an upward phase.
> Come teach me now the secret phrase,
> so that I can this planet raise.

> O Song of Life, you vitalize,
> all hearts you truly synchronize.
> O Sacred Sound, you alchemize,
> turn earth into a paradise.

Sealing:

In the name of the Divine Mother, I fully accept that the power of these calls is used to set free the Ma-ter light, so it can outpicture the perfect vision of Christ for my own life, for all people and for the planet. In the name I AM THAT I AM, it is done! Amen.

13 | CLEARING THE HEART CHAKRA

[*NOTE*: Study the dictation from the Third Ray.]

In the name I AM THAT I AM, Jesus Christ, I call to my I AM Presence to flow through the I Will Be Presence that I AM and give this invocation with full power. I call to beloved Elohim Heros and Amora, Archangel Chamuel and Charity, Paul the Venetian and Venus to help me overcome all impurities in my Heart Chakra. Help me be free from all patterns or forces within or without that oppose the free flow of love from my I AM Presence, including …

[Make personal calls]

1. Clear my Heart Chakra from anti-love

1. Archangel Chamuel, come into my Heart Chakra and clear it from all selfishness, self-centeredness and lower expressions.

> Chamuel Archangel, in ruby ray power,
> I know I am taking a life-giving shower.
> Love burning away all perversions of will,
> I suddenly feel my desires falling still.
>
> **Chamuel Archangel, descend from Above,**
> **Chamuel Archangel, with ruby-pink love,**
> **Chamuel Archangel, so often thought-of,**
> **Chamuel Archangel, o come Holy Dove.**

2. Archangel Chamuel, come into my Heart Chakra and clear it from the dualistic love that is opposed to fear, anger and hatred.

> Chamuel Archangel, a spiral of light,
> as ruby ray fire now pierces the night.
> All forces of darkness consumed by your fire,
> consuming all those who will not rise higher.
>
> **Chamuel Archangel, descend from Above,**
> **Chamuel Archangel, with ruby-pink love,**
> **Chamuel Archangel, so often thought-of,**
> **Chamuel Archangel, o come Holy Dove.**

3. Archangel Chamuel, come into my Heart Chakra and clear it from the conditions that manifest impurities in my mind and physical body.

Chamuel Archangel, your love so immense,
with clarified vision, my life now makes sense.
The purpose of life you so clearly reveal,
immersed in your love, God's oneness I feel.

**Chamuel Archangel, descend from Above,
Chamuel Archangel, with ruby-pink love,
Chamuel Archangel, so often thought-of,
Chamuel Archangel, o come Holy Dove.**

4. Archangel Chamuel, come into my Heart Chakra and clear it from the concept that I am unable or unworthy to express a higher love.

Chamuel Archangel, what calmness you bring,
I see now that even death has no sting.
For truly, in love there can be no decay,
as love is transcendence into a new day.

**Chamuel Archangel, descend from Above,
Chamuel Archangel, with ruby-pink love,
Chamuel Archangel, so often thought-of,
Chamuel Archangel, o come Holy Dove.**

5. Archangel Chamuel, come into my Heart Chakra and clear it from the possessive love that seeks to own other people or things.

Chamuel Archangel, in ruby ray power,
I know I am taking a life-giving shower.
Love burning away all perversions of will,
I suddenly feel my desires falling still.

**Chamuel Archangel, descend from Above,
Chamuel Archangel, with ruby-pink love,
Chamuel Archangel, so often thought-of,
Chamuel Archangel, o come Holy Dove.**

6. Archangel Chamuel, come into my Heart Chakra and clear it from the fear of rejection and the ego's desire to own, posses or have something in return.

> Chamuel Archangel, a spiral of light,
> as ruby ray fire now pierces the night.
> All forces of darkness consumed by your fire,
> consuming all those who will not rise higher.

**Chamuel Archangel, descend from Above,
Chamuel Archangel, with ruby-pink love,
Chamuel Archangel, so often thought-of,
Chamuel Archangel, o come Holy Dove.**

7. Archangel Chamuel, come into my Heart Chakra and clear it from the sense of lack, the illusion that I need something from any human being.

> Chamuel Archangel, your love so immense,
> with clarified vision, my life now makes sense.
> The purpose of life you so clearly reveal,
> immersed in your love, God's oneness I feel.

**Chamuel Archangel, descend from Above,
Chamuel Archangel, with ruby-pink love,
Chamuel Archangel, so often thought-of,
Chamuel Archangel, o come Holy Dove.**

8. Archangel Chamuel, come into my Heart Chakra and clear it from the deficit consciousness, the illusion that I need something from any source in the material universe.

> Chamuel Archangel, what calmness you bring,
> I see now that even death has no sting.
> For truly, in love there can be no decay,
> as love is transcendence into a new day.

> **Chamuel Archangel, descend from Above,**
> **Chamuel Archangel, with ruby-pink love,**
> **Chamuel Archangel, so often thought-of,**
> **Chamuel Archangel, o come Holy Dove.**

9. Archangel Chamuel, come into my Heart Chakra and clear it from the illusion that because of something I have done – or something I have not done – I could be unworthy to receive love.

> With angels I soar,
> as I reach for MORE.
> The angels so real,
> their love all will heal.
> The angels bring peace,
> all conflicts will cease.
> With angels of light,
> we soar to new height.

> **The rustling sound of angel wings,**
> **what joy as even matter sings,**
> **what joy as every atom rings,**
> **in harmony with angel wings.**

2. Unlock the flow of love

1. Elohim Heros, come into my Heart Chakra and release the flow of the true vibration of the Third Ray, the unconditionality of divine love.

> O Heros-Amora, in your love so pink,
> I care not what others about me may think,
> in oneness with you, I claim a new day,
> an innocent child, I frolic and play.
>
> **O Heros-Amora, a new life begun,**
> **I laugh at the devil, the serious one,**
> **I bathe in your glorious Ruby-Pink Sun,**
> **knowing my God allows life to be fun.**

2. Elohim Heros, come into my Heart Chakra and release the flow of Love as the unconditional force that wants to be expressed. I now see that I do not have to do anything in order to be an open door for the expression of unconditionality.

> O Heros-Amora, life is such a joy,
> I see that the world is like a great toy,
> whatever my mind into it projects,
> the mirror of life exactly reflects.
>
> **O Heros-Amora, I reap what I sow,**
> **yet this is Plan B for helping me grow,**
> **for truly, Plan A is that I join the flow,**
> **immersed in the Infinite Love you bestow.**

3. Elohim Heros, come into my Heart Chakra and release the vibration of unconditionality that consumes all fear of rejection.

> O Heros-Amora, conditions you burn,
> I know I AM free to take a new turn,
> Immersed in the stream of infinite Love,
> I know that my Spirit came from Above.
>
> **O Heros-Amora, awakened I see,**
> **in true love is no conditionality,**
> **the devil is stuck in his duality,**
> **but I AM set free by Love's reality.**

4. Elohim Heros, come into my Heart Chakra and release the flow of unconditional love that is self-contained because it finds its joy in being expressed and in flowing.

> O Heros-Amora, I feel that at last,
> I've risen above the trap of my past,
> in true love I claim my freedom to grow,
> forever I'm one with Love's Infinite Flow.
>
> **O Heros-Amora, conditions are ties,**
> **forming a net of serpentine lies,**
> **your love has no bounds, forever it flies,**
> **raising all life into Ruby-Pink skies.**

5. Elohim Heros, come into my Heart Chakra and release the flow of unconditional love that is everywhere present. Consume the illusion that there could be a place where the unconditional love of God is not present.

O Heros-Amora, in your love so pink,
I care not what others about me may think,
in oneness with you, I claim a new day,
an innocent child, I frolic and play.

**O Heros-Amora, a new life begun,
I laugh at the devil, the serious one,
I bathe in your glorious Ruby-Pink Sun,
knowing my God allows life to be fun.**

6. Elohim Heros, come into my Heart Chakra and release the flow of unconditional love that never seeks to restrict anyone, but only wants everyone to be *more* and to be free to flow with the River of Life.

O Heros-Amora, life is such a joy,
I see that the world is like a great toy,
whatever my mind into it projects,
the mirror of life exactly reflects.

**O Heros-Amora, I reap what I sow,
yet this is Plan B for helping me grow,
for truly, Plan A is that I join the flow,
immersed in the Infinite Love you bestow.**

7. Elohim Heros, come into my Heart Chakra and release the flow of unconditionality from my I AM Presence. Consume the illusion that I am incomplete and that because of this or that condition, I cannot love.

O Heros-Amora, conditions you burn,
I know I AM free to take a new turn,
Immersed in the stream of infinite Love,
I know that my Spirit came from Above.

**O Heros-Amora, awakened I see,
in true love is no conditionality,
the devil is stuck in his duality,
but I AM set free by Love's reality.**

8. Elohim Heros, come into my Heart Chakra and release the flow of unconditionality that consumes the illusion that something is not worthy of love. Consume all conditions, for I am willing to let love flow through me freely.

O Heros-Amora, I feel that at last,
I've risen above the trap of my past,
in true love I claim my freedom to grow,
forever I'm one with Love's Infinite Flow.

**O Heros-Amora, conditions are ties,
forming a net of serpentine lies,
your love has no bounds, forever it flies,
raising all life into Ruby-Pink skies.**

9. Elohim Heros, come into my Heart Chakra and release the flow of unconditionality, consuming the illusion that I have to fulfill a condition in order to be worthy of love. I now unconditionally accept divine love.

Accelerate into Oneness, I AM real,
Accelerate into Oneness, all life heal,
Accelerate into Oneness, I AM MORE,
Accelerate into Oneness, all will soar.

Accelerate into Oneness! (3X)
Beloved Heros and Amora.
Accelerate into Oneness! (3X)
Beloved Chamuel and Charity.

Accelerate into Oneness! (3X)
Beloved Paul the Venetian.
Accelerate into Oneness! (3X)
Beloved I AM.

3. I transcend the illusion of conditionality

1. Paul the Venetian, come into my Heart Chakra and help me transcend the illusion that I am missing something and that someone else must come in and fill that hole so that I can be complete.

> Master Paul, venetian dream,
> your love for beauty's flowing stream.
> Master Paul, in love's own womb,
> your power shatters ego's tomb.
>
> **O Holy Spirit, flow through me,**
> **I am the open door for thee.**
> **O mighty rushing stream of Light,**
> **transcendence is my sacred right.**

2. Paul the Venetian, come into my Heart Chakra and help me see that only by coming into oneness with my I AM Presence will I be complete, will I be whole.

> Master Paul, your counsel wise,
> my mind is raised to lofty skies.
> Master Paul, in wisdom's love,
> such beauty flowing from Above.

13 | Clearing the Heart Chakra

**O Holy Spirit, flow through me,
I am the open door for thee.
O mighty rushing stream of Light,
transcendence is my sacred right.**

3. Paul the Venetian, come into my Heart Chakra and help me transcend the illusion of the serious, romantic love. Help me accept that love is not to be taken seriously.

Master Paul, love is an art,
it opens up the secret heart.
Master Paul, love's rushing flow,
my heart awash in sacred glow.

**O Holy Spirit, flow through me,
I am the open door for thee.
O mighty rushing stream of Light,
transcendence is my sacred right.**

4. Paul the Venetian, come into my Heart Chakra and help me see that if I take love seriously, it can only be conditional love. Help me tune in to the unconditional love of God, so I am joyful in flowing with the River of Life.

Master Paul, accelerate,
upon pure love I meditate.
Master Paul, intentions pure,
my self-transcendence will ensure.

**O Holy Spirit, flow through me,
I am the open door for thee.
O mighty rushing stream of Light,
transcendence is my sacred right.**

5. Paul the Venetian, come into my Heart Chakra and help me transcend the illusion that there is only one person on this earth who is worthy of my love, and that I absolutely need to have that love returned.

> Master Paul, your love will heal,
> my inner light you do reveal.
> Master Paul, all life console,
> with you I'm being truly whole.

> **O Holy Spirit, flow through me,**
> **I am the open door for thee.**
> **O mighty rushing stream of Light,**
> **transcendence is my sacred right.**

6. Paul the Venetian, come into my Heart Chakra and help me laugh at my own seriousness when it comes to love. Help me become the joyful lover who realizes that I am the beloved of an even greater lover, namely the Divine Lover who loves me as its beloved.

> Master Paul, you serve the All,
> by helping us transcend the fall.
> Master Paul, in peace we rise,
> as ego meets its sure demise.

> **O Holy Spirit, flow through me,**
> **I am the open door for thee.**
> **O mighty rushing stream of Light,**
> **transcendence is my sacred right.**

7. Paul the Venetian, come into my Heart Chakra and help me experience that my I AM Presence is my personal Divine Lover who loves me as its only beloved. Help me be full in the love from my higher being.

> Master Paul, love all life free,
> your love is for eternity.
> Master Paul, you are the One,
> to help us make the journey fun.

> **O Holy Spirit, flow through me,**
> **I am the open door for thee.**
> **O mighty rushing stream of Light,**
> **transcendence is my sacred right.**

8. Paul the Venetian, come into my Heart Chakra and help me become one with the Divine Lover and *become* the Divine Lover who is the open door for the flow of love. I am the open door for the force that loves all life and seeks to raise up all life.

> Master Paul, you balance all,
> the seven rays upon my call.
> Master Paul, you paint the sky,
> with colors that delight the I.

> **O Holy Spirit, flow through me,**
> **I am the open door for thee.**
> **O mighty rushing stream of Light,**
> **transcendence is my sacred right.**

9. Paul the Venetian, come into my Heart Chakra and help me set myself and my partner free from the overlay of conditionality. Help me attain a playful, joyful, flowing relationship that is not hemmed in by boundaries, conditions, expectations, blaming and feeling that my love is not returned.

> Master Paul, your Presence here,
> filling up my inner sphere.
> Life is now a sacred flow,
> God Love I do on all bestow.

> **O Holy Spirit, flow through me,**
> **I am the open door for thee.**
> **O mighty rushing stream of Light,**
> **transcendence is my sacred right.**

4. I set my cells free to be whole

1. Beloved Venus, come into my Heart Chakra and help me see that when I begin to shut off the flow of love, my lower being becomes a closed system, generating disease in my physical body.

> O Venus, show me how to serve,
> your cosmic beauty I observe.
> What love from Venus you now bring,
> our planets do in tandem sing.

> **O Venus, service so divine,**
> **you are for earth a cosmic sign.**
> **Your selfless service is now mine,**
> **a life in service I define.**

13 | Clearing the Heart Chakra

2. Beloved Venus, come into my Heart Chakra and help me transcend the illusion that my body is working against me. Help me overcome the fear of looking at the disease and the illusion that I cannot love my body because it is ill.

> O Venus, your love is the key,
> the hardened hearts on earth are free.
> Embracing future bright and bold,
> our planet's story is retold.
>
> **O Venus, service so divine,**
> **you are for earth a cosmic sign.**
> **Your selfless service is now mine,**
> **a life in service I define.**

3. Beloved Venus, come into my Heart Chakra and help me see that my cells are out-picturing a state of consciousness that caused me to shut off the flow of love. Help me love the cells so that I help them free themselves from the condition that makes them ill.

> O Venus, loving Mother mine,
> my heart your love does now refine.
> I am the open door for love,
> descending like a Holy Dove.
>
> **O Venus, service so divine,**
> **you are for earth a cosmic sign.**
> **Your selfless service is now mine,**
> **a life in service I define.**

4. Beloved Venus, come into my Heart Chakra and help me break the vicious circle of shutting off the flow of love so that I can set my body free from disease.

O Venus, play the secret note,
that is for hatred antidote.
All poisoned hearts you gently heal,
as love's true story you reveal.

O Venus, service so divine,
you are for earth a cosmic sign.
Your selfless service is now mine,
a life in service I define.

5. Beloved Venus, come into my Heart Chakra and help me accept that the key to true healing is to restore the flow of love—and I am the one who restores it.

O Venus, love fills every need,
for truly, love is God's first seed.
O let it blossom, let it grow,
sweep earth into your loving flow.

O Venus, service so divine,
you are for earth a cosmic sign.
Your selfless service is now mine,
a life in service I define.

6. Beloved Venus, come into my Heart Chakra and help me love my cells free of all disease, setting them free to outpicture the higher pattern of oneness, of perfect health.

O Venus, music of the spheres,
heard by those who God reveres.
Our voices now as one we raise,
singing in adoring praise.

> O Venus, service so divine,
> you are for earth a cosmic sign.
> Your selfless service is now mine,
> a life in service I define.

7. Beloved Venus, come into my Heart Chakra and help me unlock the flow of unconditional love that will consume the conditions that I have subconsciously projected upon the cells of my body.

> O Venus, we are joining ranks,
> Sanat Kumara we give thanks.
> Our planet has received new life,
> to lift her out of war and strife.

> O Venus, service so divine,
> you are for earth a cosmic sign.
> Your selfless service is now mine,
> a life in service I define.

8. Beloved Venus, come into my Heart Chakra and help me unlock the wisdom in my cells, the wisdom of the Divine Mother that knows how to express perfect health—if it is only allowed to outpicture what is within it.

> O Venus, your sweet melody,
> consumes veil of duality.
> Absorbed in tones of Cosmic Love,
> all conflict we now rise above.

> O Venus, service so divine,
> you are for earth a cosmic sign.
> Your selfless service is now mine,
> a life in service I define.

9. Beloved Venus, come into my Heart Chakra and help me accept that God has written his law in my inward parts. Help me love my cells free so they can shake off all disease and outpicture their natural state of perfect health.

> O Venus, shining Morning Star,
> a cosmic herald, that you are.
> The earth set free by sacred sound,
> our planet is now heaven-bound.
>
> **O Venus, service so divine,**
> **you are for earth a cosmic sign.**
> **Your selfless service is now mine,**
> **a life in service I define.**

Sealing:

In the name of the Divine Mother, I fully accept that the power of these calls is used to set free the Ma-ter light, so it can outpicture the perfect vision of Christ for my own life, for all people and for the planet. In the name I AM THAT I AM, it is done! Amen.

14 | CLEARING THE SOLAR PLEXUS CHAKRA

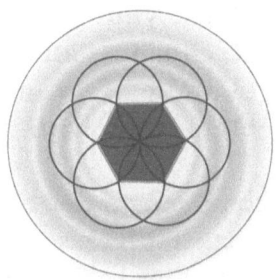

[NOTE: Study the dictation from the Sixth Ray.]

In the name I AM THAT I AM, Jesus Christ, I call to my I AM Presence to flow through the I Will Be Presence that I AM and give this invocation with full power. I call to beloved Elohim Peace and Aloha, Archangel Uriel and Aurora, and beloved Nada to help me overcome all impurities in my Solar Plexus Chakra. Help me be free from all patterns or forces within or without that oppose the free flow of peace from my I AM Presence, including ...

[Make personal calls]

1. I reestablish the flow of emotions

1. Archangel Uriel, come into my Solar Plexus Chakra and clear it from the trauma of experiencing that my spiritual light was rejected and put down.

> Uriel Archangel, immense is the power,
> of angels of peace, all war to devour.
> The demons of war, no match for your light,
> consuming them all, with radiance so bright.
>
> **Uriel Archangel, use your great sword,**
> **Uriel Archangel, consume all discord,**
> **Uriel Archangel, we're of one accord,**
> **Uriel Archangel, we walk with the Lord.**

2. Archangel Uriel, come into my Solar Plexus Chakra and clear it from the fear of rejection that caused me to decide that I have to adapt the expression of my light to the conditions found on earth.

> Uriel Archangel, intense is the sound,
> when millions of angels, their voices compound.
> They build a crescendo, piercing the night,
> life's glorious oneness revealed to our sight.
>
> **Uriel Archangel, use your great sword,**
> **Uriel Archangel, consume all discord,**
> **Uriel Archangel, we're of one accord,**
> **Uriel Archangel, we walk with the Lord.**

14 | Clearing the Solar Plexus Chakra

3. Archangel Uriel, come into my Solar Plexus Chakra and clear it from the fear, anger and sense of injustice that caused me to suppress my light.

> Uriel Archangel, from out the Great Throne,
> your millions of trumpets, sound the One Tone.
> Consuming all discord with your harmony,
> the sound of all sounds will set all life free.

> **Uriel Archangel, use your great sword,**
> **Uriel Archangel, consume all discord,**
> **Uriel Archangel, we're of one accord,**
> **Uriel Archangel, we walk with the Lord.**

4. Archangel Uriel, come into my Solar Plexus Chakra and clear it from the illusion that as a spiritual person I should not have negative emotions but should try to suppress them.

> Uriel Archangel, all war is now gone,
> for you bring a message, from heart of the One.
> The hearts of all men, now singing in peace,
> the spirals of love, forever increase.

> **Uriel Archangel, use your great sword,**
> **Uriel Archangel, consume all discord,**
> **Uriel Archangel, we're of one accord,**
> **Uriel Archangel, we walk with the Lord.**

5. Archangel Uriel, come into my Solar Plexus Chakra and clear it from all of the energy that has been produced by suppressing my negative emotions, the energy that has accumulated and blocks the flow of light.

Uriel Archangel, immense is the power,
of angels of peace, all war to devour.
The demons of war, no match for your light,
consuming them all, with radiance so bright.

Uriel Archangel, use your great sword,
Uriel Archangel, consume all discord,
Uriel Archangel, we're of one accord,
Uriel Archangel, we walk with the Lord.

6. Archangel Uriel, come into my Solar Plexus Chakra and clear it from the unwillingness to acknowledge and give expression to my negative emotions. Help me reestablish the flow of light through my four lower bodies.

Uriel Archangel, intense is the sound,
when millions of angels, their voices compound.
They build a crescendo, piercing the night,
life's glorious oneness revealed to our sight.

Uriel Archangel, use your great sword,
Uriel Archangel, consume all discord,
Uriel Archangel, we're of one accord,
Uriel Archangel, we walk with the Lord.

7. Archangel Uriel, come into my Solar Plexus Chakra and clear it from the illusion that causes me to identify with my emotions. Help me experience the freedom that my emotions are just energy and I am more than energy, more than my emotions.

Uriel Archangel, from out the Great Throne,
your millions of trumpets, sound the One Tone.
Consuming all discord with your harmony,
the sound of all sounds will set all life free.

Uriel Archangel, use your great sword,
Uriel Archangel, consume all discord,
Uriel Archangel, we're of one accord,
Uriel Archangel, we walk with the Lord.

8. Archangel Uriel, come into my Solar Plexus Chakra and clear it from all unwillingness to accept myself for having certain emotions. Help me experience that you love me for who I am regardless of my emotions.

Uriel Archangel, all war is now gone,
for you bring a message, from heart of the One.
The hearts of all men, now singing in peace,
the spirals of love, forever increase.

Uriel Archangel, use your great sword,
Uriel Archangel, consume all discord,
Uriel Archangel, we're of one accord,
Uriel Archangel, we walk with the Lord.

9. Archangel Uriel, come into my Solar Plexus Chakra and clear it from all unwillingness to accept myself unconditionally and accept myself as being more than any emotion.

With angels I soar,
as I reach for MORE.
The angels so real,
their love all will heal.
The angels bring peace,
all conflicts will cease.
With angels of light,
we soar to new height.

**The rustling sound of angel wings,
what joy as even matter sings,
what joy as every atom rings,
in harmony with angel wings.**

2. I will no longer suppress my light

1. Elohim Peace, come into my Solar Plexus Chakra and release the energy of active peace so that I can shift my perception into fully accepting my right to be on earth and to express my light here.

> O Elohim Peace, in Unity's Flame,
> there is no more room for duality's game,
> we know that all form is from the same source,
> empowering us to plot a new course.

> **O Elohim Peace, the bell now you ring,
> causing all atoms to vibrate and sing,
> I now see that there is no separate thing,
> to my ego-based self I no longer cling.**

2. Elohim Peace, come into my Solar Plexus Chakra and release the peace that gives me the foundation for making the conscious decision that I have the right to be here and that I have a right to let my light shine because my light is acceptable to God.

> O Elohim Peace, you help me to know,
> that Jesus has come your Flame to bestow,
> upon all who are ready to give up the strife,
> by following Christ into infinite life.

> O Elohim Peace, through your eyes I see,
> that only in oneness will I ever be free,
> I give up the sense of a separate me,
> I AM crossing Samsara's turbulent sea.

3. Elohim Peace, come into my Solar Plexus Chakra and release the peace that helps me see that other people do not have the right to demand that I suppress my light. I have a right to shine my light regardless of how other people choose to react.

O Elohim Peace, you show me the way,
for clearing my mind from duality's fray,
you pierce the illusions of both time and space,
separation consumed by your Infinite Grace.

> O Elohim Peace, what beauty your name,
> consuming within me duality's shame,
> It was through the vibration of your Golden Flame,
> that Christ the illusion of death overcame.

4. Elohim Peace, come into my Solar Plexus Chakra and release the peace that gives me the courage to express any emotions I have. Help me reestablish the flow of spiritual light through my emotional body.

O Elohim Peace, you bring now to earth,
the unstoppable flame of Cosmic Rebirth,
I give up the sense that something is mine,
allowing your Light through my being to shine.

> O Elohim Peace, through your tranquility,
> we are free from the chaos of duality,
> in oneness with God a new identity,
> we are raising the earth into Infinity.

5. Elohim Peace, come into my Solar Plexus Chakra and release the peace that gives me the courage to look at limiting thought patterns. Help me reestablish the flow of spiritual light through my mental body.

> O Elohim Peace, in Unity's Flame,
> there is no more room for duality's game,
> we know that all form is from the same source,
> empowering us to plot a new course.
>
> **O Elohim Peace, the bell now you ring,**
> **causing all atoms to vibrate and sing,**
> **I now see that there is no separate thing,**
> **to my ego-based self I no longer cling.**

6. Elohim Peace, come into my Solar Plexus Chakra and release the peace that gives me the courage to look at any limited sense of identity. Help me reestablish the flow of spiritual light through my identity body.

> O Elohim Peace, you help me to know,
> that Jesus has come your Flame to bestow,
> upon all who are ready to give up the strife,
> by following Christ into infinite life.
>
> **O Elohim Peace, through your eyes I see,**
> **that only in oneness will I ever be free,**
> **I give up the sense of a separate me,**
> **I AM crossing Samsara's turbulent sea.**

7. Elohim Peace, come into my Solar Plexus Chakra and help me stand centered in complete peace. I hereby release the image that I was a powerless being who was forced to respond a certain way to certain outer stimuli.

> O Elohim Peace, you show me the way,
> for clearing my mind from duality's fray,
> you pierce the illusions of both time and space,
> separation consumed by your Infinite Grace.
>
> **O Elohim Peace, what beauty your name,**
> **consuming within me duality's shame,**
> **It was through the vibration of your Golden Flame,**
> **that Christ the illusion of death overcame.**

8. Elohim Peace, come into my Solar Plexus Chakra and release the peace that helps me know that I AM real. Everything created out of the duality consciousness is unreal, and I have no obligation to let unreality affect the real me. Nor is there a natural law that says that the real me has to respond a certain way to that which is unreal.

> O Elohim Peace, you bring now to earth,
> the unstoppable flame of Cosmic Rebirth,
> I give up the sense that something is mine,
> allowing your Light through my being to shine.
>
> **O Elohim Peace, through your tranquility,**
> **we are free from the chaos of duality,**
> **in oneness with God a new identity,**
> **we are raising the earth into Infinity.**

9. Elohim Peace, come into my Solar Plexus Chakra and release the peace that gives me the experience that as a real being, I am never bound by my past choices. At any moment, I have the right to decide that I will be who I will be, I will be more than ever before.

> Accelerate into Unity, I AM real,
> Accelerate into Unity, all life heal,
> Accelerate into Unity, I AM MORE,
> Accelerate into Unity, all will soar.
>
> Accelerate into Unity! (3X)
> Beloved Peace and Aloha.
> Accelerate into Unity! (3X)
> Beloved Uriel and Aurora.
> Accelerate into Unity! (3X)
> Beloved Jesus and Nada.
> Accelerate into Unity! (3X)
> Beloved I AM.

3. My body is nurtured and healed

1. Beloved Nada, come into my Solar Plexus Chakra and help me know that a disease of any kind in the physical body began in the higher bodies as a suppression of the light that I am. It was suppression that started the chain reaction that led to the physical disease.

> Master Nada, beauty's power,
> unfolding like a sacred flower.
> Master Nada, so sublime,
> a will that conquers even time.

14 | Clearing the Solar Plexus Chakra

**O Holy Spirit, flow through me,
I am the open door for thee.
O mighty rushing stream of Light,
transcendence is my sacred right.**

2. Beloved Nada, come into my Solar Plexus Chakra and help me know that I cannot heal a disease by suppressing the light even more. I can heal only by reestablishing the flow of light through all of my chakras.

Master Nada, you bestow,
upon me wisdom's rushing flow.
Master Nada, mind so strong
rising on your wings of song.

**O Holy Spirit, flow through me,
I am the open door for thee.
O mighty rushing stream of Light,
transcendence is my sacred right.**

3. Beloved Nada, come into my Solar Plexus Chakra and help me focus on my blocked emotions, applying the heat through my conscious awareness that gets them flowing again.

Master Nada, precious scent,
your love is truly heaven-sent.
Master Nada, kind and soft
on wings of love we rise aloft.

**O Holy Spirit, flow through me,
I am the open door for thee.
O mighty rushing stream of Light,
transcendence is my sacred right.**

4. Beloved Nada, come into my Solar Plexus Chakra and help me know that I am not bound by anything in the past. Help me overcome the need to judge, evaluate and analyze everything with my outer mind.

> Master Nada, mother light,
> my heart is rising like a kite.
> Master Nada, from your view,
> all life is pure as morning dew.

> **O Holy Spirit, flow through me,**
> **I am the open door for thee.**
> **O mighty rushing stream of Light,**
> **transcendence is my sacred right.**

5. Beloved Nada, come into my Solar Plexus Chakra and help me *be* in the flow of the River of Life. I am expressing, at any moment whatever life wants to express through me. I dare to give spontaneous expression to what comes from my I AM Presence.

> Master Nada, truth you bring,
> as morning birds in love do sing.
> Master Nada, I now feel,
> your love that all four bodies heal.

> **O Holy Spirit, flow through me,**
> **I am the open door for thee.**
> **O mighty rushing stream of Light,**
> **transcendence is my sacred right.**

6. Beloved Nada, come into my Solar Plexus Chakra and help me know that my past choices have not set a pattern for my future. I hereby reject the projections that I am not free to make new choices right now.

> Master Nada, serve in peace,
> as all emotions I release.
> Master Nada, life is fun,
> my solar plexus is a sun.

**O Holy Spirit, flow through me,
I am the open door for thee.
O mighty rushing stream of Light,
transcendence is my sacred right.**

7. Beloved Nada, come into my Solar Plexus Chakra and help me fully accept my right to flow with the River of Life. Help me know that there are no rules in Christhood. There are no rules for what I should *be,* how I should express my Being. I AM flowing with the River of Life.

> Master Nada, love is free,
> with no conditions binding me.
> Master Nada, rise above,
> all human forms of lesser love.

**O Holy Spirit, flow through me,
I am the open door for thee.
O mighty rushing stream of Light,
transcendence is my sacred right.**

8. Beloved Nada, come into my Solar Plexus Chakra and help me let go of all tendencies to analyze and grumble about the past. Help me experience that no matter what I have done in the past, I AM shifting back into the flow and just *being more*.

> Master Nada, balance all,
> the seven rays upon my call.
> Master Nada, rise and shine,
> your radiant beauty most divine.

> **O Holy Spirit, flow through me,**
> **I am the open door for thee.**
> **O mighty rushing stream of Light,**
> **transcendence is my sacred right.**

9. Beloved Nada, come into my Solar Plexus Chakra and help me see what I haven't yet gotten. Help me find the particular individual key and insight that will unlock my being. Help me see the particular individual block that stands in the way of me fully accepting myself.

> Nada Dear, your Presence here,
> filling up my inner sphere.
> Life is now a sacred flow,
> God Peace I do on all bestow.

> **O Holy Spirit, flow through me,**
> **I am the open door for thee.**
> **O mighty rushing stream of Light,**
> **transcendence is my sacred right.**

4. I find joy in true service

1. Beloved Nada, come into my Solar Plexus Chakra and help me accept that my emotions are not my enemies. They are one expression that is needed to bring the fullness of life, to bring the higher vision I have into physical manifestation.

> O Nada, blessed cosmic grace,
> filling up my inner space.
> Your song is like a sacred balm,
> my mind a sea of perfect calm.
>
> **With Nada's secret melody,**
> **my mind remains forever free.**
> **Conducting Nada's symphony,**
> **eternal peace I do decree.**

2. Beloved Nada, come into my Solar Plexus Chakra and help me truly feel the vision of health, feel perfect health, feel wholeness, so that wholeness can break through to my physical body and nourish it.

> O Nada, in your Buddhic mind,
> my inner peace I truly find.
> As I your song reverberate,
> your love I do assimilate.
>
> **With Nada's secret melody,**
> **my mind remains forever free.**
> **Conducting Nada's symphony,**
> **eternal peace I do decree.**

3. Beloved Nada, come into my Solar Plexus Chakra and help me know that my body can only function by also receiving spiritual nourishment. My emotions are a vehicle to bring the spiritual light into the physical realm where my cells can absorb it and therefore be accelerated and nourished by it.

> O Nada, beauty so sublime,
> I follow you beyond all time.
> In soundless sound we do immerse,
> to recreate the universe.

> **With Nada's secret melody,**
> **my mind remains forever free.**
> **Conducting Nada's symphony,**
> **eternal peace I do decree.**

4. Beloved Nada, come into my Solar Plexus Chakra and help me make the shift so I do not seek to squash, deny or run away from what I actually feel. I listen to my feelings, acknowledge them, give them expression and get the flow going through the emotional body.

> O Nada, future we predict
> where nothing Christhood can restrict.
> With Buddhic mind we do perceive,
> a better future we conceive.

> **With Nada's secret melody,**
> **my mind remains forever free.**
> **Conducting Nada's symphony,**
> **eternal peace I do decree.**

5. Beloved Nada, come into my Solar Plexus Chakra and help me surrender the need to suppress the emotions. I hereby surrender the entire idea that I need to analyze and categorize my emotions. Instead, I let the energy be in motion.

> O Nada, future we rewrite,
> where might is never, ever right.
> Instead, the mind of Christ is king,
> we see the Christ in every thing.
>
> **With Nada's secret melody,**
> **my mind remains forever free.**
> **Conducting Nada's symphony,**
> **eternal peace I do decree.**

6. Beloved Nada, come into my Solar Plexus Chakra and help me tune in to my divine plan and my highest service. I will not let any blocked emotions stand in the way of the manifestation of my highest service to life.

> O Nada, peace is now the norm,
> my Spirit is beyond all form.
> To form I will no more adapt,
> I use potential yet untapped.
>
> **With Nada's secret melody,**
> **my mind remains forever free.**
> **Conducting Nada's symphony,**
> **eternal peace I do decree.**

7. Beloved Nada, come into my Solar Plexus Chakra and help me re-establish the flow through my being. I allow my I AM Presence to spontaneously express what other people need.

O Nada, such resplendent joy,
my life I truly can enjoy.
I am allowed to have some fun,
my solar plexus like a sun.

**With Nada's secret melody,
my mind remains forever free.
Conducting Nada's symphony,
eternal peace I do decree.**

8. Beloved Nada, come into my Solar Plexus Chakra and help me immerse myself fully in the flow of service where everything becomes a joy. My entire life is a joy because I am always serving in one capacity or another.

O Nada, service is the key,
to living in reality.
For I see now that life is one,
my highest service has begun.

**With Nada's secret melody,
my mind remains forever free.
Conducting Nada's symphony,
eternal peace I do decree.**

9. Beloved Nada, come into my Solar Plexus Chakra and help me experience that through my service God is experiencing its fullness through me. I experience the joy that is the Creator's own joy of being expressed. I follow that joy, merge with it, and I see that everything is joy. The underlying reality behind all form is unconditional, never-ending, ever-flowing, ever-creative, ever-self-transcending joy.

O Nada, we do now decree,
that life on earth shall be carefree.
With Jesus we complete the quest,
God's kingdom is now manifest.

**With Nada's secret melody,
my mind remains forever free.
Conducting Nada's symphony,
eternal peace I do decree.**

Sealing:

In the name of the Divine Mother, I fully accept that the power of these calls is used to set free the Ma-ter light, so it can outpicture the perfect vision of Christ for my own life, for all people and for the planet. In the name I AM THAT I AM, it is done! Amen.

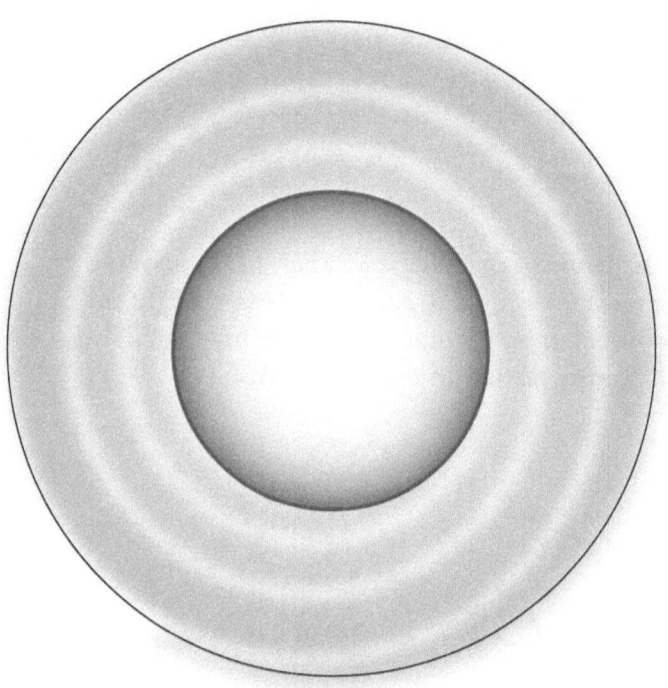

15 | CLEARING THE THROAT CHAKRA

[*NOTE*: Study the dictation from the First Ray.]

In the name I AM THAT I AM, Jesus Christ, I call to my I AM Presence to flow through the I Will Be Presence that I AM and give this invocation with full power. I call to beloved Archangel Michael and Faith, Elohim Hercules and Amazonia, Master MORE and Maraytaii to help me overcome all impurities in my Throat Chakra. Help me be free from all patterns or forces within or without that oppose the free flow of power from my I AM Presence, including …

[Make personal calls]

1. I surrender all anti-will

1. Archangel Michael, come into my Throat Chakra and clear it from the anti-will that prevents me from deciding that enough is enough and claiming my right to move on.

> Michael Archangel, in your flame so blue,
> there is no more night, there is only you.
> In oneness with you, I am filled with your light,
> what glorious wonder, revealed to my sight.
>
> **Michael Archangel, your Faith is so strong,**
> **Michael Archangel, oh sweep me along.**
> **Michael Archangel, I'm singing your song,**
> **Michael Archangel, with you I belong.**

2. Archangel Michael, come into my Throat Chakra and clear it from the very core of dishonesty, the belief that something can be hidden, the tendency to say or do certain things while thinking something different within.

> Michael Archangel, protection you give,
> within your blue shield, I ever shall live.
> Sealed from all creatures, roaming the night,
> I remain in your sphere, of electric blue light.
>
> **Michael Archangel, your Faith is so strong,**
> **Michael Archangel, oh sweep me along.**
> **Michael Archangel, I'm singing your song,**
> **Michael Archangel, with you I belong.**

3. Archangel Michael, come into my Throat Chakra and clear it from the dishonesty of anti-will that causes me to think I am trapped in a particular role and that some external force is preventing me from moving on.

> Michael Archangel, what power you bring,
> as millions of angels, praises will sing.
> Consuming the demons, of doubt and of fear,
> I know that your Presence, will always be near.
>
> **Michael Archangel, your Faith is so strong,**
> **Michael Archangel, oh sweep me along.**
> **Michael Archangel, I'm singing your song,**
> **Michael Archangel, with you I belong.**

4. Archangel Michael, come into my Throat Chakra and clear it from the anti-power that causes me to think that some external force has put me in my current situation. Help me reclaim my power to change my situation.

> Michael Archangel, God's will is your love,
> you bring to us all, God's light from Above.
> God's will is to see, all life taking flight,
> transcendence of self, our most sacred right.
>
> **Michael Archangel, your Faith is so strong,**
> **Michael Archangel, oh sweep me along.**
> **Michael Archangel, I'm singing your song,**
> **Michael Archangel, with you I belong.**

5. Archangel Michael, come into my Throat Chakra and clear it from the anti-will that causes me give away my free will to an external power.

> Michael Archangel, in your flame so blue,
> there is no more night, there is only you.
> In oneness with you, I am filled with your light,
> what glorious wonder, revealed to my sight.

Michael Archangel, your Faith is so strong,
Michael Archangel, oh sweep me along.
Michael Archangel, I'm singing your song,
Michael Archangel, with you I belong.

6. Archangel Michael, come into my Throat Chakra and clear it from the anti-will that caused me to decide that I no longer want to decide. Help me surrender the graven image that there is some external power that is ruling my life.

> Michael Archangel, protection you give,
> within your blue shield, I ever shall live.
> Sealed from all creatures, roaming the night,
> I remain in your sphere, of electric blue light.

Michael Archangel, your Faith is so strong,
Michael Archangel, oh sweep me along.
Michael Archangel, I'm singing your song,
Michael Archangel, with you I belong.

7. Archangel Michael, come into my Throat Chakra and clear it from the anti-power that causes me to think I can own and possess things for the separate self. Help me surrender all desire to raise the separate self in comparison to others or attain some prominent position in society.

Michael Archangel, what power you bring,
as millions of angels, praises will sing.
Consuming the demons, of doubt and of fear,
I know that your Presence, will always be near.

Michael Archangel, your Faith is so strong,
Michael Archangel, oh sweep me along.
Michael Archangel, I'm singing your song,
Michael Archangel, with you I belong.

8. Archangel Michael, come into my Throat Chakra and clear it from the anti-power that causes me to think I am like a God and that I have the ability and the right to define good and evil based on the dualistic thinking of the ego.

Michael Archangel, God's will is your love,
you bring to us all, God's light from Above
God's will is to see, all life taking flight,
transcendence of self, our most sacred right.

Michael Archangel, your Faith is so strong,
Michael Archangel, oh sweep me along.
Michael Archangel, I'm singing your song,
Michael Archangel, with you I belong.

9. Archangel Michael, come into my Throat Chakra and clear it from the anti-power that causes me to think the forms I see in the material world have some ultimate reality. Help me give of the ghost of thinking my Spirit is crucified in matter.

With angels I soar,
as I reach for MORE.
The angels so real,
their love all will heal.

The angels bring peace,
all conflicts will cease.
With angels of light,
we soar to new height.

**The rustling sound of angel wings,
what joy as even matter sings,
what joy as every atom rings,
in harmony with angel wings.**

2. I am honest

1. Elohim Hercules, come into my Throat Chakra and release the vibration of honesty as oneness with the will and the creative power of God.

O Hercules Blue, you fill every space,
with infinite Power and infinite Grace,
you embody the key to creativity,
the will to transcend into Infinity.

**O Hercules Blue, in oneness with thee,
I open my heart to your reality,
in feeling your flame, so clearly I see,
transcending my self is the true alchemy.**

2. Elohim Hercules, come into my Throat Chakra and release the vibration of creative freedom that helps me accept my right and ability to take off any limiting role I have chosen to play on earth.

15 | Clearing the Throat Chakra

> O Hercules Blue, I lovingly raise,
> my voice in giving God infinite praise,
> I'm grateful for playing my personal part,
> In God's infinitely intricate work of art.
>
> **O Hercules Blue, all life now you heal,**
> **enveloping all in your Blue-flame Seal,**
> **your electric-blue fire within us reveal,**
> **our innermost longing for all that is real.**

3. Elohim Hercules, come into my Throat Chakra and release the creative will that empowers me to break free from any limited sense of identity.

> O Hercules Blue, I pledge now my life,
> in helping this planet transcend human strife,
> duality's lies are pierced by your light,
> restoring the fullness of my inner sight.
>
> **O Hercules Blue, I'm one with your will,**
> **all space in my being with Blue Flame you fill,**
> **your power allows me to forge on until,**
> **I pierce every veil and climb every hill.**

4. Elohim Hercules, come into my Throat Chakra and release the vibration of honesty and realism that empowers me to accept myself as the pure Being that God created.

> O Hercules Blue, your Temple of Light,
> revealed to us all through our inner sight,
> a beacon that radiates light to the earth,
> bringing about our planet's rebirth.

**O Hercules Blue, all life you defend,
giving us power to always transcend,
in you the expansion of self has no end,
as I in God's infinite spirals ascend.**

5. Elohim Hercules, come into my Throat Chakra and release the flow of creative drive that helps me take back the full power of my will.

O Hercules Blue, you fill every space,
with infinite Power and infinite Grace,
you embody the key to creativity,
the will to transcend into Infinity.

**O Hercules Blue, in oneness with thee,
I open my heart to your reality,
in feeling your flame, so clearly I see,
transcending my self is the true alchemy.**

6. Elohim Hercules, come into my Throat Chakra and help me switch my sense of identity, switch my self-image, switch my perspective. Help me go through a seismic shift in identity where I no longer see separation but see oneness.

O Hercules Blue, I lovingly raise,
my voice in giving God infinite praise,
I'm grateful for playing my personal part,
In God's infinitely intricate work of art.

**O Hercules Blue, all life now you heal,
enveloping all in your Blue-flame Seal,
your electric-blue fire within us reveal,
our innermost longing for all that is real.**

15 | Clearing the Throat Chakra

7. Elohim Hercules, come into my Throat Chakra and help me take back my creative power. Help me reconnect to the Higher Being that I AM and say with Jesus: "I and my father are one. My father worketh hitherto and I work."

> O Hercules Blue, I pledge now my life,
> in helping this planet transcend human strife,
> duality's lies are pierced by your light,
> restoring the fullness of my inner sight.
>
> **O Hercules Blue, I'm one with your will,**
> **all space in my being with Blue Flame you fill,**
> **your power allows me to forge on until,**
> **I pierce every veil and climb every hill.**

8. Elohim Hercules, come into my Throat Chakra and help me seek first the oneness of the Christ consciousness so that the power of God can flow through me and balance my karma much more quickly.

> O Hercules Blue, your Temple of Light,
> revealed to us all through our inner sight,
> a beacon that radiates light to the earth,
> bringing about our planet's rebirth.
>
> **O Hercules Blue, all life you defend,**
> **giving us power to always transcend,**
> **in you the expansion of self has no end,**
> **as I in God's infinite spirals ascend.**

9. Elohim Hercules, come into my Throat Chakra and help me claim the power of the greater being that I AM, using it to transform my life into an upward spiral.

> Accelerate into Creativity, I AM real,
> Accelerate into Creativity, all life heal,
> Accelerate into Creativity, I AM MORE,
> Accelerate into Creativity, all will soar.
>
> Accelerate into Creativity! (3X)
> Beloved Hercules and Amazonia.
> Accelerate into Creativity! (3X)
> Beloved Michael and Faith.
> Accelerate into Creativity! (3X)
> Beloved Master MORE.
> Accelerate into Creativity! (3X)
> Beloved I AM.

3. I accept God's power within me

1. Master MORE, come into my Throat Chakra and help me claim my willingness to look at the beam in my own eye, to look at and transcend the consciousness that precipitates disease in the body.

> Master MORE, come to the fore,
> I will absorb your flame of MORE.
> Master MORE, my will so strong,
> my power center cleared by song.
>
> **O Holy Spirit, flow through me,**
> **I am the open door for thee.**
> **O mighty rushing stream of Light,**
> **transcendence is my sacred right.**

2. Master MORE, come into my Throat Chakra and help me see the reality that the foundation of disease is dishonesty, the illusion that something can be hidden.

> Master MORE, your wisdom flows,
> as my attunement ever grows.
> Master MORE, we have a tie,
> that helps me see through Serpent's lie.
>
> **O Holy Spirit, flow through me,**
> **I am the open door for thee.**
> **O mighty rushing stream of Light,**
> **transcendence is my sacred right.**

3. Master MORE, come into my Throat Chakra and help me fully accept the Omega aspect of the will of God, namely that true healing is self-healing!

> Master MORE, your love so pink,
> there is no purer love, I think.
> Master MORE, you set me free,
> from all conditionality.
>
> **O Holy Spirit, flow through me,**
> **I am the open door for thee.**
> **O mighty rushing stream of Light,**
> **transcendence is my sacred right.**

4. Master MORE, come into my Throat Chakra and help me accept that the purpose of life is the growth of the self, the growth of self-awareness. Help me embrace that this growth is self-growth, and it is not forced upon me by God.

> Master MORE, I will endure,
> your discipline that makes me pure.
> Master MORE, intentions true,
> as I am always one with you.
>
> **O Holy Spirit, flow through me,**
> **I am the open door for thee.**
> **O mighty rushing stream of Light,**
> **transcendence is my sacred right.**

5. Master MORE, come into my Throat Chakra and help me accept that I am a spiritual being who is not trapped in this universe, trapped in a particular role. Help me claim my power to heal myself.

> Master MORE, my vision raised,
> the will of God is always praised.
> Master MORE, creative will,
> raising all life higher still.

> **O Holy Spirit, flow through me,**
> **I am the open door for thee.**
> **O mighty rushing stream of Light,**
> **transcendence is my sacred right.**

6. Master MORE, come into my Throat Chakra and help me accept that my free will is truly free. At any moment I have the complete freedom to separate myself from my role—to just take it off, to let it drop from me, to let the old man die and be reborn in a new sense of self.

> Master MORE, your peace is power,
> the demons of war it will devour.
> Master MORE, we serve all life,
> our flames consuming war and strife.

> **O Holy Spirit, flow through me,**
> **I am the open door for thee.**
> **O mighty rushing stream of Light,**
> **transcendence is my sacred right.**

7. Master MORE, come into my Throat Chakra and help me dismiss the serpentine lie that I have become a limited being and thus cannot simply walk away from the limited self.

> Master MORE, I am so free,
> eternal bond from you to me.
> Master MORE, I find rebirth,
> in flow of your eternal mirth.

O Holy Spirit, flow through me,
I am the open door for thee.
O mighty rushing stream of Light,
transcendence is my sacred right.

8. Master MORE, come into my Throat Chakra and help me dismiss the serpentine lie that the power of God can only come from outside myself. Help me claim the power of God within me.

> Master MORE, you balance all,
> the seven rays upon my call.
> Master MORE, forever MORE,
> I am the Spirit's open door.

O Holy Spirit, flow through me,
I am the open door for thee.
O mighty rushing stream of Light,
transcendence is my sacred right.

9. Master MORE, come into my Throat Chakra and help me dismiss the illusion that I need to do something here on earth, as a separate self, in order to be redeemed of my sin or to balance my karma.

> Master MORE, your Presence here,
> filling up my inner sphere.
> Life is now a sacred flow,
> God Power I on all bestow.

> **O Holy Spirit, flow through me,**
> **I am the open door for thee.**
> **O mighty rushing stream of Light,**
> **transcendence is my sacred right.**

4. I surrender all dualistic conditions

1. Master MORE, come into my Throat Chakra and help me accept that there is nothing wrong with me. What is truly wrong with me is the concept that there is something wrong.

> O Cosmic Mother, sound the gong,
> that calls me home where I belong.
> I know you love me tenderly,
> and in that knowing I am free.

> **Maraytaii, I resonate**
> **with song that opens cosmic gate.**
> **Your melody makes me vibrate**
> **my sense of self I recreate.**

2. Master MORE, come into my Throat Chakra and help me accept that only that which is created in oneness is real. Anything created out of the consciousness of separation is not real and cannot affect that part of me which is real.

> O Cosmic Mother, hold me tight,
> I resonate with your own light.
> Your music purifies my heart,
> your love to all I do impart.

> **Maraytaii, I resonate**
> **with song that opens cosmic gate.**
> **Your melody makes me vibrate**
> **my sense of self I recreate.**

3. Master MORE, come into my Throat Chakra and help me see that in oneness there can be no conditions. I separate from oneness by creating two conditions that oppose each other.

> O Cosmic Mother, we are one,
> your heart is like a blazing sun.
> My being can but amplify,
> the sacred sound you magnify.

> **Maraytaii, I resonate**
> **with song that opens cosmic gate.**
> **Your melody makes me vibrate**
> **my sense of self I recreate.**

4. Master MORE, come into my Throat Chakra and help me see that I cannot neutralize, balance or negate one dualistic condition by going into the opposite. I cannot overcome a problem with the same state of consciousness that created the problem.

O Cosmic Mother, I now hear,
the subtle sound of Sacred Sphere.
As I attune to Cosmic Hum,
the lesser self I overcome.

**Maraytaii, I resonate
with song that opens cosmic gate.
Your melody makes me vibrate
my sense of self I recreate.**

5. Master MORE, come into my Throat Chakra and help me see that I created karma because I came to see myself as a separate being. I became focused on the self, and therefore I did something that was egotistical and selfish.

O Cosmic Mother, take me home,
I am in sync with Sacred OM,
The sound of sounds will raise me up,
so only light is in my cup.

**Maraytaii, I resonate
with song that opens cosmic gate.
Your melody makes me vibrate
my sense of self I recreate.**

6. Master MORE, come into my Throat Chakra and help me see that I cannot counteract my karma by doing something else through the separate self. Striving to balance the karma made by the separate self only reinforces the illusion that I am a separate self.

> O Cosmic Mother, I will be,
> a part of cosmic symphony.
> All that I AM, an instrument,
> for sound that is from heaven sent.
>
> **Maraytaii, I resonate**
> **with song that opens cosmic gate.**
> **Your melody makes me vibrate**
> **my sense of self I recreate.**

7. Master MORE, come into my Throat Chakra and help me accept that I enter the kingdom of heaven by becoming one with the power of God within me. I can only become one with that by overcoming the separate self.

> O Cosmic Mother, I now call,
> to enter sacred music hall.
> I will be part of life's ascent,
> towards the starry firmament.
>
> **Maraytaii, I resonate**
> **with song that opens cosmic gate.**
> **Your melody makes me vibrate**
> **my sense of self I recreate.**

8. Master MORE, come into my Throat Chakra and help me follow my bliss. Help me experience that what gives me the greatest joy is the sense of oneness with my inner Being, with my God Flame, with the greater spiritual Being out of which I AM come.

O Cosmic Mother, tune my strings,
my total being with you sings.
Your song I now reverberate,
as cosmic love I celebrate.

**Maraytaii, I resonate
with song that opens cosmic gate.
Your melody makes me vibrate
my sense of self I recreate.**

9. Master MORE, come into my Throat Chakra and help me come into oneness with the will and the power of God by loving the will and the power. Help me purify my motive so that the power of God will flow through me to raise all life. I hereby accept that I AM real.

O Cosmic Mother, I love you,
your love song keeps me ever true.
You fill me with your sacred tone,
and thus I never feel alone.

**Maraytaii, I resonate
with song that opens cosmic gate.
Your melody makes me vibrate
my sense of self I recreate.**

Sealing:

In the name of the Divine Mother, I fully accept that the power of these calls is used to set free the Ma-ter light, so it can outpicture the perfect vision of Christ for my own life, for all people and for the planet. In the name I AM THAT I AM, it is done! Amen.

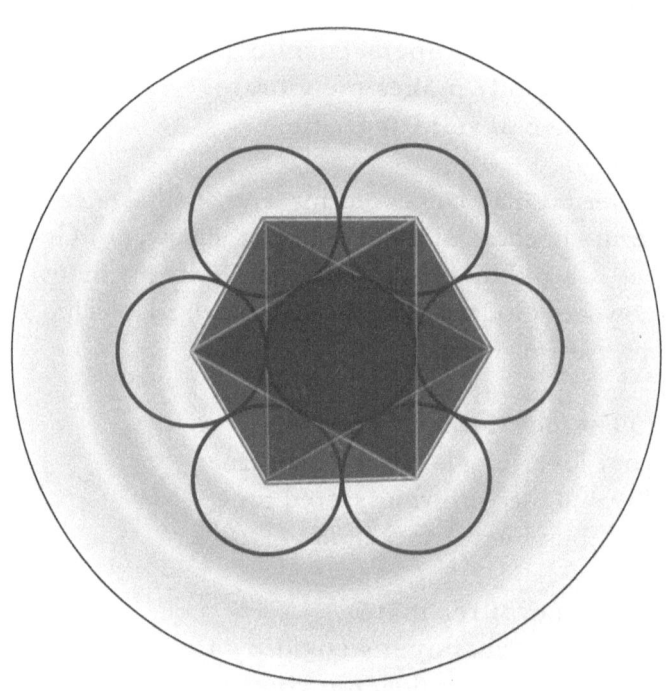

16 | CLEARING THE SOUL CHAKRA

[*NOTE*: Study the dictation from the Seventh Ray.]

In the name I AM THAT I AM, Jesus Christ, I call to my I AM Presence to flow through the I Will Be Presence that I AM and give this invocation with full power. I call to beloved Archangel Zadkiel and Amethyst, Elohim Arcturus and Victoria, Saint Germain and Kuan Yin to help me overcome all impurities in my Soul Chakra. Help me be free from all patterns or forces within or without that oppose the flow of freedom from my I AM Presence, including …

[Make personal calls]

1. I accept Divine justice

1. Archangel Zadkiel, come into my Soul Chakra and clear it from the dualistic concept of justice, especially the illusion that only after being punished enough can I be free from past choices.

> Zadkiel Archangel, your flow is so swift,
> in your violet light, I instantly shift,
> into a vibration in which I am free,
> from all limitations of the lesser me.

> **Zadkiel Archangel, encircle the earth,**
> **Zadkiel Archangel, with your violet girth,**
> **Zadkiel Archangel, unstoppable mirth,**
> **Zadkiel Archangel, our planet's rebirth.**

2. Archangel Zadkiel, come into my Soul Chakra and clear it from the belief that illness or misfortune must be God's punishment because God is the angry judge.

> Zadkiel Archangel, I truly aspire,
> to being the master of your violet fire.
> Wielding the power, of your alchemy,
> I use Sacred Word, to set all life free.

> **Zadkiel Archangel, encircle the earth,**
> **Zadkiel Archangel, with your violet girth,**
> **Zadkiel Archangel, unstoppable mirth,**
> **Zadkiel Archangel, our planet's rebirth.**

3. Archangel Zadkiel, come into my Soul Chakra and clear it from the energies of fear, especially related to the belief that illness is a punishment for having done something wrong.

> Zadkiel Archangel, your violet light,
> transforming the earth, with unstoppable might.
> So swiftly our planet, beginning to spin,
> with legions of angels, our victory we win.

> **Zadkiel Archangel, encircle the earth,**
> **Zadkiel Archangel, with your violet girth,**
> **Zadkiel Archangel, unstoppable mirth,**
> **Zadkiel Archangel, our planet's rebirth.**

4. Archangel Zadkiel, come into my Soul Chakra and clear it from all energies that pull me towards one dualistic extreme and prevent me from finding balance in all aspects of life.

> Zadkiel Archangel, your violet flame,
> the earth and humanity, never the same.
> Saint Germain's Golden Age, is a reality,
> what glorious wonder, I joyously see.

> **Zadkiel Archangel, encircle the earth,**
> **Zadkiel Archangel, with your violet girth,**
> **Zadkiel Archangel, unstoppable mirth,**
> **Zadkiel Archangel, our planet's rebirth.**

5. Archangel Zadkiel, come into my Soul Chakra and clear it from the illusion that God wants me to be punished for having made a mistake, or that by suffering I can compensate for my past choices.

Zadkiel Archangel, your flow is so swift,
in your violet light, I instantly shift,
into a vibration in which I am free,
from all limitations of the lesser me.

**Zadkiel Archangel, encircle the earth,
Zadkiel Archangel, with your violet girth,
Zadkiel Archangel, unstoppable mirth,
Zadkiel Archangel, our planet's rebirth.**

6. Archangel Zadkiel, come into my Soul Chakra and clear it from the death consciousness that makes me believe matter is permanent and difficult to change, even that matter is real and has some independent existence.

Zadkiel Archangel, I truly aspire,
to being the master of your violet fire.
Wielding the power, of your alchemy,
I use Sacred Word, to set all life free.

**Zadkiel Archangel, encircle the earth,
Zadkiel Archangel, with your violet girth,
Zadkiel Archangel, unstoppable mirth,
Zadkiel Archangel, our planet's rebirth.**

7. Archangel Zadkiel, come into my Soul Chakra and clear it from the black cloud of the death consciousness, so I can see that behind the matter that seems so solid, there is consciousness, and consciousness can change in an instant.

Zadkiel Archangel, your violet light,
transforming the earth, with unstoppable might.
So swiftly our planet, beginning to spin,
with legions of angels, our victory we win.

**Zadkiel Archangel, encircle the earth,
Zadkiel Archangel, with your violet girth,
Zadkiel Archangel, unstoppable mirth,
Zadkiel Archangel, our planet's rebirth.**

8. Archangel Zadkiel, come into my Soul Chakra and clear it from the death consciousness that says once I have made the mistake of partaking of the duality consciousness, I can never overcome separation. Help me accept that something which is unreal cannot permanently affect that which is real.

Zadkiel Archangel, your violet flame,
the earth and humanity, never the same.
Saint Germain's Golden Age, is a reality,
what glorious wonder, I joyously see.

**Zadkiel Archangel, encircle the earth,
Zadkiel Archangel, with your violet girth,
Zadkiel Archangel, unstoppable mirth,
Zadkiel Archangel, our planet's rebirth.**

9. Archangel Zadkiel, come into my Soul Chakra and help me experience that no illusion can hold me any longer than the moment when I decide that I am no longer the person who accepted the death consciousness. I now accept that I am free to *be* what I want to be. God within says: "I will be who I will be. And now I choose to be *more* than I was before."

With angels I soar,
as I reach for MORE.
The angels so real,
their love all will heal.

The angels bring peace,
all conflicts will cease.
With angels of light,
we soar to new height.

**The rustling sound of angel wings,
what joy as even matter sings,
what joy as every atom rings,
in harmony with angel wings.**

2. I am a creative being

1. Elohim Arcturus, come into my Soul Chakra and release the energies of rebirth so I can accept that no matter how far I have descended into the death consciousness, I can, at any moment, reach for the Christ. I now accept Christ the Redeemer.

Beloved Arcturus, release now the flow,
of Violet Flame to help all life grow,
in ever-expanding circles of Light,
it pulses within every atom so bright.

**Beloved Arcturus, thou Elohim Free,
I open my heart to your reality,
expanding my heart into Infinity,
your flame is the key to my God-victory.**

2. Elohim Arcturus, come into my Soul Chakra and release the unconditionality of God. Help me see that whatever mistake I have made was an expression of the state of consciousness I was in at the time. I now let that consciousness die and I accept that I am reborn into a new sense of self.

Beloved Arcturus, be with me alway,
reborn, I am ready to face a new day,
I have no attachments to life here on earth,
I claim a new life in your Flame of Rebirth.

Beloved Arcturus, your Violet Flame pure,
is for every ailment the ultimate cure,
against it no darkness could ever endure,
my freedom it will forever ensure.

3. Elohim Arcturus, come into my Soul Chakra and help me accept that any condition I face in the material universe is the outpicturing of a mental image. I now accept that when I truly change my consciousness, I change the image that creates the physical condition.

Beloved Arcturus, your bright violet fire,
now fills every atom, raising them higher,
the space in each atom all filled with your light,
as matter itself is shining so bright.

Beloved Arcturus, your transforming Grace,
empowers me now every challenge to face,
as your violet light floods my inner space,
towards my ascension I willingly race.

4. Elohim Arcturus, come into my Soul Chakra and help me see that my separate self believes matter is solid and unchangeable because the ego is made out of the same frequencies as the material universe. Yet I am made out of the vibrations of Spirit.

Beloved Arcturus, bring in a new age,
help earth and humanity turn a new page,
your transforming light gives me certainty,
Saint Germain's Golden Age is a reality.

**Beloved Arcturus, I surrender all fear,
I AM feeling your Presence so tangibly near,
with your Freedom's Song filling my ear,
I know that to God I AM ever so dear.**

5. Elohim Arcturus, come into my Soul Chakra and help me experience that matter is infinitely changeable. I now accept that I do not deserve punishment. I accept that I am instantly free of illness. I accept healing, I accept wholeness.

Beloved Arcturus, release now the flow,
of Violet Flame to help all life grow,
in ever-expanding circles of Light,
it pulses within every atom so bright.

**Beloved Arcturus, thou Elohim Free,
I open my heart to your reality,
expanding my heart into Infinity,
your flame is the key to my God-victory.**

6. Elohim Arcturus, come into my Soul Chakra and help me accept the realization that Jesus came to, namely that it – truly, honestly, absolutely, realistically – is possible to change any condition in matter in an instant—when I switch the mind.

Beloved Arcturus, be with me alway,
reborn, I am ready to face a new day,
I have no attachments to life here on earth,
I claim a new life in your Flame of Rebirth.

> **Beloved Arcturus, your Violet Flame pure,**
> **is for every ailment the ultimate cure,**
> **against it no darkness could ever endure,**
> **my freedom it will forever ensure.**

7. Elohim Arcturus, come into my Soul Chakra and help me face my fear of death. Help me experience that even death is an illusion, for I am more than the physical body.

> Beloved Arcturus, your bright violet fire,
> now fills every atom, raising them higher,
> the space in each atom all filled with your light,
> as matter itself is shining so bright.

> **Beloved Arcturus, your transforming Grace,**
> **empowers me now every challenge to face,**
> **as your violet light floods my inner space,**
> **towards my ascension I willingly race.**

8. Elohim Arcturus, come into my Soul Chakra and help me take responsibility for experiencing the conditions that I create in the mind. Help me experience and accept the unlimited creative power within me.

> Beloved Arcturus, bring in a new age,
> help earth and humanity turn a new page,
> your transforming light gives me certainty,
> Saint Germain's Golden Age is a reality.

> **Beloved Arcturus, I surrender all fear,**
> **I AM feeling your Presence so tangibly near,**
> **with your Freedom's Song filling my ear,**
> **I know that to God I AM ever so dear.**

9. Elohim Arcturus, come into my Soul Chakra and release the energies of total creative freedom. I am willing to decide who I am and how I express my creative power. I accept that I am in oneness with my I AM Presence and I express the spontaneous flow of Being.

> Accelerate into Freedom, I AM real,
> Accelerate into Freedom, all life heal,
> Accelerate into Freedom, I AM MORE,
> Accelerate into Freedom, all will soar.

> Accelerate into Freedom! (3X)
> Beloved Arcturus and Victoria.
> Accelerate into Freedom! (3X)
> Beloved Zadkiel and Amethyst.
> Accelerate into Freedom! (3X)
> Beloved Saint Germain.
> Accelerate into Freedom! (3X)
> Beloved I AM.

3. I am a co-creator with God

1. Saint Germain, come into my Soul Chakra and help me accept that the reason I am in a certain state of consciousness is that I made certain choices. I can only be free of that state of consciousness by transcending those choices.

> Saint Germain, your alchemy,
> with violet fire now sets me free.
> Saint Germain, I ever grow,
> in freedom's overpowering flow.

16 | Clearing the Soul Chakra

> O Holy Spirit, flow through me,
> I am the open door for thee.
> O mighty rushing stream of Light,
> transcendence is my sacred right.

2. Saint Germain, come into my Soul Chakra, for I am willing to let the old man die and put on the new man. Help me recognize and accept that I am reborn, I am a new person. Help me accept that I did not make the mistake and thus I do not deserve the punishment.

> Saint Germain, your mastery,
> of violet flame geometry.
> Saint Germain, in you I see,
> the formulas that set me free.

> O Holy Spirit, flow through me,
> I am the open door for thee.
> O mighty rushing stream of Light,
> transcendence is my sacred right.

3. Saint Germain, come into my Soul Chakra and help me accept that the harder I strive to compensate for a past error, the more I confirm the reality of the separate self.

> Saint Germain, in Liberty,
> I feel the love you have for me.
> Saint Germain, I do adore,
> the violet flame that makes all more.

> O Holy Spirit, flow through me,
> I am the open door for thee.
> O mighty rushing stream of Light,
> transcendence is my sacred right.

4. Saint Germain, come into my Soul Chakra and help me accept that when I truly change my consciousness, I will also change my physical body and any condition in it. I accept that I can instantly change the manifestation in my physical body by changing the image in my mind.

> Saint Germain, in unity,
> I will transcend duality.
> Saint Germain, my self so pure,
> your violet chemistry so sure.
>
> **O Holy Spirit, flow through me,**
> **I am the open door for thee.**
> **O mighty rushing stream of Light,**
> **transcendence is my sacred right.**

5. Saint Germain, come into my Soul Chakra and help me overcome the ego's illusion that I should never look at how I came to be where I am. Help me accept my right to undo any choice. Help me take back my power and willingness to make choices as to who I am as a co-creator with God.

> Saint Germain, reality,
> in violet light I am carefree.
> Saint Germain, my aura seal,
> your violet flame my chakras heal.
>
> **O Holy Spirit, flow through me,**
> **I am the open door for thee.**
> **O mighty rushing stream of Light,**
> **transcendence is my sacred right.**

6. Saint Germain, come into my Soul Chakra and help me accept death so that I can move into it and see that it is an illusion.

Saint Germain, your chemistry,
with violet fire set atoms free.
Saint Germain, from lead to gold,
transforming vision I behold.

**O Holy Spirit, flow through me,
I am the open door for thee.
O mighty rushing stream of Light,
transcendence is my sacred right.**

7. Saint Germain, come into my Soul Chakra and help me emerge on the other side of death and see that what seems so real from the viewpoint of the separate self is completely unreal. I now know and accept that I am an extension of the infinite Creator who can never die.

Saint Germain, transcendency,
as I am always one with thee.
Saint Germain, from soul I'm free,
I so delight in being me.

**O Holy Spirit, flow through me,
I am the open door for thee.
O mighty rushing stream of Light,
transcendence is my sacred right.**

8. Saint Germain, come into my Soul Chakra and help me see that I switch my perspective only by looking at any limitation, by not seeking to hide anything from God or myself. I now accept the very reality that by confessing a limitation, by acknowledging it, I have already started separating myself from it.

Saint Germain, nobility,
the key to sacred alchemy.
Saint Germain, you balance all,
the seven rays upon my call.

**O Holy Spirit, flow through me,
I am the open door for thee.
O mighty rushing stream of Light,
transcendence is my sacred right.**

9. Saint Germain, come into my Soul Chakra and help me re-establish my true sense of identity. I say: "I did not make that error in the past. I was a different person back then. The person I was when I made the error, I have allowed that sense of self to die. I have been reborn and I am now a new being in Christ."

Saint Germain, your Presence here,
filling up my inner sphere.
Life is now a sacred flow,
God Freedom I on all bestow.

**O Holy Spirit, flow through me,
I am the open door for thee.
O mighty rushing stream of Light,
transcendence is my sacred right.**

4. I am in total surrender

1. Saint Germain, come into my Soul Chakra and help me realize that I am crucified by my own mental images. I cannot take myself down from the cross by using the same state of consciousness that is nailing me to the cross. I now give up the ghost in a final act of total, unconditional surrender of all mental images and conditions.

> O Kuan Yin, what sacred name,
> fill me now with Mercy's Flame.
> In giving mercy I am free,
> forgiving all is magic key.
>
> **In Kuan Yin's sweet melody,**
> **I am set free my Self to be.**
> **In Kuan Yin's vitality,**
> **I claim my immortality.**

2. Saint Germain, come into my Soul Chakra and help me experience that it is such a release, such a freedom, such a joy to go through that unconditional surrender where I surrender any condition, any illusion.

> O Kuan Yin, I now let go,
> of all attachments here below.
> All pent-up feelings I release,
> free from emotional disease.
>
> **In Kuan Yin's sweet melody,**
> **I am set free my Self to be.**
> **In Kuan Yin's vitality,**
> **I claim my immortality.**

3. Saint Germain, come into my Soul Chakra and help me experience that instead of running away from that which I fear, I can embrace it. Help me experience a sense that if I died at this moment, I can leave the earth with no regrets, no pulls, no sense of unfulfilled work.

> O Kuan Yin, why must I feel,
> that life falls short of my ideal?
> All expectations I give up,
> my mind is now an empty cup
>
> **In Kuan Yin's sweet melody,**
> **I am set free my Self to be.**
> **In Kuan Yin's vitality,**
> **I claim my immortality.**

4. Saint Germain, come into my Soul Chakra and help me be reborn as a Bodhisattva, who is now serving to help people see that it is possible to transcend the entire consciousness represented by the scales. It is possible to transcend duality, to move out of it and into the total freedom expressed by God to Moses: "I will be who I will be."

> O Kuan Yin, transcend the past,
> as all resentment gone at last.
> From future nothing I expect,
> eternal now I won't reject.
>
> **In Kuan Yin's sweet melody,**
> **I am set free my Self to be.**
> **In Kuan Yin's vitality,**
> **I claim my immortality.**

5. Saint Germain, come into my Soul Chakra and help me accept that I am real and that death – unreality – cannot affect life. I now see that death has lost its sting. Death where is thy victory, for I accept my freedom, the total freedom to *be* God's Being through me.

> O Kuan Yin, uplifting me,
> beyond Samsara's raging sea.
> All safe inside your Prajna boat,
> the farther shore no more remote.
>
> **In Kuan Yin's sweet melody,**
> **I am set free my Self to be.**
> **In Kuan Yin's vitality,**
> **I claim my immortality.**

6. Saint Germain, come into my Soul Chakra and help me accept that freedom is not freedom from any condition, for freedom is not relative to any condition. Freedom is a vibration that is beyond conditions—it is unconditional freedom. It is a state of consciousness; it is a stream of consciousness that is constantly transcending itself. In that transcendence, it can never be pinned down or held back in any limited expression, for it is always more, it is free to express that *more* and become more at any moment.

> O Kuan Yin, your alchemy,
> with miracles you set me free.
> As I forgive, I am forgiven,
> by guilt I am no longer driven.

**In Kuan Yin's sweet melody,
I am set free my Self to be.
In Kuan Yin's vitality,
I claim my immortality.**

7. Saint Germain, come into my Soul Chakra and help me become one with that flow, that spirit of consciousness, that conscious being that *is* freedom—and that you represent to the earth. I accept your assistance in becoming one with you, for I desire to be truly free. Saint Germain, I accept your total Being, your Spirit of Freedom. I merge with it, I AM one with Freedom, and I know that no conditions can limit me whatsoever.

> O Kuan Yin, all worries gone,
> with nothing done, no thing undone.
> Through separate self I will not do,
> and thus I rest, all one with you.

**In Kuan Yin's sweet melody,
I am set free my Self to be.
In Kuan Yin's vitality,
I claim my immortality.**

8. Saint Germain, come into my Soul Chakra, for I AM willing to experience that ultimate healing, that ultimate wholeness, of giving up even the fear of death, giving up any condition. I stand here on earth and declare that I AM a free being and I do not accept any condition that limits my Spirit and the Spirit's expression through me in seeking to raise all life.

> O Kuan Yin, your sanity,
> now sets me free from vanity.
> For truly, what is that to me;
> I just let go and follow thee.

**In Kuan Yin's sweet melody,
I am set free my Self to be.
In Kuan Yin's vitality,
I claim my immortality.**

9. Saint Germain, come into my Soul Chakra and help me realize that I came here to work with Christ to set the captives free. I do not set them free by seeking to change them. I set them free by changing myself. I accept that I AM free, and therefore I AM that torch of freedom that shows people that there is light outside the prison of their minds.

> O Kuan Yin, so sweet the sound,
> that emanates from holy ground.
> As I let go of ego's chore,
> I find myself on farther shore.

**In Kuan Yin's sweet melody,
I am set free my Self to be.
In Kuan Yin's vitality,
I claim my immortality.**

Sealing:

In the name of the Divine Mother, I fully accept that the power of these calls is used to set free the Ma-ter light, so it can outpicture the perfect vision of Christ for my own life, for all people and for the planet. In the name I AM THAT I AM, it is done! Amen.

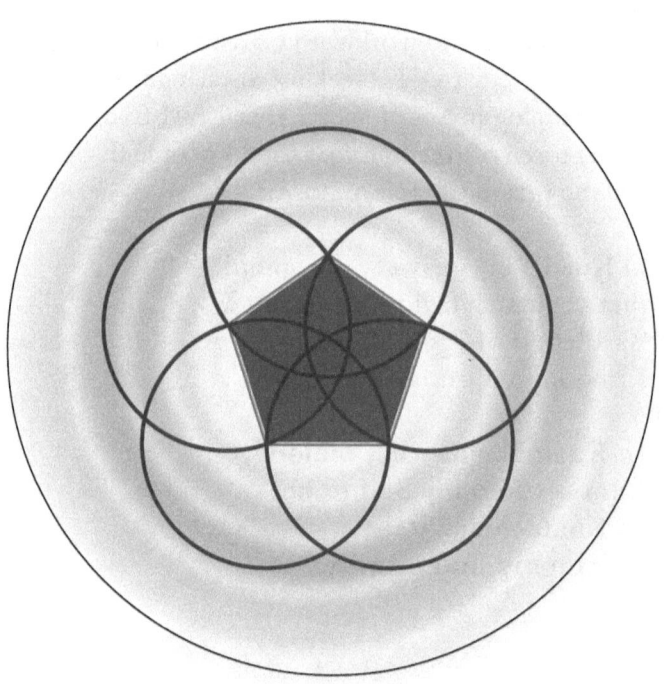

17 | CLEARING THE THIRD EYE CHAKRA

[*NOTE*: Study the dictation from the Fifth Ray.]

In the name I AM THAT I AM, Jesus Christ, I call to my I AM Presence to flow through the I Will Be Presence that I AM and give this invocation with full power. I call to beloved Archangel Raphael and Mother Mary, Elohim Cyclopea and Virginia and Hilarion to help me overcome all impurities in my Third Eye Chakra. Help me be free from all patterns or forces within or without that oppose the free flow of truth from my I AM Presence, including …

[Make personal calls]

I. I know God accepts me

1. Archangel Raphael, come into my Third Eye Chakra and clear it from the illusion of separation that makes me feel alone or abandoned by God.

> Raphael Archangel, your light so intense,
> raise me beyond all human pretense.
> Mother Mary and you have a vision so bold,
> to see that our highest potential unfold.
>
> **Raphael Archangel, for vision I pray,**
> **Raphael Archangel, show me the way,**
> **Raphael Archangel, your emerald ray,**
> **Raphael Archangel, my life a new day.**

2. Archangel Raphael, come into my Third Eye Chakra and clear it from spiritual pride, the arrogance of rebellion against God and the illusion that beings can oppose God and turn the earth into a place where God is not present.

> Raphael Archangel, in emerald sphere,
> to immaculate vision I always adhere.
> Mother Mary enfolds me in her sacred heart,
> from Mother's true love, I am never apart.
>
> **Raphael Archangel, for vision I pray,**
> **Raphael Archangel, show me the way,**
> **Raphael Archangel, your emerald ray,**
> **Raphael Archangel, my life a new day.**

3. Archangel Raphael, come into my Third Eye Chakra and clear it from the serpentine lie that I could have done something or could ever do something that would make God or the Divine Mother turn away from me.

> Raphael Archangel, all ailments you heal,
> each cell in my body in light now you seal.
> Mother Mary's immaculate concept I see,
> perfection of health is real now for me.
>
> **Raphael Archangel, for vision I pray,**
> **Raphael Archangel, show me the way,**
> **Raphael Archangel, your emerald ray,**
> **Raphael Archangel, my life a new day.**

4. Archangel Raphael, come into my Third Eye Chakra and clear it from the lie that the material world is an enemy of my spiritual growth and that I need to escape the material world instead of expressing my Christhood here.

> Raphael Archangel, your light is so real,
> the vision of Christ in me you reveal.
> Mother Mary now helps me to truly transcend,
> in emerald light with you I ascend.
>
> **Raphael Archangel, for vision I pray,**
> **Raphael Archangel, show me the way,**
> **Raphael Archangel, your emerald ray,**
> **Raphael Archangel, my life a new day.**

5. Archangel Raphael, come into my Third Eye Chakra and clear it from the illusion that it is possible to use a spiritual teaching to "perfect" the separate self and make it acceptable in the eyes of God.

> Raphael Archangel, your light so intense,
> raise me beyond all human pretense.
> Mother Mary and you have a vision so bold,
> to see that our highest potential unfold.
>
> **Raphael Archangel, for vision I pray,**
> **Raphael Archangel, show me the way,**
> **Raphael Archangel, your emerald ray,**
> **Raphael Archangel, my life a new day.**

6. Archangel Raphael, come into my Third Eye Chakra and clear it from the lie that I, as a spiritual person, have to fight and destroy the forces of anti-christ. I refuse to let them pull me into the dualistic struggle.

> Raphael Archangel, in emerald sphere,
> to immaculate vision I always adhere.
> Mother Mary enfolds me in her sacred heart,
> from Mother's true love, I am never apart.
>
> **Raphael Archangel, for vision I pray,**
> **Raphael Archangel, show me the way,**
> **Raphael Archangel, your emerald ray,**
> **Raphael Archangel, my life a new day.**

7. Archangel Raphael, come into my Third Eye Chakra and clear it from the dualistic sense that I have to be right, that others are wrong, that I have to be validated and that I have to force others to change.

> Raphael Archangel, all ailments you heal,
> each cell in my body in light now you seal.
> Mother Mary's immaculate concept I see,
> perfection of health is real now for me.
>
> **Raphael Archangel, for vision I pray,**
> **Raphael Archangel, show me the way,**
> **Raphael Archangel, your emerald ray,**
> **Raphael Archangel, my life a new day.**

8. Archangel Raphael, come into my Third Eye Chakra and clear it from the illusion that I am here to validate the ego illusions of other people by responding to them through my own ego illusions.

> Raphael Archangel, your light is so real,
> the vision of Christ in me you reveal.
> Mother Mary now helps me to truly transcend,
> in emerald light with you I ascend.
>
> **Raphael Archangel, for vision I pray,**
> **Raphael Archangel, show me the way,**
> **Raphael Archangel, your emerald ray,**
> **Raphael Archangel, my life a new day.**

9. Archangel Raphael, come into my Third Eye Chakra and help me accept that I am here to demonstrate that I am not trapped in illusions. I am here to demonstrate that whatever people throw at me, they cannot pull me into their state of consciousness.

> With angels I soar,
> as I reach for MORE.
> The angels so real,
> their love all will heal.
> The angels bring peace,
> all conflicts will cease.
> With angels of light,
> we soar to new height.
>
> **The rustling sound of angel wings,**
> **what joy as even matter sings,**
> **what joy as every atom rings,**
> **in harmony with angel wings.**

2. I switch my perspective

1. Elohim Cyclopea, come into my Third Eye Chakra and release the vision that it is possible to instantly switch my perspective on life. I recognize that God is here with me, the Divine Mother is here with me. I am never alone, for all life is one.

> Cyclopea so dear, the truth you reveal,
> the truth that duality's ailments will heal,
> your Emerald Light is like a great balm,
> my emotional body is perfectly calm.

**Cyclopea so dear, in Emerald Sphere,
to vision so clear I always adhere,
in raising perception I shall persevere,
as deep in my heart your truth I revere.**

2. Elohim Cyclopea, come into my Third Eye Chakra and release the acceleration of power, wisdom and love in that intensity of the white light that propels me beyond my present state of consciousness.

Cyclopea so dear, with you I unwind,
all negative spirals clouding my mind,
I know pure awareness is truly my core,
the key to becoming the wide-open door.

**Cyclopea so dear, clear my inner sight,
empowered, I pierce the soul's fearful night,
through veils of duality I now take flight,
bathed in your penetrating Emerald Light.**

3. Elohim Cyclopea, come into my Third Eye Chakra and release the sense of truth that the Law of Free Will makes me one hundred percent responsible for my own state of mind, and one hundred percent *not* responsible for the state of mind of any other human being.

Cyclopea so dear, life can only reflect,
the images that my mind does project,
the key to my healing is clearing the mind,
from the images my ego is hiding behind.

> Cyclopea so dear, I want to aim high,
> to your healing flame I ever draw nigh,
> I now see my life through your single eye,
> beyond all disease I AM ready to fly.

4. Elohim Cyclopea, come into my Third Eye Chakra and release the vibration of truth to consume all false sense of responsibility. Consume the illusion that I should allow my life experience to be dependent on the choices made by other people.

> Cyclopea so dear, your Emerald Flame,
> exposes every subtle, dualistic power game,
> including the game of wanting to say,
> that truth is defined in only one way.

> Cyclopea so dear, I am feeling the flow,
> as your Living Truth upon me you bestow,
> I know truth transcends all systems below,
> immersed in your light, I continue to grow.

5. Elohim Cyclopea, come into my Third Eye Chakra and release the vibration of truth to consume the ego illusion that for me to attain inner peace, all other people must become like me.

> Cyclopea so dear, the truth you reveal,
> the truth that duality's ailments will heal,
> your Emerald Light is like a great balm,
> my emotional body is perfectly calm.

> Cyclopea so dear, in Emerald Sphere,
> to vision so clear I always adhere,
> in raising perception I shall persevere,
> as deep in my heart your truth I revere.

6. Elohim Cyclopea, come into my Third Eye Chakra and help me experience the surrender of that false responsibility, the sense that my state of mind depends on material conditions in this universe.

> Cyclopea so dear, with you I unwind,
> all negative spirals clouding my mind,
> I know pure awareness is truly my core,
> the key to becoming the wide-open door.
>
> **Cyclopea so dear, clear my inner sight,**
> **empowered, I pierce the soul's fearful night,**
> **through veils of duality I now take flight,**
> **bathed in your penetrating Emerald Light.**

7. Elohim Cyclopea, come into my Third Eye Chakra and help me overcome the sense that I descended to save one person or save humankind as a whole, and that I am responsible for the salvation of others.

> Cyclopea so dear, life can only reflect,
> the images that my mind does project,
> the key to my healing is clearing the mind,
> from the images my ego is hiding behind.
>
> **Cyclopea so dear, I want to aim high,**
> **to your healing flame I ever draw nigh,**
> **I now see my life through your single eye,**
> **beyond all disease I AM ready to fly.**

8. Elohim Cyclopea, come into my Third Eye Chakra and help me recognize the reality of free will, namely that no one can save anyone else. I am only here to demonstrate how all can attain salvation within themselves by releasing the illusion that they are separated from their Source.

> Cyclopea so dear, your Emerald Flame,
> exposes every subtle, dualistic power game,
> including the game of wanting to say,
> that truth is defined in only one way.
>
> **Cyclopea so dear, I am feeling the flow,**
> **as your Living Truth upon me you bestow,**
> **I know truth transcends all systems below,**
> **immersed in your light, I continue to grow.**

9. Elohim Cyclopea, come into my Third Eye Chakra, for I hereby make a conscious decision to actively surrender all false sense of responsibility. I now breathe out all false sense of responsibility. I feel lighter, I feel a release and I accept that I am free.

> Accelerate into Wholeness, I AM real,
> Accelerate into Wholeness, all life heal,
> Accelerate into Wholeness, I AM MORE,
> Accelerate into Wholeness, all will soar.

17 | Clearing the Third Eye Chakra

>Accelerate into Wholeness! (3X)
>Beloved Cyclopea and Virginia.
>Accelerate into Wholeness! (3X)
>Beloved Raphael and Mary.
>Accelerate into Wholeness! (3X)
>Beloved Master Hilarion.
>Accelerate into Wholeness! (3X)
>Beloved I AM.

3. I take Christ down from the cross

1. Hilarion, come into my Third Eye Chakra and help me see that the illusion of separation creates an image that is projected upon my physical body. Trying to run away from the condition in my body or the consciousness behind it will not set me free.

>Hilarion, on emerald shore,
>I'm free from all that's gone before.
>Hilarion, I let all go,
>that keeps me out of sacred flow.

>**O Holy Spirit, flow through me,**
>**I am the open door for thee.**
>**O mighty rushing stream of Light,**
>**transcendence is my sacred right.**

2. Hilarion, come into my Third Eye Chakra and help me reach the point of truth and realism, where I realize that I am not happy in my present state of mind. Help me escape the twilight zone where I continue doing the same thing while expecting different results.

Hilarion, the secret key,
is wisdom's own reality.
Hilarion, all life is healed,
the ego's face no more concealed.

**O Holy Spirit, flow through me,
I am the open door for thee.
O mighty rushing stream of Light,
transcendence is my sacred right.**

3. Hilarion, come into my Third Eye Chakra and help me see that the Ma-ter light springs from the Logos of the Christ consciousness. Therefore, my physical body has the Christ consciousness embedded within it.

Hilarion, your love for life,
helps me surrender inner strife.
Hilarion, your loving words,
thrill my heart like song of birds.

**O Holy Spirit, flow through me,
I am the open door for thee.
O mighty rushing stream of Light,
transcendence is my sacred right.**

4. Hilarion, come into my Third Eye Chakra and help me see that the Christ in me has been crucified by the lower images projected through duality. Yet nothing can limit or confine the Christ, thus my body has the potential to be resurrected from all imperfections.

Hilarion, invoke the light,
your sacred formulas recite.
Hilarion, your secret tone,
philosopher's most sacred stone.

**O Holy Spirit, flow through me,
I am the open door for thee.
O mighty rushing stream of Light,
transcendence is my sacred right.**

5. Hilarion, come into my Third Eye Chakra and help me come up higher by giving up the ghost of my ego so that the Christ is resurrected in me.

Hilarion, with love you greet,
me in your temple over Crete.
Hilarion, your emerald light,
my third eye sees with Christic sight.

**O Holy Spirit, flow through me,
I am the open door for thee.
O mighty rushing stream of Light,
transcendence is my sacred right.**

6. Hilarion, come into my Third Eye Chakra and help me see how my choices have nailed the Christ to the cross of matter. Help me see how I can personally take Christ down from the cross.

Hilarion, you give me fruit,
of truth that is so absolute.
Hilarion, all stress decrease,
as my ambitions I release.

> O Holy Spirit, flow through me,
> I am the open door for thee.
> O mighty rushing stream of Light,
> transcendence is my sacred right.

7. Hilarion, come into my Third Eye Chakra and help me see that what I do onto others, I have already done to myself. Help me take the Mother and her children down from the cross, reconnecting to the Mother who always knows who she is.

> Hilarion, my chakras clear,
> as I let go of subtlest fear.
> Hilarion, I am sincere,
> as freedom's truth I do revere.

> **O Holy Spirit, flow through me,**
> **I am the open door for thee.**
> **O mighty rushing stream of Light,**
> **transcendence is my sacred right.**

8. Hilarion, come into my Third Eye Chakra and help me overcome the illusion that I can perfect the ghost of the ego. Instead, help me know how to give up the ghost.

> Hilarion, you balance all,
> the seven rays upon my call.
> Hilarion, you keep me true,
> as I remain all one with you.

> **O Holy Spirit, flow through me,**
> **I am the open door for thee.**
> **O mighty rushing stream of Light,**
> **transcendence is my sacred right.**

9. Hilarion, come into my Third Eye Chakra and clear it from the consciousness of competition and war. Help me step onto the true path of total surrender.

> Hilarion, your Presence here,
> filling up my inner sphere.
> Life is now a sacred flow,
> God Vision I on all bestow.

> **O Holy Spirit, flow through me,**
> **I am the open door for thee.**
> **O mighty rushing stream of Light,**
> **transcendence is my sacred right.**

4. I see my true service

1. Hilarion, come into my Third Eye Chakra and help me overcome the illusion that surrender is a passive act of giving up. Help me learn surrender as an active process of giving *up* the ghost, for I am willing to give *up* the separate self in order to become whole.

> O Blessed Mary's Song of Life,
> consuming every form of strife.
> As I attune to sound so fair,
> each cell is healthy, I declare.

> **O Mother Mary, generate,**
> **the song that does accelerate,**
> **my cells into a higher state,**
> **in perfect health they scintillate.**

2. Hilarion, come into my Third Eye Chakra and help me see and surrender my personal dramas. I no longer want to play the dualistic game where I win or lose, or where I am right or wrong compared to others. I want wholeness within myself.

> As life's own song I ever hear,
> it does consume all sense of fear.
> In tune with Mother's symphony,
> from all diseases I AM free.
>
> **O Mother Mary, generate,**
> **the song that does accelerate,**
> **my cells into a higher state,**
> **in perfect health they scintillate.**

3. Hilarion, come into my Third Eye Chakra and help me quickly become aware of the qualities I have that can help other people. I am willing to use those qualities more consciously for the selfless service of raising other parts of life.

> In Mother's love I do transcend,
> and all my struggles hereby end.
> For when with Mother's eye I see,
> no imperfection touches me.
>
> **O Mother Mary, generate,**
> **the song that does accelerate,**
> **my cells into a higher state,**
> **in perfect health they scintillate.**

4. Hilarion, come into my Third Eye Chakra and help me become more aware of my potential to give service—not by using my own internal qualities alone but by being the open door. I desire to be the open door, which no man can shut.

I see that healing must begin
by finding Living Christ within.
For as I see with single eye,
each cell the light does amplify.

**O Mother Mary, generate,
the song that does accelerate,
my cells into a higher state,
in perfect health they scintillate.**

5. Hilarion, come into my Third Eye Chakra and help me come to the point where I know that I am the open door which no man can shut. Neither my own ego nor the reactions of other people can cause me to withhold my light, love and service.

In Mother's music I am free,
from memories of a lesser me.
My vision in a perfect state,
that all my cells regenerate.

**O Mother Mary, generate,
the song that does accelerate,
my cells into a higher state,
in perfect health they scintillate.**

6. Hilarion, come into my Third Eye Chakra and help me see that I am not here to battle and engage others. I am here to stand and *be* and radiate my light and demonstrate that whatever they throw at me cannot touch me, cannot change my self-image.

O Mother's Love, sweet melody,
from imperfections I AM free.
O Mother Mary, sound of sounds,
within my heart your love abounds.

**O Mother Mary, generate,
the song that does accelerate,
my cells into a higher state,
in perfect health they scintillate.**

7. Hilarion, come into my Third Eye Chakra and help me pass the initiation of the Fifth Ray of not letting others pull me into the dualistic battle. Help me see that the way to heal my lower bodies is by reaching beyond the ego and seeking to heal others, seeking to bring the light.

Through Mother's beauty so sublime,
transcending bounds of space and time.
All cells beyond the mortal tomb,
as they are whole in Mother's womb.

**O Mother Mary, generate,
the song that does accelerate,
my cells into a higher state,
in perfect health they scintillate.**

8. Hilarion, come into my Third Eye Chakra and help me know the truth that the wounds I have left, the unresolved substance in my own being, is what I will encounter from others. Help me depersonalize my relationships with people and remain non-attached.

In resonance with life's own song,
in life's harmonics I belong.
The blueprint of my perfect state
does every cell reconsecrate.

**O Mother Mary, generate,
the song that does accelerate,
my cells into a higher state,
in perfect health they scintillate.**

9. Hilarion, come into my Third Eye Chakra and help me apply this truth and feel the release that I do not have to react the way I have always reacted. Help me step outside of my previous reactionary pattern. I now say: "I have had enough of playing that role in the drama of life. This role no longer reflects who I AM."

The tuning fork in every cell
is now attuned to Mother's bell.
From curse of death I AM now free,
I claim my immortality.

**O Mother Mary, generate,
the song that does accelerate,
my cells into a higher state,
in perfect health they scintillate.**

Sealing:

In the name of the Divine Mother, I fully accept that the power of these calls is used to set free the Ma-ter light, so it can outpicture the perfect vision of Christ for my own life, for all people and for the planet. In the name I AM THAT I AM, it is done! Amen.

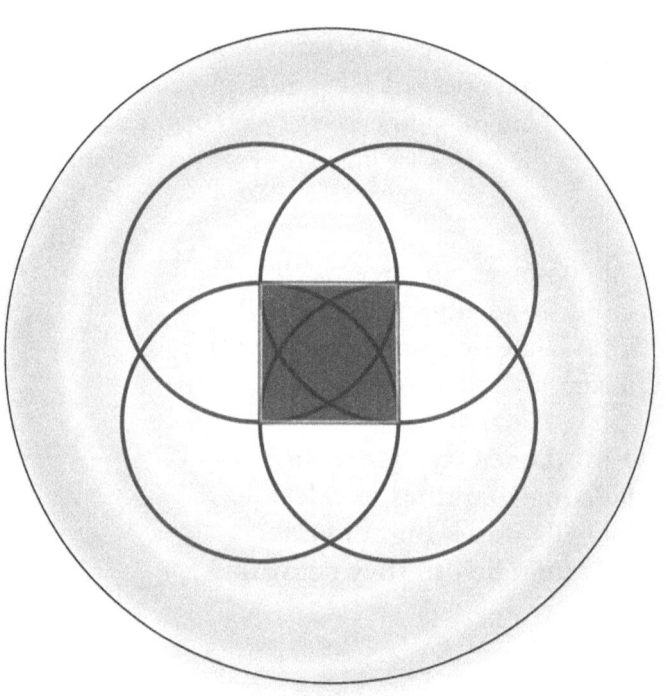

18 | CLEARING THE BASE CHAKRA

[*NOTE*: Study the dictation from the Fourth Ray.]

In the name I AM THAT I AM, Jesus Christ, I call to my I AM Presence to flow through the I Will Be Presence that I AM and give this invocation with full power. I call to beloved Archangel Gabriel and Hope, Elohim Purity and Astrea, Serapis Bey and Goddess of Liberty to help me overcome all impurities in my Base Chakra. Help me be free from all patterns or forces within or without that oppose the free flow of purity from my I AM Presence, including …

[Make personal calls]

1. I tune in to the vibration of purity

1. Archangel Gabriel, come into my Base Chakra and clear it from all tendency to be focused on outer symbols. Help me see beyond the outer forms and symbols and tune in to the Christ vibration behind all appearances.

> Gabriel Archangel, your light I revere,
> immersed in your Presence, nothing I fear.
> A disciple of Christ, I do leave behind,
> the ego's desire for responding in kind.

> **Gabriel Archangel, of this I am sure,**
> **Gabriel Archangel, Christ light is the cure.**
> **Gabriel Archangel, intentions so pure,**
> **Gabriel Archangel, in you I'm secure.**

2. Archangel Gabriel, come into my Base Chakra and clear it from the dualistic concept of purity as the opposite of impurity. Help me overcome the illusion that in order to attain purity, I have to overcome, destroy, run away from or cover over my impurities.

> Gabriel Archangel, I fear not the light,
> in purifications' fire, I delight.
> With your hand in mine, each challenge I face,
> I follow the spiral to infinite grace.

> **Gabriel Archangel, of this I am sure,**
> **Gabriel Archangel, Christ light is the cure.**
> **Gabriel Archangel, intentions so pure,**
> **Gabriel Archangel, in you I'm secure.**

3. Archangel Gabriel, come into my Base Chakra and clear it from the state of mind in which I do not want God to see my impurities. Help me see that in seeking to hide anything from God, I cannot look at it myself, and then I cannot accelerate it out of impurity by raising its vibration.

> Gabriel Archangel, your fire burning white,
> ascending with you, out of the night.
> My ego has nowhere to run and to hide,
> in ascension's bright spiral, with you I abide.
>
> **Gabriel Archangel, of this I am sure,**
> **Gabriel Archangel, Christ light is the cure.**
> **Gabriel Archangel, intentions so pure,**
> **Gabriel Archangel, in you I'm secure.**

4. Archangel Gabriel, come into my Base Chakra and clear it from the illusion that when my body gets ill I cannot simply accelerate away from the illness. Help me accept that I can escape the illness because it is impermanent, it is ultimately unreal and has no power over me.

> Gabriel Archangel, your trumpet I hear,
> announcing the birth of Christ drawing near.
> In lightness of being, I now am reborn,
> rising with Christ on bright Easter morn.
>
> **Gabriel Archangel, of this I am sure,**
> **Gabriel Archangel, Christ light is the cure.**
> **Gabriel Archangel, intentions so pure,**
> **Gabriel Archangel, in you I'm secure.**

5. Archangel Gabriel, come into my Base Chakra and help me see the reality that no matter how burdened I feel, I am more than these burdens. I now decide to unleash the full power of my I AM Presence and accelerate my being, accelerate my cells, accelerate my very atoms, and rise above the vibration—even raising the vibration of the burdened cells and atoms.

> Gabriel Archangel, your light I revere,
> immersed in your Presence, nothing I fear.
> A disciple of Christ, I do leave behind,
> the ego's desire for responding in kind.

> **Gabriel Archangel, of this I am sure,**
> **Gabriel Archangel, Christ light is the cure.**
> **Gabriel Archangel, intentions so pure,**
> **Gabriel Archangel, in you I'm secure.**

6. Archangel Gabriel, come into my Base Chakra and clear it from the conditions that I have come to accept as being real and having power over me. I now make the decision to accelerate beyond the limitations and tune in to the vibration of purity. I am absorbing the vibration of purity and I know I can accelerate beyond any condition.

> Gabriel Archangel, I fear not the light,
> in purifications' fire, I delight.
> With your hand in mine, each challenge I face,
> I follow the spiral to infinite grace.

> **Gabriel Archangel, of this I am sure,**
> **Gabriel Archangel, Christ light is the cure.**
> **Gabriel Archangel, intentions so pure,**
> **Gabriel Archangel, in you I'm secure.**

7. Archangel Gabriel, come into my Base Chakra and clear it from the curse of perfectionism, the lie that perfection means that I live up to certain conditions. Any condition can exist only in the mind of duality. Any condition in the mind of duality has an opposite polarity, or it would not exist. Thus, any condition has no reality in the Christ mind.

> Gabriel Archangel, your fire burning white,
> ascending with you, out of the night.
> My ego has nowhere to run and to hide,
> in ascension's bright spiral, with you I abide.
>
> **Gabriel Archangel, of this I am sure,**
> **Gabriel Archangel, Christ light is the cure.**
> **Gabriel Archangel, intentions so pure,**
> **Gabriel Archangel, in you I'm secure.**

8. Archangel Gabriel, come into my Base Chakra and clear it from the dualistic concept of perfection that is in opposition to imperfection. Help me overcome the lie that what makes me imperfect is a certain condition, and in order to become perfect I have to take on another condition. I now see that both "imperfect" and "perfect" conditions affirm the reality of the separate self.

> Gabriel Archangel, your trumpet I hear,
> announcing the birth of Christ drawing near.
> In lightness of being, I now am reborn,
> rising with Christ on bright Easter morn.
>
> **Gabriel Archangel, of this I am sure,**
> **Gabriel Archangel, Christ light is the cure.**
> **Gabriel Archangel, intentions so pure,**
> **Gabriel Archangel, in you I'm secure.**

9. Archangel Gabriel, come into my Base Chakra and help me experience that purity is not the absence of impurity. It is a particular vibration, a frequency, a living stream of consciousness. I now to tune in to and absorb that stream so that I attain a sense of co-measurement and oneness with the vibration of purity.

> With angels I soar,
> as I reach for MORE.
> The angels so real,
> their love all will heal.
> The angels bring peace,
> all conflicts will cease.
> With angels of light,
> we soar to new height.

> **The rustling sound of angel wings,**
> **what joy as even matter sings,**
> **what joy as every atom rings,**
> **in harmony with angel wings.**

2. I can accelerate any condition

1. Elohim Astrea, come into my Base Chakra and help me take responsibility for the energy that is truly a reflection of my consciousness. I will stop the process of coloring light with a lower vibration. I will look at the illusions in my own consciousness that have added to the accumulation of misqualified energy in my four lower bodies.

> Beloved Astrea, your heart is so true,
> your Circle and Sword of white and blue,
> cut all life free from dramas unwise,
> on wings of Purity our planet will rise.

> **Beloved Astrea, in God Purity,**
> **accelerate all of my life energy,**
> **raising my mind into true unity**
> **with the Masters of love in Infinity.**

2. Elohim Astrea, come into my Base Chakra and help me change my consciousness so I stop misqualifying light. Help me see the message in the disease manifest in my physical body and surrender the consciousness behind it. I will then purify the energy I have already misqualified.

> Beloved Astrea, from Purity's Ray,
> send forth deliverance to all life today,
> acceleration to Purity, I AM now free
> from all that is less than love's Purity.

> **Beloved Astrea, in oneness with you,**
> **your circle and sword of electric blue,**
> **with Purity's Light cutting right through,**
> **raising within me all that is true.**

3. Elohim Astrea, come into my Base Chakra and help me switch out of the self-centered perspective. Help me reach the ultimate clarity of recognizing that the way to purify energy is not by destroying the energy. It is to accelerate it so that it shakes off the imperfect vibration and is again raised to the level of love, the level of purity.

> Beloved Astrea, accelerate us all,
> as for your deliverance I fervently call,
> set all life free from vision impure
> beyond fear and doubt, I AM rising for sure.

**Beloved Astrea, I AM willing to see,
all of the lies that keep me unfree,
I AM rising beyond every impurity,
with Purity's Light forever in me.**

4. Elohim Astrea, come into my Base Chakra and help me recognize my full potential and to truly accelerate myself out of the problems, out of the wounds, out of the setbacks, out of the diseases, out of any condition that is holding me back.

Beloved Astrea, accelerate life
beyond all duality's struggle and strife,
consume all division between God and man,
accelerate fulfillment of God's perfect plan.

**Beloved Astrea, I lovingly call,
break down separation's invisible wall,
I surrender all lies causing the fall,
forever affirming the oneness of All.**

5. Elohim Astrea, come into my Base Chakra and help me decide to shift away from confirming the reality of the separate self. This is not about me and how bad and burdened I feel. This is about why I actually came to this earth, namely to serve the ascended masters, serve God, serve other people, serve to bring forth the Golden Age of Saint Germain.

Beloved Astrea, your heart is so true,
your Circle and Sword of white and blue,
cut all life free from dramas unwise,
on wings of Purity our planet will rise.

**Beloved Astrea, in God Purity,
accelerate all of my life energy,
raising my mind into true unity
with the Masters of love in Infinity.**

6. Elohim Astrea, come into my Base Chakra and help me avoid going into the dualistic reaction of either trying to take flight from the trouble or to fight and destroy the trouble. Help me learn how to accelerate my way out of trouble.

Beloved Astrea, from Purity's Ray,
send forth deliverance to all life today,
acceleration to Purity, I AM now free
from all that is less than love's Purity.

**Beloved Astrea, in oneness with you,
your circle and sword of electric blue,
with Purity's Light cutting right through,
raising within me all that is true.**

7. Elohim Astrea, come into my Base Chakra and help me overcome both the unworthiness and the pride of the ego. Help me see the illogical nature of the dualistic conditions and realize that I cannot set up any condition that defines perfection. Neither conditional imperfection nor conditional perfection is real.

Beloved Astrea, accelerate us all,
as for your deliverance I fervently call,
set all life free from vision impure
beyond fear and doubt, I AM rising for sure.

**Beloved Astrea, I AM willing to see,
all of the lies that keep me unfree,
I AM rising beyond every impurity,
with Purity's Light forever in me.**

8. Elohim Astrea, come into my Base Chakra and help me recognize that it is not possible to define perfection by setting up any condition whatsoever. Perfection means unconditionality. Unconditionality does not mean the loss of individuality. I do not become nothing by becoming unconditional. I become free of being tied to any thing, any sense of identity in the dualistic realm.

> Beloved Astrea, accelerate life
> beyond all duality's struggle and strife,
> consume all division between God and man,
> accelerate fulfillment of God's perfect plan.

**Beloved Astrea, I lovingly call,
break down separation's invisible wall,
I surrender all lies causing the fall,
forever affirming the oneness of All.**

9. Elohim Astrea, come into my Base Chakra and help me make the essential switch from local to global awareness. I will not let any conditions stand in the way of my service to God. I love this *more*. I am willing to look my separate self straight in the eye and say: "You are not right when you tell me I cannot. My God within me tells me that I *can,* for with God, all things are possible."

> Accelerate into Purity, I AM real,
> Accelerate into Purity, all life heal,
> Accelerate into Purity, I AM MORE,
> Accelerate into Purity, all will soar.
>
> Accelerate into Purity! (3X)
> Beloved Elohim Astrea.
> Accelerate into Purity! (3X)
> Beloved Gabriel and Hope.
> Accelerate into Purity! (3X)
> Beloved Serapis Bey.
> Accelerate into Purity! (3X)
> Beloved I AM.

3. I do not seek to hide impurities

1. Serapis Bey, come into my Base Chakra and help me pass the initiation of the Fourth Ray of purity. Help me see that in order to reach the fullness of wholeness I need to accelerate my being.

> Serapis Bey, what power lies,
> behind your purifying eyes.
> Serapis Bey, it is a treat,
> to enter your sublime retreat.
>
> **O Holy Spirit, flow through me,**
> **I am the open door for thee.**
> **O mighty rushing stream of Light,**
> **transcendence is my sacred right.**

2. Serapis Bey, come into my Base Chakra and help me overcome the sense that I am too tired, too sick and that I cannot possibly accelerate. Help me see that I have come to identify myself with a role. By focusing my mind on that image, I make it a manifest, but temporary, reality in my physical temple.

> Serapis Bey, what wisdom found,
> your words are always most profound.
> Serapis Bey, I tell you true,
> my mind has room for naught but you.

> **O Holy Spirit, flow through me,**
> **I am the open door for thee.**
> **O mighty rushing stream of Light,**
> **transcendence is my sacred right.**

3. Serapis Bey, come into my Base Chakra and help me overcome the illusion that because of this or that condition I cannot accelerate. Help me recognize that it is not rest that I need at this particular stage in the healing process—it is acceleration.

> Serapis Bey, what love beyond,
> my heart does leap, as I respond.
> Serapis Bey, your life a poem,
> that calls me to my starry home.

> **O Holy Spirit, flow through me,**
> **I am the open door for thee.**
> **O mighty rushing stream of Light,**
> **transcendence is my sacred right.**

18 | Clearing the Base Chakra

4. Serapis Bey, come into my Base Chakra and help me see that I cannot walk away from anything. I cannot rise above the duality consciousness by using the duality consciousness. The act of transmuting energy is not the same as removing energy.

> Serapis Bey, your guidance sure,
> my base is clear and white and pure.
> Serapis Bey, no longer trapped,
> by soul in which my self was wrapped.
>
> **O Holy Spirit, flow through me,**
> **I am the open door for thee.**
> **O mighty rushing stream of Light,**
> **transcendence is my sacred right.**

5. Serapis Bey, come into my Base Chakra and help me see that as I receive light from my I AM Presence, I color the light with a higher or lower vibration. The light that is colored with a lower vibration will eventually accumulate and burden the cells so they cannot function properly, and thus disease will manifest.

> Serapis Bey, what healing balm,
> in mind that is forever calm.
> Serapis Bey, my thoughts are pure,
> your discipline I shall endure.
>
> **O Holy Spirit, flow through me,**
> **I am the open door for thee.**
> **O mighty rushing stream of Light,**
> **transcendence is my sacred right.**

6. Serapis Bey, come into my Base Chakra and help me see that what has caused the coloring of the light is the illusion of a separate self. Help me surrender the lie that I have a right to do what is best for me even if it harms other forms of life.

> Serapis Bey, what secret test,
> for egos who want to be best.
> Serapis Bey, expose in me,
> all that is less than harmony.

> **O Holy Spirit, flow through me,**
> **I am the open door for thee.**
> **O mighty rushing stream of Light,**
> **transcendence is my sacred right.**

7. Serapis Bey, come into my Base Chakra and help me rise above the instinctive response of wanting to get rid of the disease and the energies. Help me see that it is not enough to get rid of the impure energies, for I also need to resolve the state of consciousness that corresponds to the energies that burden my cells.

> Serapis Bey, what moving sight,
> my self ascends to sacred height.
> Serapis Bey, forever free,
> in sacred synchronicity.

> **O Holy Spirit, flow through me,**
> **I am the open door for thee.**
> **O mighty rushing stream of Light,**
> **transcendence is my sacred right.**

8. Serapis Bey, come into my Base Chakra and help me rise above being self-focused, self-centered. Help me rise above the reaction of wanting to be healed no matter what, the desire to suppress the symptoms. Help me develop a desire for true healing through a transformation of consciousness.

> Serapis Bey, you balance all,
> the seven rays upon my call.
> Serapis Bey, in space and time,
> the pyramid of self, I climb.

> **O Holy Spirit, flow through me,**
> **I am the open door for thee.**
> **O mighty rushing stream of Light,**
> **transcendence is my sacred right.**

9. Serapis Bey, come into my Base Chakra and help me tune in to your heart and accept that you do not require me to attain a certain level of purity before you will work with me. Help me know that your task is to help me overcome impurity, so I can accept you instead of seeking to hide my impurities from you.

> Serapis Bey, your Presence here,
> filling up my inner sphere.
> Life is now a sacred flow,
> God Purity I do bestow.

> **O Holy Spirit, flow through me,**
> **I am the open door for thee.**
> **O mighty rushing stream of Light,**
> **transcendence is my sacred right.**

4. I accept my healing

1. Serapis Bey, come into my Base Chakra and help me experience that it is your deepest love to help me become pure. You are willing to work with me at my present level because to you no impurity is real.

> O Liberty now set me free
> from devil's curse of poverty.
> I blame not Mother for my lack,
> O Blessed Mother, take me back.
>
> **O Cosmic Mother Liberty,**
> **conduct Abundance Symphony.**
> **My highest service I now see,**
> **abundance is now real for me.**

2. Serapis Bey, come into my Base Chakra and help me see beyond all impurity and experience the pure being that was created out of the mind of God. Help me see that I am real and thus you never condemn me or look down upon me.

> O Liberty, from distant shore,
> I come with longing to be More.
> I see abundance is a flow,
> abundance consciousness I grow.
>
> **O Cosmic Mother Liberty,**
> **conduct Abundance Symphony.**
> **My highest service I now see,**
> **abundance is now real for me.**

3. Serapis Bey, come into my Base Chakra and help me know the reality that I can overcome any impurity that I have taken on in the material universe. Help me come into oneness with the vibration of purity, so I know that it is so high that there is nothing of the lower vibrations of the material universe that it cannot accelerate back into purity.

> O Liberty, expose the lie,
> that limitations can me tie.
> The Ma-ter light is not my foe,
> true opulence it does bestow.

> **O Cosmic Mother Liberty,**
> **conduct Abundance Symphony.**
> **My highest service I now see,**
> **abundance is now real for me.**

4. Serapis Bey, come into my Base Chakra and help me experience the extreme realism that you bring. Help me overcome the illusion that there are certain things I cannot overcome, certain problems I must remove or destroy, even the idea that I need a certain insight to overcome the illusion.

> O Liberty, expose the plot,
> projected by the fallen lot.
> O Cosmic Mother, I now see,
> that Mother's not my enemy.

> **O Cosmic Mother Liberty,**
> **conduct Abundance Symphony.**
> **My highest service I now see,**
> **abundance is now real for me.**

5. Serapis Bey, come into my Base Chakra and help me go through a shift of self-image and accept that I AM a spiritual being. I AM more than these material conditions, and therefore I have the potential to raise my vibration. I can raise the vibration of any condition that I have outpictured in my four lower bodies.

> O Liberty, with opened eyes,
> I now reject the devil's lies.
> I now embrace the Mother realm,
> for I see Father at the helm.

> **O Cosmic Mother Liberty,**
> **conduct Abundance Symphony.**
> **My highest service I now see,**
> **abundance is now real for me.**

6. Serapis Bey, come into my Base Chakra and help me see that giving up the ghost of the ego is the Omega side of the equation. The Alpha side is that I deliberately and willfully accelerate my sense of self to that higher vibration of the purity of the spiritual being that was never confined to the lower sense of self.

> O Liberty, a chalice pure,
> my lower bodies are for sure.
> Release through me your symphony,
> your gift of Cosmic Liberty.

> **O Cosmic Mother Liberty,**
> **conduct Abundance Symphony.**
> **My highest service I now see,**
> **abundance is now real for me.**

7. Serapis Bey, come into my Base Chakra and help me reach the point where I have given up enough that I can make that final push away from the gravitational pull of the separate self and the mass consciousness. I now unleash the Alpha thrust of accelerating my sense of self, and I accept that I have shifted my identity.

> O Liberty, the open door,
> I am for Symphony of More.
> In chakras mine light you release,
> the flow of love shall never cease.

> **O Cosmic Mother Liberty,**
> **conduct Abundance Symphony.**
> **My highest service I now see,**
> **abundance is now real for me.**

8. Serapis Bey, come into my Base Chakra and help me see that the true key to healing is the acceptance of who I AM. Acceptance has an active quality of deliberately and consciously making the decision to choose to accelerate my sense of self. I AM accelerating it, I AM experiencing it, and in experiencing it, I am accepting my healing fully.

> O Liberty, release the flow,
> of opulence that you bestow.
> For I am willing to receive,
> the Golden Fleece that you now weave.

> **O Cosmic Mother Liberty,**
> **conduct Abundance Symphony.**
> **My highest service I now see,**
> **abundance is now real for me.**

9. Serapis Bey, come into my Base Chakra and help me see that the key to healing is the acceptance, but more than the passive acceptance. I hereby accelerate my sense of self and I accept that I am no longer the ill person who started this invocation. I AM the healed person who is finishing it.

> O Liberty, release the cure,
> to free the tired and the poor.
> The huddled masses are set free,
> by loving Song of Liberty.
>
> **O Cosmic Mother Liberty,**
> **conduct Abundance Symphony.**
> **My highest service I now see,**
> **abundance is now real for me.**

Sealing:

In the name of the Divine Mother, I fully accept that the power of these calls is used to set free the Ma-ter light, so it can outpicture the perfect vision of Christ for my own life, for all people and for the planet. In the name I AM THAT I AM, it is done! Amen.

19 | CLEARING THE CROWN CHAKRA

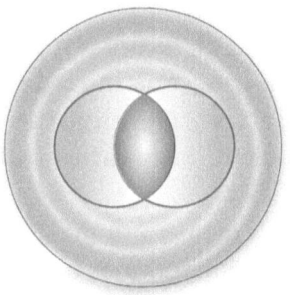

[NOTE: Study the dictation from the Second Ray.]

In the name I AM THAT I AM, Jesus Christ, I call to my I AM Presence to flow through the I Will Be Presence that I AM and give this invocation with full power. I call to beloved Archangel Jophiel and Christine, Elohim Apollo and Lumina, Lord Lanto and Portia to help me overcome all impurities in my Crown Chakra. Help me be free from all patterns or forces within or without that oppose the free flow of wisdom from my I AM Presence, including …

[Make personal calls]

1. I transcend all false wisdom

1. Archangel Jophiel, come into my Crown Chakra and clear it from the worldly wisdom, the illusion that because I have acquired such great wisdom, I am now self-sufficient, self-contained, and I know everything that I need to know.

> Jophiel Archangel, in wisdom's great light,
> all serpentine lies exposed to my sight.
> So subtle the lies that creep through the mind,
> yet you are the greatest teacher I find.

> **Jophiel Archangel, exposing all lies,**
> **Jophiel Archangel, cutting all ties.**
> **Jophiel Archangel, clearing the skies,**
> **Jophiel Archangel, my mind truly flies.**

2. Archangel Jophiel, come into my Crown Chakra and clear it from the false wisdom that causes me to isolate myself, not only from society but from the River of Life.

> Jophiel Archangel, your wisdom I hail,
> your sword cutting through duality's veil.
> As you show the way, I know what is real,
> from serpentine doubt, I instantly heal.

> **Jophiel Archangel, exposing all lies,**
> **Jophiel Archangel, cutting all ties.**
> **Jophiel Archangel, clearing the skies,**
> **Jophiel Archangel, my mind truly flies.**

3. Archangel Jophiel, come into my Crown Chakra and clear it from the false wisdom that causes my ego to feel that it has my surroundings, even the entire world, under control.

> Jophiel Archangel, your reality,
> the best antidote to duality.
> No lie can remain in your Presence so clear,
> with you on my side, no serpent I fear.

Jophiel Archangel, exposing all lies,
Jophiel Archangel, cutting all ties.
Jophiel Archangel, clearing the skies,
Jophiel Archangel, my mind truly flies.

4. Archangel Jophiel, come into my Crown Chakra and clear it from the false wisdom that forms a graven image. Help me see through all false wisdom even if the experts in society claim it is true.

> Jophiel Archangel, God's mind is in me,
> and through your clear light, its wisdom I see.
> Divisions all vanish, as I see the One,
> and truly, the wholeness of mind I have won.

Jophiel Archangel, exposing all lies,
Jophiel Archangel, cutting all ties.
Jophiel Archangel, clearing the skies,
Jophiel Archangel, my mind truly flies.

5. Archangel Jophiel, come into my Crown Chakra and clear it from the false wisdom promoted by the institutions of the world. Help me see that the elaborate structures that accumulate massive amounts of information simply demonstrate the insecurity of the ego and its failure to explain the River of Life.

> Jophiel Archangel, in wisdom's great light,
> all serpentine lies exposed to my sight.
> So subtle the lies that creep through the mind,
> yet you are the greatest teacher I find.

> **Jophiel Archangel, exposing all lies,**
> **Jophiel Archangel, cutting all ties.**
> **Jophiel Archangel, clearing the skies,**
> **Jophiel Archangel, my mind truly flies.**

6. Archangel Jophiel, come into my Crown Chakra and clear it from the desire to be a teacher in order to be thought wise among men and raise up the separate self. Help me constantly strive for oneness, so I can be an open door for the fount of wisdom to flow through me.

> Jophiel Archangel, your wisdom I hail,
> your sword cutting through duality's veil.
> As you show the way, I know what is real,
> from serpentine doubt, I instantly heal.

> **Jophiel Archangel, exposing all lies,**
> **Jophiel Archangel, cutting all ties.**
> **Jophiel Archangel, clearing the skies,**
> **Jophiel Archangel, my mind truly flies.**

7. Archangel Jophiel, come into my Crown Chakra and help me go beyond the structure that serves to maintain the ego's sense of security and control. Help me absorb your unconditional wisdom and transcend the sense of separation. Help me see that which I cannot see right now.

> Jophiel Archangel, your reality,
> the best antidote to duality.
> No lie can remain in your Presence so clear,
> with you on my side, no serpent I fear.

> **Jophiel Archangel, exposing all lies,**
> **Jophiel Archangel, cutting all ties.**
> **Jophiel Archangel, clearing the skies,**
> **Jophiel Archangel, my mind truly flies.**

8. Archangel Jophiel, come into my Crown Chakra and clear it from everything that takes my attention away from what is the true key to healing, namely that there is energy flowing from outside the material universe.

> Jophiel Archangel, God's mind is in me,
> and through your clear light, its wisdom I see.
> Divisions all vanish, as I see the One,
> and truly, the wholeness of mind I have won.

> **Jophiel Archangel, exposing all lies,**
> **Jophiel Archangel, cutting all ties.**
> **Jophiel Archangel, clearing the skies,**
> **Jophiel Archangel, my mind truly flies.**

9. Archangel Jophiel, come into my Crown Chakra and help me accept a healing miracle, even though it cannot be explained by worldly wisdom.

> With angels I soar,
> as I reach for MORE.
> The angels so real,
> their love all will heal.
> The angels bring peace,
> all conflicts will cease.
> With angels of light,
> we soar to new height.
>
> **The rustling sound of angel wings,**
> **what joy as even matter sings,**
> **what joy as every atom rings,**
> **in harmony with angel wings.**

2. I immerse myself in the fount of wisdom

1. Elohim Apollo, come into my Crown Chakra and unleash the vibration of spring, the vitality of the unstoppable force, the Fountain of Youth. I now feel this fountain of youth flowing into my body, flowing up through my legs, into the torso, into the head and creating a golden ring of light around my head.

> Beloved Apollo, with your Second Ray,
> you open my eyes to see a new day,
> I see through duality's lies and deceit,
> transcending the mindset producing defeat.

19 | Clearing the Crown Chakra

**Beloved Apollo, thou Elohim Gold,
your radiant light my eyes now behold,
as pages of wisdom you gently unfold,
I feel I am free from all that is old.**

2. Elohim Apollo, come into my Crown Chakra and help me absorb the wisdom behind the miracle of spring, the vital, ever-flowing wisdom that is forever transcending itself, becoming more in oneness with the River of Life.

Beloved Apollo, in your flame I know,
that your living wisdom is always a flow,
in your light I see my own highest will,
immersed in the stream that never stands still.

**Beloved Apollo, your light makes it clear,
why we have taken embodiment here,
working to raise our own cosmic sphere,
together we form the tip of the spear.**

3. Elohim Apollo, come into my Crown Chakra and help me immerse myself in the River of Life and flow with that wisdom—instead of using the worldly wisdom to build some kind of palace where the separate self can feel important and enthroned.

Beloved Apollo, exposing all lies,
I hereby surrender all ego-based ties,
I know my perception is truly the key,
to transcending the serpentine duality.

> Beloved Apollo, we heed now your call,
> drawing us into Wisdom's Great Hall,
> exposing all lies causing the fall,
> you help us reclaim the oneness of all.

4. Elohim Apollo, come into my Crown Chakra and help me absorb the living wisdom that challenges my current perception, my current self-image, and magnetically draws me to reconnect to that ever-flowing fount of wisdom that is always transcending itself.

> Beloved Apollo, your wisdom so clear,
> in oneness with you, no serpent I fear,
> the beam in my eye I'm willing to see,
> I'm free from the serpent's own duality.

> Beloved Apollo, my eyes now I raise,
> I see that the earth is in a new phase,
> I willingly stand in your piercing gaze,
> empowered, I exit duality's maze.

5. Elohim Apollo, come into my Crown Chakra and help me experience that wisdom is alive. Wisdom is a living, vital force that tells all life how to become more. I tune in to the vibration, the flow, the fount of wisdom. I immerse myself in the living waters of wisdom and in flowing with it, I experience healing.

> Beloved Apollo, with your Second Ray,
> you open my eyes to see a new day,
> I see through duality's lies and deceit,
> transcending the mindset producing defeat.

19 | Clearing the Crown Chakra

Beloved Apollo, thou Elohim Gold,
your radiant light my eyes now behold,
as pages of wisdom you gently unfold,
I feel I am free from all that is old.

6. Elohim Apollo, come into my Crown Chakra and help me see that disease is caused when the ego blocks the flow and my energy field becomes a closed system. Help me accept the force that breaks down this closed system, thereby setting me free to again flow with the River of Life in constant self-transcendence.

Beloved Apollo, in your flame I know,
that your living wisdom is always a flow,
in your light I see my own highest will,
immersed in the stream that never stands still.

Beloved Apollo, your light makes it clear,
why we have taken embodiment here,
working to raise our own cosmic sphere,
together we form the tip of the spear.

7. Elohim Apollo, come into my Crown Chakra and help me see that for every dualistic argument there is a counter-argument that will negate it, which means that any form of dualistic wisdom is relative. I want absolute wisdom, I want unconditional wisdom.

Beloved Apollo, exposing all lies,
I hereby surrender all ego-based ties,
I know my perception is truly the key,
to transcending the serpentine duality.

> **Beloved Apollo, we heed now your call,**
> **drawing us into Wisdom's Great Hall,**
> **exposing all lies causing the fall,**
> **you help us reclaim the oneness of all.**

8. Elohim Apollo, come into my Crown Chakra and help me see that it is not by seeking an outer, structured wisdom that I will go further. I am in a catch-22 because I see myself as not having wisdom. I overcome the catch-22 by being willing to let go of all I think I know, to have the childlike mind that is not asking but that simply observes.

> Beloved Apollo, your wisdom so clear,
> in oneness with you, no serpent I fear,
> the beam in my eye I'm willing to see,
> I'm free from the serpent's own duality.

> **Beloved Apollo, my eyes now I raise,**
> **I see that the earth is in a new phase,**
> **I willingly stand in your piercing gaze,**
> **empowered, I exit duality's maze.**

9. Elohim Apollo, come into my Crown Chakra and help me walk away from all that the ego thinks it knows about the spiritual path. Help me absorb my own Higher Being and switch my focus, so I experience oneness with something beyond the separate self. In that experience of oneness, I am whole, I AM healed.

> Accelerate my Awakeness, I AM real,
> Accelerate my Awakeness, all life heal,
> Accelerate my Awakeness, I AM MORE,
> Accelerate my Awakeness, all will soar.

Accelerate my Awakeness! (3X)
Beloved Apollo and Lumina.
Accelerate my Awakeness! (3X)
Beloved Jophiel and Christine.
Accelerate my Awakeness! (3X)
Beloved Master Lanto.
Accelerate my Awakeness! (3X)
Beloved I AM.

3. I want to live my spiritual teaching

1. Lord Lanto, come into my Crown Chakra and help me see that there is something missing, that there is more to understand about the miracle of life, and that life cannot be reduced to a machine that follows mechanical laws.

Master Lanto, golden wise,
expose in me the ego's lies.
Master Lanto, will to be,
I will to win my mastery.

O Holy Spirit, flow through me,
I am the open door for thee.
O mighty rushing stream of Light,
transcendence is my sacred right.

2. Lord Lanto, come into my Crown Chakra and help me overcome the belief that in order to reach my spiritual goal I need to get some kind of wisdom, some kind of secret formula from a source outside myself.

Master Lanto, balance all,
for wisdom's balance I do call.
Master Lanto, help me see,
that balance is the Golden key.

**O Holy Spirit, flow through me,
I am the open door for thee.
O mighty rushing stream of Light,
transcendence is my sacred right.**

3. Lord Lanto, come into my Crown Chakra and help me see that it is not a matter of seeking knowledge from without, it is a matter of realizing that I have access to the kingdom of God within me. I am willing to go within and connect to the fount of wisdom and to have my consciousness raised.

Master Lanto, from Above,
I call forth discerning love.
Master Lanto, love's not blind,
through love, God vision I will find.

**O Holy Spirit, flow through me,
I am the open door for thee.
O mighty rushing stream of Light,
transcendence is my sacred right.**

4. Lord Lanto, come into my Crown Chakra and help me know that the Christ consciousness is oneness with the River of Life that is constant self-transcendence. The Christ is constantly transcending itself and becoming *more*.

Master Lanto, pure I am,
intentions pure as Christic lamb.
Master Lanto, I will transcend,
acceleration now my truest friend.

**O Holy Spirit, flow through me,
I am the open door for thee.
O mighty rushing stream of Light,
transcendence is my sacred right.**

5. Lord Lanto, come into my Crown Chakra and help me go beyond understanding something intellectually. Help me stand in front of the mirror and see a particular aspect of duality in myself, so that I can apply and live my spiritual teaching.

Master Lanto, I am whole,
no more division in my soul.
Master Lanto, healing flame,
all balance in your sacred name.

**O Holy Spirit, flow through me,
I am the open door for thee.
O mighty rushing stream of Light,
transcendence is my sacred right.**

6. Lord Lanto, come into my Crown Chakra and help me see that when wisdom is approached only from the intellect, my mind becomes a closed system. This is when I become trapped by my database, wanting wisdom to fit into some category in the database so that the ego can feel it is in control.

Master Lanto, serve all life,
as I transcend all inner strife.
Master Lanto, peace you give,
to all who want to truly live.

**O Holy Spirit, flow through me,
I am the open door for thee.
O mighty rushing stream of Light,
transcendence is my sacred right.**

7. Lord Lanto, come into my Crown Chakra and help me see that the intellect cannot help me connect to the fount of wisdom, for this happens only in the heart. Therefore, I cannot intellectually understand what it takes to transcend the separate self.

Master Lanto, free to be,
in balanced creativity.
Master Lanto, we employ,
your balance as the key to joy.

**O Holy Spirit, flow through me,
I am the open door for thee.
O mighty rushing stream of Light,
transcendence is my sacred right.**

8. Lord Lanto, come into my Crown Chakra and help me see that as long as I think I am missing some crucial piece of information, I am subconsciously affirming the image that I am separated from Christhood, from the kingdom of God, from enlightenment.

> Master Lanto, balance all,
> the seven rays upon my call.
> Master Lanto, I take flight,
> my threefold flame a blazing light.
>
> **O Holy Spirit, flow through me,**
> **I am the open door for thee.**
> **O mighty rushing stream of Light,**
> **transcendence is my sacred right.**

9. Lord Lanto, come into my Crown Chakra and help me see that the crucial piece of information that I have not yet found is the realization that what is wrong with me is the sense that there is something I do not know, something that I do not have access to within myself and must find from an outer source.

> Lanto dear, your Presence here,
> filling up my inner sphere.
> Life is now a sacred flow,
> God Wisdom I on all bestow.
>
> **O Holy Spirit, flow through me,**
> **I am the open door for thee.**
> **O mighty rushing stream of Light,**
> **transcendence is my sacred right.**

4. I acquire true wisdom

1. Lord Lanto, come into my Crown Chakra and help me see that I *do* need something from outside the closed circle of my separate sense of identity. I need the guru to demonstrate that there is something beyond my current state of consciousness.

O Portia, in your own retreat,
with Mother's Love you do me greet.
As all my tests I now complete,
old patterns I no more repeat.

**O Portia, opportunity,
I am beyond duality.
I focus now internally,
with you I grow eternally.**

2. Lord Lanto, come into my Crown Chakra and help me see when I am at the point where I cannot progress by only listening to the outer teaching given by or through the teacher. I must go beyond the teaching and absorb the vibration that is coming through the guru.

O Portia, Justice is your name,
upholding Cosmic Honor Flame,
No longer will I play the game,
of seeking to remain the same.

**O Portia, opportunity,
I am beyond duality.
I focus now internally,
with you I grow eternally.**

3. Lord Lanto, come into my Crown Chakra and help me open my mind and heart to receiving the vibration of a particular master. I now say: "Drink me, while I am drinking thee." I am willing to give up anything in this world, any part of the separate self, in order to come into oneness with the master.

> O Portia, in the cosmic flow,
> one with you, I ever grow.
> I am the chalice here below,
> of cosmic justice you bestow.
>
> **O Portia, opportunity,**
> **I am beyond duality.**
> **I focus now internally,**
> **with you I grow eternally.**

4. Lord Lanto, come into my Crown Chakra and help me accept that there is no secret formula that will enable me to know and master all things. God hides the secret of life from those who are approaching it from the consciousness of separation. I only discover the secret of life by becoming one with the River of Life.

> O Portia, cosmic balance bring,
> eternal hope, my heart does sing.
> Protected by your Mother's wing,
> I feel at one with everything.
>
> **O Portia, opportunity,**
> **I am beyond duality.**
> **I focus now internally,**
> **with you I grow eternally.**

5. Lord Lanto, come into my Crown Chakra and help me accept that I am worthy to receive your unconditional love with a tint of the unconditional, infinite wisdom of God. Help me absorb the true wisdom that you are and with which you have become one. I know this wisdom cannot be reduced to words, formulas, rituals or teachings, for it is alive and defies any structure whatsoever.

O Portia, bring the Mother Light,
to set all free from darkest night.
Your Love Flame shines forever bright,
with Saint Germain now hold me tight.

**O Portia, opportunity,
I am beyond duality.
I focus now internally,
with you I grow eternally.**

6. Lord Lanto, come into my Crown Chakra and help me discover the message behind any disease in my body or mind. Help me see what kind of illusion is outpictured in the disease. Help me walk right into it, look at it and seek oneness with it.

O Portia, in your mastery,
I feel transforming chemistry.
In your light of reality,
I find the golden alchemy.

**O Portia, opportunity,
I am beyond duality.
I focus now internally,
with you I grow eternally.**

7. Lord Lanto, come into my Crown Chakra and help me see that in seeking separation from the disease, I only reinforce the illusion of separation. Separation is running away from oneness, and I cannot come back to oneness by seeking to run away from that which is created out of separation.

19 | Clearing the Crown Chakra

> O Portia, in the cosmic stream,
> I am awake from human dream.
> Removing now the ego's beam,
> I earn my place on cosmic team.
>
> **O Portia, opportunity,**
> **I am beyond duality.**
> **I focus now internally,**
> **with you I grow eternally.**

8. Lord Lanto, come into my Crown Chakra and help me see that the only way to progress is to stop running away from anything and walk right into it. In merging with it, I see that beyond this imperfect image is the reality of the Ma-ter light, which is an expression of God. I see oneness behind the separate images, and I see that the separate images are unreal.

> O Portia, you come from afar,
> you are a cosmic avatar.
> So infinite your repertoire,
> you are for earth a guiding star.
>
> **O Portia, opportunity,**
> **I am beyond duality.**
> **I focus now internally,**
> **with you I grow eternally.**

9. Lord Lanto, come into my Crown Chakra and help me receive your vibration of victory. In oneness with true wisdom, I know I can overcome any condition in the material world. They are all unreal, they are all projections of an unreal image. I AM real, and when I stop running away from that which is unreal – but instead merge with everything – I merge with that which is real. I know that I AM real, and I am more than any unreal appearance.

> O Portia, I am confident,
> I am a cosmic instrument.
> I came to earth from heaven sent,
> to help bring forward her ascent.
>
> **O Portia, opportunity,**
> **I am beyond duality.**
> **I focus now internally,**
> **with you I grow eternally.**

Sealing:

In the name of the Divine Mother, I fully accept that the power of these calls is used to set free the Ma-ter light, so it can outpicture the perfect vision of Christ for my own life, for all people and for the planet. In the name I AM THAT I AM, it is done! Amen.

About the Author

Kim Michaels is an accomplished writer and author. He has conducted spiritual conferences and workshops in 14 countries, has counseled hundreds of spiritual students and has done numerous radio shows on spiritual topics. Kim has been on the spiritual path since 1976. He has studied a wide variety of spiritual teachings and practiced many techniques for raising consciousness. Since 2002 he has served as a messenger for Jesus and other ascended masters. He has brought forth extensive teachings about the mystical path, many of them available for free on his websites: *www.askrealjesus.com, www.ascendedmasteranswers.com, www.ascendedmasterlight.com* and *www.transcendencetoolbox.com*. For personal information, visit Kim at *www.KimMichaels.info*.

Transcendence Toolbooks, vol 1

Flowing with the River of Life Exercise Book

This book is the companion to "Flowing With the River of Life" and contains four unique invocations based on the teachings by the Maha Chohan. The invocations are designed to help you accomplish the following:
- Rise above the death consciousness,
- Attain freedom from aggressive spirits seeking to influence you,
- Expose the spirit in your own being that is holding you back right now,
- Help you let go of spirits in your own being.

This book also contains abbreviated teachings on the death consciousness and how you create and transcend spirits.

Part two of the book contains all of the decrees you use in the seven-month vigil to the spiritual rays. This vigil is designed to help you become familiar with the creative energies of the seven rays and thus unlock your creative potential. You will also find short descriptions of the pure qualities and the perversions of each ray.

Transcendence Toolbooks, vol 2

The Song of Life Healing Matrix

Every day we experience situations where we are exposed to uncertainties, mental or emotional disturbances, positive or negative stress. Everything we go through leaves a mark on our personal story. Some are uplifting positive memories, others are painful to a degree that we suppress them in order to escape the trauma. Each detail of our personal story reveals part of who we are and what blocks our growth. In these spheres of our personal stories we hide our deepest beliefs, concepts, feelings and thoughts that all affect the way we look at life, each other and ourselves. This often generates diseases in our mental, emotional or physical bodies.

The Song of Life Healing Matrix provides you with the unique tools to bring to light the deepest details of your of own song of life. This highly effective tool contains the teachings from eight representatives of the Divine Mother–the ascended masters who represent the Divine Feminine for planet earth. They address the blocks to your personal healing and introduce a highly effective tool for sound healing in the form of the Song Life. The eight invocations that you can easily learn, allow you to call forth the following types of healing:
- The transformation of your sense of identity so you realize you are a spiritual being in a human body.
- The clearing of your mental body from all blocking illusions and destructive thought patterns.

The healing of emotional wounds and the release of the accumulated negative feelings that reinforce self-destructive reactionary patterns.
- The healing of the organs and systems in your physical body from any disease.
- The healing of all lack of balance that prevents you from manifesting your goals in life.
- The healing of all sense of lack that block the manifestation of a spiritually and materially abundant life.
- The healing of all blocks to your acceptance of unconditional love and the flow of love through your being.
- The healing of the denial of your true identity as a co-creator with God and the fact that we are all are part of the Divine Feminine.

Transcendence Toolbooks, vol 3

How to Communicate from the Heart

In all human relationships communication is the biggest block to peace and cooperation. Unfortunately, most communication happens at a level where superficial human perceptions create conflict and disharmony.

The mystical teachings revealed in this book by the ascended masters help you develop a higher form of communication. You will learn how create peace and harmony within our own soul and mind, connect to your higher self and use the seven spiritual energies. The connection with your higher self opens the gates for communication from the heart, and this will help you heal both your own psyche and your relationships.

Through its unique combination of teachings and practical exercises, this book will help you boost your communication skills beyond the perceptions of the ego. You will learn:

- How to respect the free will of others and yourself
- How to give with wisdom
- How to let unconditional love flow through you
- How to purify your intentions
- How to avoid control games and manipulations
- How to serve others from a state of peace
- How to find true freedom in your relationships

www.ingramcontent.com/pod-product-compliance
Lightning Source LLC
Chambersburg PA
CBHW030101170426
43198CB00009B/449